ARMIES OF THE RAJ

ARMIES
OF THE RAJ

From the Mutiny to Independence, 1858–1947

BYRON FARWELL

W · W · NORTON & COMPANY
New York   London

The text of this book is composed in Aster. Composition and manufacturing by The Maple-Vail Book Manufacturing Group.

First published as a Norton paperback 1991

Library of Congress Cataloging-in-Publication Data

Farwell, Byron.
Armies of the Raj / Byron Farwell. — 1st ed.
p. cm.
Bibliography: p.
Includes index.
1. Great Britain. Army. Indian Army—History.   2. Sociology,
Military—India.   3. India—History, Military.   I. Title.
UA842.F37   1989
306'.27'0954–dc19   88–29362

ISBN 0-393-30802-2

W. W. Norton & Company, Inc.
500 Fifth Avenue, New York, N. Y. 10110
W. W. Norton & Company Ltd.
10 Coptic Street, London WC1A 1PU

   3 4 5 6 7 8 9 0

For Jim and Liz Moore,
the finest of friends

Contents

ILLUSTRATIONS   9

ACKNOWLEDGMENTS   11

FOREWORD   13

INTRODUCTION   15

CHAPTER 1   The Great Indian Army   25

CHAPTER 2   From Company to Crown   43

CHAPTER 3   Britons and Indians   57

CHAPTER 4   First Wars and Troubles Under
             the Crown   65

CHAPTER 5   A "Moral and Social Question"   78

CHAPTER 6   British Officers   90

CHAPTER 7   Playing the Great Game   105

CHAPTER 8   The Imperial Assemblage   120

CHAPTER 9   Chota Sahib and Burra Sahib   128

CHAPTER 10   Sex and the Other Ranks   143

CHAPTER 11   Sport   155

CHAPTER 12   Sepoy and Sowar   168

CHAPTER 13   The Martial Races of India   179

CHAPTER 14   The Frontiers   191

CHAPTER 15   Kitchener and Curzon   204
CHAPTER 16   Indian Princes and Their Armies   220
CHAPTER 17   The Singapore Mutiny   236
CHAPTER 18   World War I   248
CHAPTER 19   Amritsar   267
CHAPTER 20   Indianization   292
CHAPTER 21   World War II   303
CHAPTER 22   War and Peace in South-East Asia   318
CHAPTER 23   The Indian National Army   329
CHAPTER 24   Last Days of the Raj   348

APPENDIX A   Indian Army Ranks and Badges   367
APPENDIX B   The Indian Salute States in 1931   368
SELECTED BIBLIOGRAPHY   372
INDEX   381

Illustrations

Sepoys and officers of various Indian Army regiments	33
A soldier's life on board a troopship in 1880	49
The home of the Surveyor General of Madras	58
A home away from home in India	60
"The Fishing Fleet"	61
Troops on the march at night	68
In search of dacoits	72
Soldiers of the 2nd Goorkhas	73
A sowar in the Queen's Own Corps of Guides	76
An officer takes his ease on his veranda	91
An officers' coffee party after parade	92
"How my baggage travelled in India"	94
"Our Ball"	95
"Save Me from My Friends!"	107
The British camp at Kandahar in 1879	110
"How India Kept Her Word"	117
Entry of the Prince of Wales into Baroda	124
Survivors of the Mutiny	126
Caricatures of life in Madras	130
The dinner party	132

An Indian cantonment   133
A picnic in the country   134
A memsahib with her child   136
Horse racing   139
Jackal hunting   160
Pigsticking   162
"Missed!"   163
Tiger hunting   165
A sowar of the 10th Bengal Lancers   171
A sepoy in the 3rd Beluch Regiment   172
Sappers and Miners hauling on a hawser   173
The 7th Bengal native infantry on parade   175
A sepoy of the 14th Sikhs   184
A scene from the Tirah campaign of 1897–98   202
The Duke of Connaught, the Viceroy, and native
    princes   208
A sowar of the 25th Punjab Cavalry   229
An Indian lancer in France in 1915   232
Indian soldiers in World War I   255
A subaltern and the colonel of the 7th Bengal
    Native Infantry   305
[A sketch of] A Jat lance daffadar   307
Major Premindra Singh Bhagat   315

Acknowledgments

I wish to acknowledge and thank those who have been helpful to me in the preparation of this book, including Colonel James H. Jefferies III, Major E. R. B. Hudson, and Angus MacLean Thuermer. I am particularly grateful to Lieutenant-Colonel A. "Tony" Mains, late 9th Gurkha Rifles, and to my wife Ruth.

I also wish to thank Mr. Leonard Mosley for permission to quote from his book, *The Last Days of the Raj.*

Foreword

This is not a history of the Indian Army or of the British Army in India; no attempt is made here to tell the story of every war and campaign on India's frontiers, or to tell of the many engagements of the Indian Army outside India throughout the period bracketed by the Indian Mutiny and the partition of India into independent Pakistan and India. I have tried to illustrate, sometimes through little known incidents, some of the characteristics of the soldiers in India—Indian, Nepalese and British—and to describe a few of the historical events which shaped their lives through changes in organization, recruiting, arms, equipment and morale.

I have retained the old, more familiar spellings. We English speakers still call Roma Rome, Firenze Florence, Praha Prague, and Moskva Moscow. There seemed no compelling reason to change Lucknow to Laknao or Peking to Beijing.*

In the last half of the nineteenth century and the early part of this century those Europeans who had lived long in India were called Anglo-Indians; as the number of children

---

* The "A" in Roman Urdu script is pronounced "soft," e.g., "Laknao" is "Lucknow" and spelled as such. On the other hand, "Bangladesh" is properly pronounced "Bungladesh." Throughout the book, unless the "U" spelling is used (e.g., "Ahmednugger"), the "A" should be pronounced "U"; e.g., "Darsi" (meaning "tailor") is "Dursi," "Razmak" in Waziristan is "Ruzmuk," "Tank" is "Tonk," and "Daffadar" (equivalent to Sergeant) is pronounced "Duffadar."

of mixed European and Indian parentage increased and grew to occupy increasingly important niches in the social structure, they, too, were called Anglo-Indians. To avoid confusion and misunderstanding, the term "English-Indian" or "British-Indian" is here usually used for the former, except in quoted extracts.

The Indian subcontinent which Britain once ruled is now (1989) divided into three countries—India, Pakistan and Bangladesh—or four, if one counts Burma as having been part of British India; there may come to be even more if Sikhs, Pathans and other discontented communal groups have their way. A somewhat expanded Aden is also a separate country: its official name is the People's Democratic Republic of Yemen, but it is popularly called South Yemen, although most of the country is north of the Yemen Arabic Republic, which is popularly called North Yemen. We live in a confusing world. But then the world has always been a confusing place.

Introduction

F or most of recorded time much of India has been ruled by aliens. Successive waves of invaders have swept into it, usually from the north-east—Bactrian Greeks, Scythians, Persians and Turks. Early in the sixteenth century a descendant of Tamerlane and Genghis Khan, Zahīr-ud-Dīn Muhammad (1483–1530), better known as Babur (or Baber or Babar), led a Mongol army into India from Afghanistan, occupied Delhi and Agra, extended his power eastward, and founded the Mogul dynasty, which was still extant when a little noticed event occurred in distant London.

On 31 December 1600 Queen Elizabeth I by Royal Charter incorporated a trading company for "The Governor and Company of Merchants of London trading into the East Indies," and thus was founded that remarkable establishment which became the Honourable East India Company. Granted the exclusive right to trade with all the countries beyond the Cape of Good Hope for fifteen years, the company, with one hundred and twenty-five shareholders and a capital of £72,000, was a success from the start.

In 1609 King James I renewed the Company's charter "for ever," though with the proviso that it could be revoked on three years notice. Within the next two years the first "factories," i.e., trading stations, were established on the mainland of India, on the Bay of Bengal. Soon two ships a month were offloading exotic cargoes in English ports. Profits were sometimes as high as 200 percent, but they were not always easily earned for the commercial aggression of the English was much resented by the Dutch, who claimed prior rights. At times actual warfare was waged between the Dutch and English traders.

In 1619, when the Netherlands and Britain signed a "treaty of defence," the eastern fleets of the two nations dutifully dressed their ships: flags were flown, yardarms were manned, and salutes were fired. For the space of an hour peace reigned. The ceremonies over, the rivals took up the fight as bitterly as before.

The French and Portuguese were competitors as well, and throughout the seventeenth century the British company struggled to claw its way to a dominant position. Originally it was required to confine its trading to the coast, but in 1634 the Great Mogul granted the English permission to trade throughout Bengal. King Charles I muddied the waters by licensing a rival company, but under Cromwell the two companies were amalgamated. Later, the new, expanded Company acquired almost sovereign powers when Charles II gave it the right to coin money, command forts, raise an army, form alliances, make war and peace, and exercise criminal and civil jurisdictions. In 1668 he presented it with the newly acquired island of Bombay.

By the end of the seventeenth century several British trading companies, known as interlopers, were challenging the right of the Crown to establish a monopoly in the East, but in the early eighteenth century all were amalgamated and the East India Company reigned supreme. A Court of Directors, a committee of twenty-four, ruled over it from India House in Leadenhall Street, London.

After the death of Aurungzeb, sixth Mogul emperor of Hindustan, in 1707, India began a slide into anarchy, and many ambitious, strong governors transmuted their provinces into independent states and themselves into rajas. The Company seized the opportunity to acquire as many pieces of the old empire as it conveniently could, but it faced competition within and without India, not only for trade but for dominion. Inevitably the Company's officers found themselves entangled in Indian politics.

As long as the East India Company had concerned itself primarily with trade, it had received no interference from the Crown, but when Clive's great victory over a treacherous Nawab of Bengal at Plassey in 1757 made it a ruling power in India, Parliament decided to exercise some control. In 1773 it raised the governor in Bengal, Warren Hastings, to the rank of Governor-General, and although the Governor-General continued to be appointed by the Court of Directors, usually for a five-year term, his appointment was thereafter subject to approval by the Crown. Legislative power was vested in the Governor-General and his council, but a supreme court was established whose judges were appointed by the Crown. In 1784 the government appointed a Board of Control in London to supervise military, political and financial matters, and in 1813 the Board was given authority over the Company's commercial transactions as well. In 1858, following the Great Indian Mutiny, the rule of the Honourable East India Company ended and its domain passed into the care of Her Majesty's Government, becoming a part of the still growing British Empire. The Governor-General took on the additional title of Viceroy of India and became answerable to a Secretary of State for India, who was a member of the Cabinet and responsible to Parliament.*

There was never a legal or constitutional basis for the British Empire. It was a fiction with just enough reality to make it believable. Just as gold has value only because people think it has, so the Empire had substance only because people believed that it had. In reality it was, as Jan Smuts said, merely "a system of nations," a mixed bag of domin-

---

* In 1865, when India and England became linked by a direct telegraph line overland via Teheran, the independence and power of the Viceroy was eroded. Five years later, when London was linked by cable to Bombay via Suez, the control of the Secretary of State for India over the Viceroy became immediate and complete.

ions, protectorates, dependencies and colonies—plus India, which was none of these. By 1860 the degree of control exercised by Parliament in London over the various parts of the Empire varied considerably, from very little in the case of Canada to a great deal indeed for India.

For convenience the British raj is here considered to have begun when the Crown replaced the Company in November 1858. Actually, before this date the word *raj*, meaning "rule," was rarely used—although there were *rajas*, rulers, and *maharajas*, great rulers. The Indian word *sirkar* or *sarcar*, meaning "government," was usually employed by Indians and Britons alike, and it continued to be used under the Crown.

From the early days of the East India Company, when it first required some soldiers as guards, until 1 November 1858, when the armies, soldiers, civil servants, powers and territories of the Honourable East India Company were transferred to the Crown, the Indian Army, the largest mercenary army in the world, was the property of a chartered British company, and in large part it was engaged in expanding the boundaries of the Company's property.

By 1858 the area under British rule or protection was enormous: nearly 1.6 million square miles (six times larger than Texas; eighteen times larger than the United Kingdom). Under the Company, most of British India had been divided into three parts, called presidencies; these were maintained for forty years after the transfer of power to the Crown. Each had its own governor and its own army under its own commander-in-chief. The Bengal Presidency, with its capital at Calcutta, was the largest, and its chief, entitled the Governor-General of India, had, in theory, general supervision over the governors of the Madras and Bombay presidencies. Although the commander-in-chief of the Bengal Army was termed the Commander-in-Chief, India, he exercised little control over the commanders-in-chief of the Bombay and Madras armies. Thus, prior to the amalgamation of the presidential armies, the "Indian Army" was an abstraction. In the days when communications were slow, this division of an immense territory, with near-autonomous governors and military commanders, made sense.

As British rule expanded and fresh provinces were added, mostly in the Bengal Presidency, they were placed under chief commissioners or lieutenant-governors. In 1862, British Burma was put under a chief commissioner, and in 1897, after more of the country had been conquered, under a lieutenant-governor. Ceylon (today's Sri Lanka) became a Crown colony administered by the Colonial Office, but the Andaman Islands and the little enclave of Aden on the Red Sea were placed under the Indian government. Under the British raj, all local governments were financially controlled by the Viceroy.

Under the Company and under the Crown provinces were divided into districts, each about the size of an English county, administered by district officers, often remarkably young men, numbers of whom were seconded from the Indian Army. Many exercised enormous powers, and if they were conscientious, as most of them appear to have been, they came as close to knowing and understanding the people of India as was possible for a European. In a culture where power was customarily used to bilk the peasants, an honest British administrator—and nearly all were honest—often took on demigod status and was looked up to as the "supreme incarnation of power, wisdom and goodness." John Nicholson, "Lion of the Punjab," was actually apotheosized by a brotherhood of fakirs in Hazara, who took to worshipping "Nikkul Seyn." Nicholson, who did not conceal his distaste for Indians, ordered some of his worshippers imprisoned and whipped, without shaking the steadfastness of their devotion.

ARMIES OF THE RAJ

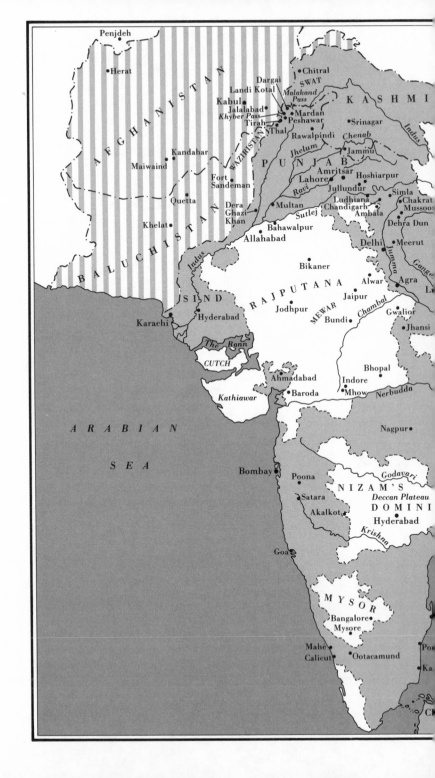

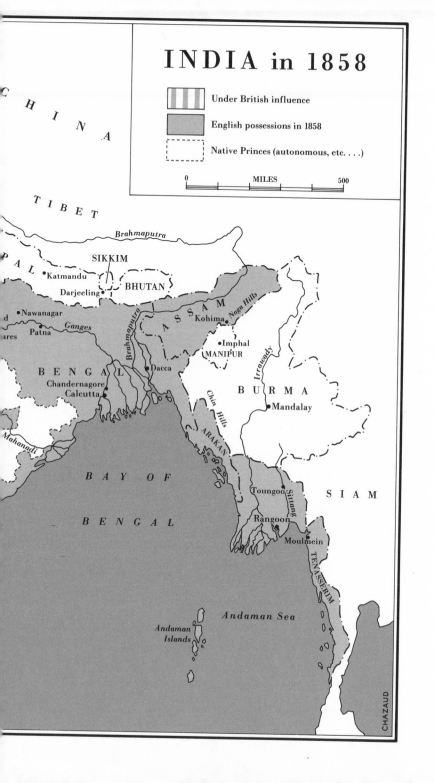

INDIA in 1858

|||||| Under British influence

▓ English possessions in 1858

⌐ ¬ Native Princes (autonomous, etc. . . .)
└ ┘

0   MILES   500

CHINA

TIBET

Brahmaputra

SIKKIM

•Katmandu   BHUTAN

Darjeeling•

•Nawanagar   ASSAM   Kohima•   Naga Hills

Patna   Ganges   Imphal
ares   •   MANIPUR

Brahmaputra   Irrawady

BENGAL   •Dacca   BURMA

Chandernagore   •Mandalay
Calcutta•

Chin Hills

Mahanadi   ARAKAN

BAY OF   Toungoo•   Siitang   SIAM

BENGAL   Rangoon•

Moulmein•   TENASSERIM

Andaman Sea

Andaman
Islands

CHAZAUD

1

The Great Indian Army

M ajor Stringer Lawrence, who formed the first military units of the East India Company in Madras in 1748, is regarded as the father of the Indian Army, an army which became, in the words of Major George MacMunn in 1911, "one of the marvels of modern times." Soon after Major Lawrence's initial efforts in Madras, the other two presidencies formed their own armies. Bengal, which eventually developed the largest army, began with "an ensign and thirty men" plus "a gunner and his crew"; in Madras, companies were formed from doorkeepers and watchmen; and the beginnings of the Bombay Army arrived as a detachment sent to garrison the fort there when Bombay passed to the British as part of the dowry Catherine of Braganza brought to her marriage to Charles II.

Because of the great distances separating the capitals of the three presidencies, their armies developed separately along different lines, but all were initially a mixture of sailors who had jumped ship, men from disbanded French units, Swiss, Hanoverians, prisoners of war, and "any other white material in search of a livelihood."

In the same year that Major Lawrence formed his first

companies of Europeans, the French in India raised several battalions of Indian troops. Soon after, the British did the same. In 1754 the first British regulars, the 39th Foot, arrived, and so began that strange amalgamation of the East India Company's Indian Army, composed of both European and Indian troops and Royal British regulars who were, in effect, rented from the Crown and constituted the British Army in India. All—British and Indian, Company and Royal troops—were officered by Britons.

More or less constant wars with the French, the Mahrattas and with Mysore led to the growth of the presidential armies. The fall of Pondichéry, the French enclave on the Coromandel Coast, in 1793 ended French expansion in India; and although Pondichéry was later restored to France, captured again in 1803 and again restored, by the end of the eighteenth century France had ceased to be a major threat.

Lord Cornwallis (1738–1805), defeated by the American revolutionaries and their French allies at Yorktown, Virginia, in 1781, found victory in India, defeating Tippoo (or Tipu) Sahib, the "Lion of Mysore," at Seringapatam in 1791 and depriving him of half his realm. He then began a general restructuring of the Company's Indian armies, based on European models; even so, for another century each presidential army continued to go its own way, retaining its own characteristics and developing its own traditions.

The British finally managed to prise the Dutch, Portuguese and French from India's shores or to reduce their holdings to minor enclaves. One by one the Indian states were absorbed into British India or reduced to feudatory status. This was possible in large part because the British learned two important facts: that Indians taken into the Company's armies were readily amenable to military discipline and that small but well-disciplined bodies of European-trained troops could defeat larger, undisciplined native forces. Indian peasants of all creeds, customs and temperament were, prior to the Great Mutiny, drilled and trained to European standards and introduced to the constrictions of stiff, uncomfortable European-style uniforms.

Termed "His Excellency" and with the resounding title of "Commander-in-Chief, India," the head of the Bengal Army was supposed to exercise supervisory control over the armies of Madras and Bombay, but he had minimal influence outside Bengal. Prior to 1886 he had no authority over the Punjab Irregular (later Frontier) Field Force—known as the "Piffers"—on the North-West Frontier, which was controlled by the Lieutenant-Governor of the Punjab. Also, of course, he had no direct control over the armies of the princely states. In fact, no officer exercised control over all of the Indian land forces.

In order of precedence the Commander-in-Chief, India, ranked second only to the Governor-General, who was his sole superior, for he did not report to the Commander-in-Chief of the British Army at the Horse Guards in London. His pay was a lakh (100,000) of rupees* per annum, making him the highest paid British soldier in the Empire. Commanders-in-Chief were usually selected from senior generals in the British regular army. (Between 1822 and 1930 only seven out of twenty-three came from the Indian Army.)

As in the British Army, most staff work in the presidential armies was undertaken by two prinicipal staff officers: the Quartermaster General (QMG) and the Adjutant-General (AG). At the highest level these were major-generals; the deputies (DQMG and DAG) were usually colonels; and the deputy assistants (DAQMG and DAAG) were majors. Adjutants were responsible for discipline, training, and administration; quartermasters were responsible for the gear, equipment, barracks, and other necessities. The commanders-in-chief of the Madras and Bombay armies were usually one rank below that of the Commander-in-Chief, India; their staffs were smaller and one grade lower in rank.

---

* A rupee was worth about 1/10 of a pound until 1870, when it began steadily to fall, reaching a low of 1/20 of a pound in the 1890s. Then it stabilized at 1/15 of a pound (about a dime), which it held until Independence in 1947.

There were four distinguishing features of the Indian Army under the raj: its soldiers were always all volunteers; it used a unique tier of ranks for Indian officers; after the Mutiny it organized and administered its cavalry regiments on what was called an "irregular" system; and each of its combatant units carried with it an enormous number of civilian servants and followers.

Not even in Britain's darkest days during World War II was conscription considered for the Indian Army. There was never the need. It enjoyed such prestige and soldiering was regarded as such an honourable, even profitable, profession that recruiting was seldom a problem and desertions were rare events. Old soldiers who retired to their villages with their small pensions were admired and respected, even envied. When, during World War II, the favoured classes, the so-called martial races, could not produce enough men and enlistment was opened to nearly all castes, races and religions, the sirkar (Indian government) was able to raise an army of more than two million men—the largest all-volunteer army in the history of the world.

The special tier of ranks for the Indian Army constituted a category of officers found in no other army in the world. Indian officers, called "native" officers before the Mutiny, afterwards were renamed Viceroy's Commissioned Officers (VCOs), indicating that their commissions came from the Viceroy rather than the British sovereign. They formed a vital link between British officers and Indian other ranks. The oldest and most senior VCOs ranked below the most junior British officer, but they carried swords, were saluted by other ranks and addressed as "sahib."*

There were three levels of VCO ranks, and their titles varied. In the cavalry the senior officer was the rissaldar-major and in the infantry he was the subedar-major; there was one to each battalion of infantry or regiment of cav-

---

* The present Indian Army has retained this tier of authority; such officers are now called junior commissioned officers.

alry. Both wore a crown as their badge of rank, as did a major in the British Army or Indian Army. Although junior to British subalterns, the senior Indian officer enjoyed enormous prestige. For the young soldiers he served as the village patriarch; for the commanding officer he was an adviser on Indian customs and personnel matters. He was treated with respect by junior British officers, who addressed him as "sahib" and took care not to offend him.

Next in rank were the rissaldars in the cavalry and subedars in the infantry, who commanded companies of infantry and troops, sometimes squadrons, of cavalry; they wore two stars as their insignia of rank. Below them, in both cavalry and infantry, were jemadars, who wore a single star and served as platoon leaders or assistant squadron commanders. One VCO usually served as assistant quartermaster and another an assistant adjutant; the latter, whatever his rank, was known as the woordy (or wurrdy) major. Many ambitious young British officers found service in the Indian Army attractive because the work of the VCOs, tasks performed by subalterns elsewhere, allowed junior officers to be given far more responsibilities than their rank would otherwise have enjoyed.

Noncommissioned officer ranks resembled a simplified British system, although different names were used for each grade. The senior noncommissioned officer in the cavalry was the daffadar-major and in the infantry the havildar-major, a rank corresponding to sergeant-major. In the infantry, sergeants were called havildars, corporals were naiks, and lance corporals were lance naiks. The equivalent ranks in the cavalry were daffadar, lance daffadar, and unpaid lance daffadar. Troopers were called sowars and privates were sepoys.*

Strictly speaking, there were no warrant officers or noncommissioned ranks above havildar or daffadar; all higher ranks were appointments. Although additional pay was

---

* See Appendix A for a table of ranks and badges.

given for a battalion quartermaster havildar or a company havildar-major, these grades were not substantive. A havildar or daffadar could be reduced only by a court-martial, but his appointment could be terminated at the discretion of the commanding officer. Positions such as drum major, mess havildar, colour havildar, bugle naik and kote naik* were also appointments.

The first Indians to obtain the King's Commission were doctors who, in 1912, were permitted to hold regular commissions in the Indian Medical Service of the Indian Army. Not until 1917 were Indians admitted to the Royal Military College, Sandhurst, and not until 1918 were Indians given commissions in the combatant arms. VCOs were always promoted from the ranks and were usually elderly men who had spent their lives in a single regiment. Their grasp of English was uncertain, if they spoke it at all, and many came from the lower ranks of Indian society. It was not men of this stamp who were expected to hold a King's Commission; they were unlikely even to desire entrance to the British officers' mess as subalterns. The King's Commissions for Indians were designed for "selected representatives of families of fighting classes which have rendered valuable services to the State during the war." A reward for services rendered, such commissions were not part of an Indianization program—that came a few years later.

Most Indian cavalry regiments were raised and maintained by the "silladar" system. (The word *silladar* comes from the Persian and means "bearer of arms.") Originally, regiments of irregular horse were raised by enlisting men who applied for service with their own horses. Each was paid a sum calculated to cover the feeding of himself and his horse with something left over for a salary. The sirkar provided only weapons and ammunition. Such recruits were

---

* Arms and ammunition were kept in locked racks or armories called "kotes." The kote naik, or kote havildar, was the noncommissioned officer responsible for the issue and receipt of weapons and ammunition.

usually wealthier than the peasants who enlisted in the infantry and many were the sons of landowners. Some were of such standing that they rode in with as many as fifty retainers, their bargirs, whom they had provided with horses; they thus became military contractors supplying recruits. This was the original silladar system, but by the 1860s it had evolved into something rather more complicated.

As all of the regular Bengal cavalry regiments had either mutinied or been disbanded as being suspected of disaffection in 1857–58, they were replaced by irregular units, mostly from the Punjab, using the silladar system, but bargirs were no longer permitted. The system proved popular, and by 1903 only three light cavalry regiments in the Madras Army were non-silladar.

In most regiments the silladar system worked in this fashion: Each regiment was assigned so many places or slots, usually about eight hundred, and these were known as *asamis*. For each asami, the sirkar paid a certain sum each month. This would be drawn by the holder or owner of the asami, who might be the sowar himself, or who might be a retired soldier, a moneylender, or a widow who paid a sowar to serve. Sometimes a rissaldar or jemadar might own several asamis and mount his sons or nephews. This system was abolished in 1871.

The regiment became in some ways similar to a family business as sons succeeded fathers—and this was true of British officers as well as Indian other ranks. It also grew to be almost a private company with a variety of operating funds. In some regiments a sowar would be assigned a horse, which he then purchased by monthly payments, one of many "cuttings" taken out of his pay. If a horse not on active service died, the sowar was responsible. If a horse was killed in battle, the regiment supplied a new one from a special fund to which all contributed.

The colonel of such a regiment had to be a good accountant and businessman, for from the lump sum given him he had to procure fodder, uniforms, food and all else except arms and ammunition. Some regiments, through good luck and wise management, became rich and were superbly mounted and dressed. Probyn's Horse and Fane's Horse (later 11th and 19th Bengal Lancers) were said to have made fortunes through loot acquired in the China War of 1859–60. The 11th Bengal Lancers even had its own horse-breeding farm.

Although uniforms varied, those of silladar regiments were loose and comfortable, well suited to the climate and the habits of the troopers; dress uniforms were gorgeous. 1st Skinner's Horse, the senior regiment, wore canary yellow kirtas or jackets, the only unit in the army to wear that colour. Fewer British officers were assigned to silladar than to non-silladar regiments, sometimes only three or four— the commanding officer (commandant), second-in-command, adjutant, and perhaps a medical officer—but discipline was usually strict; in units such as Jacob's Horse it was comparable to that of the Horse Guards.

Only three regiments were of a single class composition: 1st Skinner's Horse, composed entirely of Muslims from Hindustan and the southern Punjab; 14th Murray's Horse, composed of Jats; and 15th Curetan's Multanis, which enlisted only Pathans from Multan and related neighbouring classes. In all other regiments only squadrons were composed of men from one social, racial, or religious class. In the cavalry the principal classes were Sikhs, Dogras, Pathans, Punjabi Muslims (PMs), Rajputs, and Hindustani or Dekhani Muslims, each readily distinguished by its method of tying its lungis (turbans).

British officers assigned to Indian cavalry assumed considerable responsibilities and were inclined to regard themselves as an elite group. Lieutenant-Colonel M. A. R. Skinner, a descendant of the Anglo-Indian founder of Skinner's Horse and himself once its commandant, wrote: "Basically, by virtue of being a small corps, the Indian Cavalry were a tight knit body, whose officers knew each

The two horsemen are (l. to r.) a daffadar of the 13th Duke of Connaught's Bengal Lancers in marching order and a sowar of the 15th (Fane's Horse) Bengal Lancers in service dress. Standing are (l. to r.) a native officer of the Queen's Own Corps of Guides in full dress, a sepoy of the 4th Gurkha Rifles in marching order, a sowar of 45th Rattray's Sikhs in full dress, a sowar of the 3rd Bengal Cavalry in field service dress, a sowar of the 1st Punjab Cavalry in full dress, a sepoy of the 1st Sikh Infantry in full dress, a sepoy of the Viceroy's Bodyguard in full dress, a native officer of the 18th Bengal Infantry in full dress, a sowar of the 15th Multani Cavalry in full dress, and a sowar of the 1st Bengal Cavalry in full dress. (National Army Museum)

other well by constant meetings, either sporting or military. These conditions produced a life-style fundamentally different from other arms of the Indian Army." Differences were sometimes deliberately accentuated. One colonel refused to permit his men to march in step when dismounted, reasoning that this was alien to the cavalry spirit.

Others arms and services did not universally admire the cavalry. A fusilier subaltern named his tom cat "Indian Cavalry" because, he said, the cat spent his life eating, sleeping, playing games, and fornicating.

After seven years service noncommissioned officers and certain specialists were allowed to re-enlist for another five years. Then, if they were lucky, they might be permitted to re-engage for a further six years. If they were promoted and became rissaldars or jemadars, they could serve for twenty-five years; rissaldar-majors for two years more. One of the severest punishments which could be given a sowar was dismissal, a humiliation and a disgrace.

Sowars were often allowed to take their horses home when they went on furlough, though this was not always a happy arrangement. A sowar of Skinner's Horse who was the proud possessor of a splendid white horse, while on furlough loaned his charger to a friend for a wedding. For the happy occasion the horse was painted with large spots of vibrant green, red and yellow. Unfortunately, after the ceremony, the paint resisted all efforts to remove it. The fury of the wretched sowar's squadron commander is unrecorded but can easily be imagined.

The silladar system, which worked so well in peace-time, for internal security and for fighting on the North-West Frontier, broke down when wars were long and distant. During World War I regiments sent to France and the Middle East, far from their sources of men, horses, and special foods, were unable to maintain themselves. Replacements for fallen officers were nearly impossible to find. Britons who knew the right languages and the customs of the sowars, as well as the peculiarities of the silladar system, were few.

Not long after World War I, in the early 1920s, it was decided to abandon the silladar system and at the same time to economize by drastically reducing the number of cavalry regiments to little more than half of the pre-war establishment, from thirty-nine to twenty-one. This was done by allowing three regiments to remain whole: the 27th and

28th Light Cavalry, which were the oldest cavalry regiments in the Indian Army, and the cavalry of the Corps of Guides, a frontier regiment which had before contained both cavalry and infantry. The remaining regiments were paired off and ordered to amalgamate and produce single, nonsilladar cavalry regiments. When this was done, the twenty-one regiments were arranged into seven groups of three regiments each and the class composition of all regiments was adjusted so that the three regiments in each of the seven groups became identical in their class composition. As a further blow to the instincts and pride of the old cavalrymen, one of the three regiments in each group was to serve as little more than a depot and training center.

So ended the silladar system. Gone, too, except for ceremonial purposes, were the lances with their colourful pennons. Sowars were trained to fight as mounted infantry with the short Lee Enfield .303 magazine rifle. The next world war saw the demise of the horse in battle, but "cavalry" regiments continued to recruit from those classes which had produced the best horsemen, even though, except to train polo ponies, their skills were no longer required.

The ratio of cavalry to infantry in India tended to be high during most of the raj. In 1800 there were eight regiments of cavalry to fifty-nine battalions of infantry, a ratio of one to seven and a half. By 1824 this ratio had increased to one cavalry regiment to five and two-thirds infantry battalions, and on the eve of World War I, when they were least needed, the ratio was one to three and a half. After the war the proportion became more reasonable, falling to one to six and a half.

Part and parcel of the Indian Army was the number of noncombatants who were integrated into all units, the crowds of civilians who followed units on the march, even accompanying them to war, and the number of non-integrated followers who were attached to each cantonment. These included servants, traders, artisans, prostitutes, soldiers' families—a vast separate army that far outnumbered the soldiers themselves. Rudyard Kipling's "Gunga Din" has made the regimental bhisti (water carrier) famous. And justly so. One Indian Army officer wrote: "I have never heard of a grumbling, or impatient, or morose bhisti, or of one whose name has been associated actively or passively with violence, or provocation, or crime."

Swarms of servants and helpers, including *langris* (cooks), *mehtahs* (sweepers and latrine cleaners), *darzis* (tailors), *mochis* (cobblers), and *syces* (grooms) were employed. In World War I many of these even accompanied their units to Mesopotamia and to France, and the *drabi* and *kahar* (stretcher bearers) were elevated to combatant status and became eligible for decorations.

The batteries of Royal Artillery in India were the only units to have Indians and British mixed in the same unit, for the gun *lascars* and drivers were Indian soldiers. Of course, this destroyed much of the raison d'être for keeping the artillery in British hands, for if the Indian drivers deserted or mutinied, taking their horses, the guns could not be moved.

Just as regular army units have chaplains, so each regiment of the Indian Army had its religious instructor: maulvis for Muslims, pandits for Hindus and granthis for Sikhs. In a mixed regiment all three might be present. Except when their unit was on active service, they were not subject to military law, but a commanding officer could dismiss them.

Each regiment had its own contractor who was responsible for organizing the bazaar at each station and at each camp site. Before World War I they marched with the regiment and regularly set up shop to supply the troops with necessities and little luxuries. After that war they no longer accompanied troops on active service but continued to go as far as frontier stations in tribal territories.

Although the Commissariat Department of the Indian Army was responsible for the supply of food, fodder, fuel, bedding and clothing, no integrated system for the maintenance of troops in the field existed; even when in cantonments, units normally made their own local arrangements for food. On active service, the commissariat supplied basic rations, but these were generally supplemented from local sources purchased through the regimental bazaars and paid for by deductions from the sepoy's pay or by the sepoy himself, who usually prepared and cooked his own meals.

The diet of Indian soldiers varied greatly, depending upon where the men came from and the taboos of their religion, but staple ingredients included *atta* (a kind of flour), *dahl* (pulse or lentils), *bhat* (rice) and *ghi* (clarified butter). British soldiers ate large quantities of beef, but when meat was issued to those Indian troops who were not vegetarian, it was mutton or goat. European-style bread was supplied to British troops, but most Indians preferred chapatties (unleavened bread).

In spite of its importance in every campaign, the Indian Army had no permanent transport until 1884. (Five years later the Transport and Commissariat departments amalgamated into what was popularly called the "Rice Corps" and more British officers were assigned. Eventually this became the Royal Indian Army Service Corps.) Whenever a move was contemplated or a campaign begun, units had to hire whatever kind of transport they could find. Such arrangements made the marching order of any unit, British or Indian, a colourful spectacle that could include camels, elephants, donkeys, mules, ponies, bullocks, carts and wagons of every description, as well as drivers, mahouts, and long lines of men and women carrying goods on their heads or shoulders. As animals and people travelled at different speeds,* the elements of a column could stretch over many miles of roads.

The British Army in India was dependent upon the Indian Army for supporting arms (except artillery) and for administrative services. The Indian Army relied on the Royal

---

* On good, dry, level roads, infantry averaged 3 mph, cavalry 7 mph, pack mules and ponies 5 mph, camels, pack bullocks and coolies 2 mph, and bullock carts and pack donkeys 1½ mph.

Regiment of Artillery for guns; engineer and signal officers, unlike the cavalry and infantry officers, were not part of the Indian Army but were seconded to it for limited terms, as were some specialist British warrant officers and noncommissioned officers.

Until 1940, infantry brigades were almost always ad hoc formations and were usually formed by combining two or three battalions of Indian infantry with one battalion of British infantry of the line. (Guards regiments never served in India.)

British military hospitals were staffed by medical officers and noncommissioned officers of the Royal Army Medical Corps and by nurses from Queen Alexandra's Indian Military Nursing Service. Assistant surgeons and menials came from the Indian Hospital Corps. Indian military hospitals had both British and Indian medical officers from the Indian Medical Services, sub-assistants from the Indian Medical Department and nurses from the Indian Military Nursing Service. Even after they received the King's Commission, Indian doctors were forbidden to examine European women. In at least one instance a pregnant officer's wife was examined behind a screen by a British orderly following the oral instructions of an Indian medical officer. British arrogancy and complacency was such that most Britons saw nothing odd in such a procedure. Not until 1857 and the outbreak of the Great Mutiny was that complacency shaken, and the shock was all the greater because of what was perceived as a sudden, almost instantaneous eruption.

Only a little more than a year earlier Lord Canning, just before leaving London to take up his duties as Governor-General of India, made a prophetic statement: "We must not forget that in the sky of India, serene as it is, a small cloud may arise, at first no bigger than a man's hand, but which, growing bigger and bigger, may at last threaten to overwhelm us with ruin." At the time, however, such a cloud was discernible to almost no one, and the steady buildup of discontent in the Bengal Army went undetected.

The spark that ignited the tinder was the issuance of cartridges (which had to be bitten open) that were greased with substances made from the fat of cattle or pigs, the former being abhorrent to Hindus and the latter to Muslims. It was a stupid, administrative mistake, but the sepoys and sowars of the Bengal Army, many of whom were Brahmans, did not think so. They thought it was an attempt to suborn them from their faith.

Many Indians, not only soldiers, were disturbed by the increasing number of Christian missionaries who had come to India to convert the heathen. To make India a Christian country was the avowed ambition of numerous zealots, and some officers joined them in their religious zeal: the colonel of the 34th Bengal Native Infantry freely admitted that he tried to convert his sepoys. And few British officials scrupled to pull down a temple or mosque if it stood in the way of a telegraph line or a new road.

Officers had grown distant from their men and had grown careless of their trust. One old subedar complained: "I know that many officers nowadays only speak to their men when obliged to do so, and they show that the business is irksome and try to get rid of the sepoys as quickly as possible." Many officers, even colonels of regiments and battalions, were so ignorant of the feelings of their men that they refused to believe their loyalty had eroded. Some of these officers were killed by their own troops, even by their own orderlies.

Many grievances, great and small, had gone unattended. Men no longer fit for duty were not pensioned but required to work in the cantonment. When it was decided that soldiers should be required to pay postage on their letters, another grievance was added. Extra pay (batta) was given when Indian soldiers served outside of British territory, but as soon as the new territory they had won was annexed, the batta was stopped, a difference in status that the sepoy found difficult to understand.

The first serious rising was at the large cantonment of Meerut, when eighty-five sowars of the 3rd Light Cavalry refused to accept what they believed (wrongly) were the new polluting cartridges. They were court-martialled and all were sentenced to ten years of hard labour. (Eleven of the youngest had this sentence reduced to five years.) On 9 May 1857 they were paraded before the entire garrison of seventeen hundred British and Indian troops, the British carrying loaded muskets. Their uniforms and boots were taken from them and they were fettered with chains. The next morning, while the British were at church, the remaining sowars of the 3rd Light Cavalry with the sepoys of the 11th and 20th Bengal Native Infantry mutinied. They freed the prisoners and set out to murder every European in sight. Before the British could collect their wits, the mutineers marched to Delhi, where they were reinforced by others as regiment after regiment of cavalry and battalion after battalion of infantry joined the rising.

Not all Indian units of the Bengal Army rose. The Gurkhas and many Sikh units remained "true to their salt" and the mutineers received little support from Indian princes or the civilians in the villages, but the mutineers were strong enough to capture Delhi, Cawnpore, Lucknow and other cities, and it took the British a year and a half of vicious, no-quarter fighting to restore order in northern India.

It was natural, then, that at Mutiny's end there should be a shake-up. The reorganization that resulted was the first of four major changes the Indian Army underwent before the end of the British raj. In 1895 the three presidential armies which had constituted the Indian Army were abolished and were replaced by four area commands: the Punjab, which included the Frontier Force; Madras, including Burma; Bombay, which took in Sind and Baluchistan; and Bengal. Each was commanded by a lieutenant-general who reported directly to the Commander-in-Chief, India. In 1902 Lord Kitchener instituted sweeping changes, including the renumbering of regiments, and he wiped out the last vestiges of the old presidential armies. Kitchener's tenure as Commander-in-Chief (28 November 1902–10 September 1909) was so dramatic and traumatic that its shock was felt far beyond the Indian Army and it must be given a chapter of its own.

The last major upheaval before World War II occurred in 1922, when the sirkar's insistence on saving money caused major reductions in personnel and a degradation in the quality of arms and equipment. It was at this time that infantry battalions were linked together in groups of six, one of which acted as the training battalion and administrative unit for the others. It was this framework which held the army together for the remainder of the raj.

There remained many anomalies in the Indian Army, and many garrisons were stuck in out-of-the-way places—such as the Andaman Islands, which were used as a penal colony on the order of France's Devil's Island, and Aden, which was administered from India. The 33rd Punjabis once spent a year in Somaliland fighting a "Mad Mullah." The second oldest unit in the Indian Army was the Escort for His (and Her) Britannic Majesty's Envoy Extraordinary and Minister Plenipotentiary at the Court of Nepal. The Escort was first raised in 1816 and consisted of one company. It lasted until the end of the raj, when it consisted of seventy-five men, all Brahmans or Rajputs.

While this handful of Indian soldiers served in Nepal, thousands of Nepalese from certain tribes in eastern Nepal, called Gurkhas in the Indian and British armies, served—and still serve—as mercenaries in India. Under the raj they were officered only by selected British officers and their regiments were numbered separately from all others.

Since 1816 they have fought on the side of the British in every major and most minor wars. Their reputation for bravery and loyalty to their foreign masters has earned them the highest military reputation. When the very best troops were required, the request was often for "British or Gurkha."

The weakness of the Indian Army as a fighting force

emerged in World War I. It had existed simply as little more than a collection of infantry battalions (600–1,000 men) or cavalry regiments (300–600 men), with squadrons and companies of differing class composition, eating different food and speaking different languages. The logistics and personnel requirements became too complex and there were no experienced higher staffs to cope. The unique Indian Army had grown too peculiar.

2

From Company to Crown

The mutiny in the Bengal Army that shook the British Empire in 1857–58 was not, as many Indian writers now claim, a mass rising of the Indian people to throw off the British yoke. Indian patriots sometimes refer to the Mutiny as the "First Indian War of Independence," and this was the title of a book of essays by Marx and Engels published in Moscow in 1860. To hold such a view, to believe that hundreds of millions of Indians, more than 100,000 of whom were armed and trained soldiers, could not easily have overcome fewer than 200,000 civilian men, women and children who were protected by only 60,000 British bayonets, is either to credit Britain with a far greater military puissance than it was capable of exercising or shamefully to discredit the puissance and capabilities of the Indian peoples.

It was, as Dr. Tara Chand wrote in a history of the Independence movement in India, "a transient intoxication and not a settled permanent transformation of the will of the people." So far was the Mutiny from a general uprising that the British never lacked for recruits or for willing Indian hands to assist in its suppression. Indeed, as George MacMunn, an old India soldier and scholar, pointed out (1911): "It is only necessary for a feeling to arise that it is impious and disgraceful to serve the British, for the whole of our fabric to tumble like a house of cards without a shot being fired or a sword unsheathed." Such was indeed the case just thirty-one years later. The notion of nationhood for all of India scarcely existed in nineteenth-century India. There was not, and still has never been, a united India under Indian rule. In the Victorian era, personal identification with a tribe, a religion or a caste was far more meaningful than national sentiments.

During the Mutiny the mutineers did not look for political guidance from modern democratic systems of government, but backward to the Mogul Empire. The first mutineers ran to Delhi to seek out leaders among the descendants of the last Mogul emperor. They sought a king, not an elected president.

The causes of the Mutiny were not political and they were not of concern to all Indians; they were inherent in the Bengal Army itself. The armies of the other two presidencies, Madras and Bombay, were scarcely affected and even many regiments in the Bengal Army remained "true to their salt." Except in the province of Oudh (today part of Uttar Pradesh) the mutineers received scant support from the civilian population. Most peasants in their villages feared equally the depredations of the mutineers and the fury of the British.

Of the more than five hundred Indian princes, only a handful saw political advantage in siding with the disgruntled Bengal soldiery. Indeed, the Mutiny fostered in the British an increasingly friendly attitude towards the princes who, taken together, were seen as a valuable bulwark against future emeutes.

The Mutiny began at Meerut on 10 May 1857 and may be said to have effectively ended with the fall of Gwalior on

20 June 1858. Soon after, in language that was generous to their employees and complimentary to themselves, the directors of the Honourable East India Company turned over the government of India to the Crown:

> The Company has the great privilege of transferring to Her Majesty such a body of civil and military officers as the world has never seen before. A government cannot be base, cannot be feeble, cannot be wanting in wisdom, that has reared two such services as the civil and military services of the Company.

On 1 November 1858 Queen Victoria issued a proclamation taking upon herself "the government of the territories of India, hithertofore administered in trust for us by the Honourable East India Company."* It was, she said "our earnest desire to stimulate the peaceful industry of India, to promote works of public utility and improvement, and to administer the government for the benefit of all our subjects resident therein. In their prosperity will be our strength, in their contentment our security, and in their gratitude our best reward."

In general, the transfer of power from the Honourable East India Company to the Crown was made with remarkable smoothness. The honourific of "Viceroy" was bestowed on the Governor-General, who retained his same powers. Political changes were few at first; most of the changes occurred in the army, and the conversion of the Company's army was not simple. Recognizing that the basic causes of the Mutiny lay in the inefficiencies, maladministration, and misguided policies of the Bengal Army, the authorities set about drastically revising the baroque military organization the Company had structured. This is not to say that the old edifice was pulled down and replaced with a new, simpler, more efficient structure; that has never been the

---

* The Company retained a formal existence as a shadow of its former self until 1874 for the purpose of financial liquidation in accordance with the Charter Act of 1833.

British way. The new organization rose to even more fantastic heights than the old. Administration became ever more complex and cumbersome.

In 1858 it was decreed that "the military and naval forces of the East India Company shall be deemed to be the Indian military and naval forces of Her Majesty, and shall be under the same obligations to serve Her Majesty as they would have been under to serve the Company." The language was clear and the intent plain, but the transition created entanglements and confusions no one had foreseen, and it was far from the smooth and orderly process London had anticipated, for the transfer produced many anomalies.

The transfer of the large cadre of British officers from the Company to the Crown proved difficult. All of the Company officers accepted the Queen's Commission, making more officers than could be used in the newly reduced Indian Army. (In the Bengal Army, only fifteen out of seventy battalions of infantry and only a few regiments of the pre-Mutiny cavalry remained, and the number of British officers in each infantry battalion was reduced from twenty-two to six.)

Because British officers in the Indian Army did not purchase their commissions or promotions, as did most officers in the cavalry and infantry in the Queen's army, a separate promotion list had to be maintained until the 1870s when "purchase" was abolished in the British Army. In the British caste system, Queen's officers had always been considered socially a cut above British officers in the Indian Army and, in fact, Company officers had always ranked below all Queen's officers of the same grade. This inequality, long a sore subject with Company officers, was now corrected. Former Company officers took their place by date of rank in grade along with all other British officers.

There had existed a system of regimental promotions in the Company's army, a right to promotion by seniority within the regiment, and it was said that nothing except a sentence by court-martial could deprive an officer of this right. Under this system, officers of one regiment could be promoted more speedily than those of another regiment simply through the vagaries of attrition. A marked disparity in the rate of promotion was also found in the three presidential armies, an anomaly only partially rectified in 1861 by the creation of a peculiarly British piece of fiction: All officers in the Indian Army, even those serving in combatant units, were said to hold staff appointments in their presidential armies and were cited in Army Lists, not as members of their regiment or corps, but as members of the Bengal, Madras or Bombay Staff Corps. As a final step, Sir Hugh Rose, who became Commander-in-Chief, India, in June 1860, announced that all promotions would be based on merit alone.

It was decreed that there would be no more European troops, other than officers, in the Indian Army and that the European troops who had been in the Company's service would simply be transferred to the British Army. But it was not that simple. European troops who had been in the Company's service, faced with transfer to the Crown, proved intransigent. They maintained, quite rightly, that they had not enlisted in the Queen's army and that it was grossly unjust to shift them about as if they were so much merchandise, "transferred like guns or bullocks to the Queen."

"Why," one said darkly, "we might be transferred again to the Americans tomorrow."

Irate soldiers demanded their discharge—or at least a bounty. The Military Member of the Governor-General's Council as well as the Commander-in-Chief, India, General Sir Colin Campbell (later Lord Clyde), sided with them. It was Sir Colin's view that "the free consent of the individual must be obtained before he can be transferred from one part of the service to another." His opinion was passed on to the government, but the law officers of the Crown disagreed, arguing that it was perfectly proper to transfer the troops en masse from the Company to the Crown. The Viceroy, Lord Canning, and the Secretary of State for India agreed with the lawyers, and so on 8 April 1859 a general order for the transfer was issued. There ensued much grumbling, many memorials and numerous petitions, and finally what came to be called the "White Mutiny."

On 24 May at a ceremonial parade to celebrate the Queen's Birthday, the Madras Fusiliers refused to cheer their sovereign and new employer. At the cantonment in Meerut where the Indian Mutiny had begun, an ominous sign appeared on a wash-house wall: "John Company is dead. We will not soldier for the Queen." Stations throughout India saw numerous acts of insubordination, and in October the 5th European Infantry Regiment actually mutinied at Dinapur. A court of inquiry was held; the chief ringleader was speedily executed by a firing squad, others were sent to prison and the regiment was disbanded, but the alarm had been sounded and officers and government officials were apprehensive.

A general mutiny of European troops so soon after the Indian Mutiny was a fearful prospect. Some officers doubted that regulars would fire on their own countrymen, even mutineers, and, of course, the use of Indian troops against Europeans was unthinkable. An uncomfortable Lord Canning changed his mind and offered to discharge all those who wanted out. From a total of some 16,000 Europeans, most of them Irish, 10,116 took their discharge and were shipped back to Britain. After a short spell at home, 2,809 enlisted in the British Army and many soon returned to India as soldiers of the Queen.

A tragic sequel came to some who boarded ship for home. The clipper *Great Tasmania*, overloaded with 1,043 discharged soldiers and dependents, sailed from Calcutta provisioned with insufficient water, contaminated food, and an inadequate number of blankets. It carried only one doctor. The passengers in their light tropical clothing suffered greatly from the cold and by the time the ship anchored in

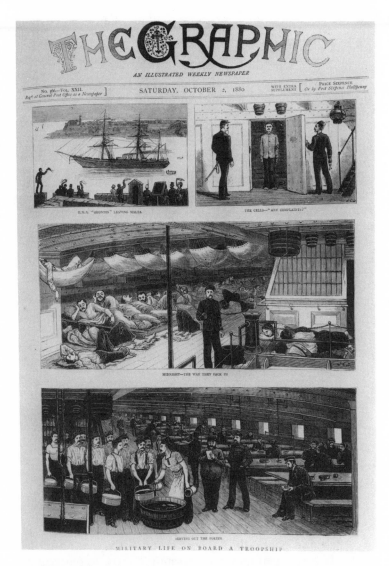

A soldier's life on board a troopship in 1880. (*The Graphic,* 2 October 1880)

the Mersey in March 1860, more than fifty had been buried at sea. Many, too weak to walk, had to be carried off the ship on stretchers.

There was a public outcry. Even the great Charles Dickens interested himself in the case and newspapers vied for stories of shipboard horror. An official inquiry was initiated, but by the time it came to an end, all of the Company's European troops who wanted their discharge had come home. The findings were moot. The tragedy was soon forgotten.

Soon after the transfer of the Indian Army was completed, a commission under fifty-nine-year-old the Right Hon. Major-General Jonathan Peel (1799–1879), Secretary of State for War, was appointed to suggest how that army should be reorganized. Although tens of thousands of Indian soldiers had fought for the British against their rebellious countrymen, the Mutiny had instilled in British hearts a distrust in all, and this was apparent in every recommendation made by the Peel Commission.

General Sir Colin Campbell gave the commission his views: "We should never again rely upon their [Indians'] *feelings* of dependence on Europeans, or on any other of their supposed *feelings*, but place it altogether out of their power to do serious mischief." Lieutenant-General Sir Patrick Grant, Commander-in-Chief of the Madras Army, went further: "I am of the opinion that there is in the heart of every black man an inherent dislike of the white man, which will always lead him to sympathize with those of his own colour, however they may differ in race, creed or country." The commission agreed. It recommended that the proportion of Indian to British soldiers in India, which before the Mutiny had been nearly nine to one, should in future not be greater than three to one. The proportion was accepted and generally adhered to until the beginning of World War II, when Indian representation rose to more than four to one, as is shown in the following table:

	Indians	*British*	*Totals*
1863	205,000	65,000	270,000
1887	153,000	73,000	226,000
1903	142,000	77,000	219,000
1923	139,000	66,000	205,000
1939	177,000	43,000	220,000

The method by which soldiers from various classes or communities—men with differing customs, speaking different languages—would be distributed in the Indian Army was one of the most troublesome issues faced by the Peel Commission. Some argued that regiments should consist of men drawn from a single race, religion, tribe or location; others that only companies should be exclusive, and that regiments should contain a variety of single-class companies. While the committee wanted to develop "clan emulation and martial characteristics to the full," it also desired to make mutiny on a large scale difficult. Consequently, the majority of the new regiments were made class-company. The 62nd Punjabis, for example, had companies of Punjabi Muslims (called PMs), Sikhs, Pathans and Rajputs. Only a few Sikh and Gurkha regiments remained homogeneous.

It was this system of dividing regiments into class companies which led the army to study closely the many diverse peoples in India and to classify them according to their assumed martial characteristics. From this sprang the theory of the "martial races of India," which was to have—even into World War II—so strong an influence on the Indian Army.

As it was principally the Poorbeahs (men of the eastern provinces of Bengal), and particularly the despised urban upper-caste Bengali, generally regarded as being too clever by half, who had mutinied, they were no longer recruited. They were replaced by stolid peasant types or rugged hillmen.

Under the reorganization scheme recommended by the

Peel Commission, each silladar cavalry regiment consisted of four hundred and twenty sowars organized into six troops with six British officers: commandant, second-in-command, two squadron officers, an adjutant and a general duty officer. Infantry battalions consisted of six hundred sepoys, NCOs and Indian officers with six British officers: commandant, two wing commanders, adjutant, quartermaster, and general duty officer. By 1865, when the reorganization was complete, the Indian forces of consequence were as shown on Chart 1.

In 1860 and 1861 the numbering of the regiments was altered several times and the resulting confusion and resentment was enormous. Soldiers become attached to the names or numbers of their units. A man who would willingly risk his life for the 15th Punjab Rifles might be reluctant to do so for the 14th or the 16th Punjab Rifles. Because the authorities found it irresistible to try to arrange regimental numbers in an orderly, logical way, and strove mightily to arrive at a system that provided a reasonable explanation of the sequences, assigning numbers to the regiments proved difficult.

A low number was often felt to be significant—as in the 1st Something Regiment, for example—so regiments were often numbered sequentially according to the date of their formation; but no one wanted to be the 20th, for it was the 20th Bengal Native Infantry that had been the first to mutiny at Meerut. Units such as the Punjab Irregular Force contained units not under the control of the Commander-in-Chief, India, but of the Punjab government, and they wanted a different system, while units such as the Gurkhas insisted upon their own idiosyncratic numbering sequence.

There is, of course, little practical value to any system of numbering regiments other than to keep two or more from having the same numbers, yet the military authorities failed even to accomplish this. All of their efforts to create order ended in a hash. By the 1930s no one not intimately concerned with the army could fathom the basis for the num-

Chart 1: Indian Ground Forces—1865

	Battalions of Infantry	Regiments of Cavalry	Batteries of Artillery	Corps of Sappers and Miners
Bengal Army	49	19	—	1
Madras Army	40	4	—	1
Bombay Army	30	7	2	1
Punjab Frontier Force	12	6	5	—
Hyderabad Contingent	6	4	4	—
Other local corps	5	2	—	—
Totals:	142	42	11	3

bers—or the absence of numbers—in Indian Army cavalry and infantry regiments.

A few of the changes recommended by the Peel Commission met with general approval. Infantry uniforms, which before the Mutiny had followed impractical European patterns—stiff leather stocks at the neck, tight tunics and overalls—were simplified and made looser and more comfortable. Promotion of Indians which had been determined by length of service was henceforth by selection on the basis of merit and capability; there would be no more sixty- or seventy-year-old jemadars, subedars or rissaldars.

A significant change which seems to have been accepted without rancour was the requirement that the weapons in the hands of Indian troops should always be inferior to the weapons carried by British troops. The Indian Army received the hand-me-downs of the British regulars, and Indian troops were as a rule kept a weapons generation behind British troops.

A change which many predicted would inhibit recruiting was the requirement that upon enlistment soldiers must promise to serve in any country. The plea of Hindu soldiers that they would lose caste if they served overseas (crossed the *kala pani,* the black water) was to be ignored. Many were astonished to find that recruiting was in no way inhibited, for high-caste Brahmans—the most meticulous observers of caste rituals, who had composed the bulk of the pre-Mutiny Bengal Army—were no longer recruited.

Begun in 1858, the reorganization was not completed until 1861. There is no one word or phrase that can describe the entire multi-faceted force that served the Empire in India during the last ninety years of the British raj. At its core was the Indian Army, but when on military campaigns it had interlarded with it battalions of infantry and regiments of cavalry from the British Army in India.

Not considered part of the regular establishment, and for most of the period between the Mutiny and Independence not even subject to the authority of the Commander-in-Chief,

India, although led by officers seconded from the Indian Army, were those colourful and romantic units known as the Frontier Scouts: the Khyber Rifles, Tochi Scouts, Zhob Militia, Gilgit Scouts, Kurram Militia, South Waziristan Scouts, and other such military units which served as the armies of British political officers on the frontiers.

Many, perhaps most, of the princely states maintained some sort of military presence. A number of the smaller states boasted only a brightly costumed bodyguard for ceremonial purposes, but the larger states maintained effective units, many of which were put at the service of the Crown in times of great need, as during the two world wars. Most of the larger units came to be trained by selected British officers and some were brought up to efficient standards.

These four military formations—the Indian Army, the British Army in India, the Frontier Scouts, and the armies of the princely states—constituted the backbone of the armed forces of the raj. But there were also many strata of police, some of whom—for example, the Military Police of Assam, which became the Assam Rifles in 1917—constituted a gendarmerie that was almost indistinguishable from regular forces and was, in fact, absorbed into the Indian Army in World War II.

In the course of the many reorganizations, various auxiliary units, territorial forces similar to the American National Guard, were created. The Peel Commission had first recommended the raising of an auxiliary force of part-time soldiers. When this was done, it was thrown open to Anglo-Indians, many of whom worked on the railways, and it soon became a condition of their employment that they enlist in the Auxiliary.

In the ninety years following the Mutiny the Indian Army's missions changed, for the days of growth and expansion were over; the borders of India with Burma, Persia, Afghanistan, Russia, China, Tibet, Bhutan, Siam, Nepal, and French possessions in Indo-China were now fairly well defined. Except for the campaigns fought on the North-West and North-East frontiers, all wars were fought outside the subcontinent, often in such faraway places as China, Abyssinia, Egypt, Mesopotamia, and France.

The Indian Army also changed in subtler ways: in the relationships which existed between British officers and Indian other ranks, between British soldiers and sepoys, and, in general, between the rulers and the ruled.

3

Britons and Indians

From first to last Britain had an economic interest in India. Even after the Honourable East India Company's commercial activities ended, British businessmen and industrialists continued to invest millions of pounds sterling in the area. In the early nineteenth century nearly 20 percent of all British exports were destined for Indian ports.

More than profits came back. India was sometimes called the "milch cow of the Empire," and indeed at times it seemed to be so regarded by the politicians and bureaucrats in London. Educated Indians and conscientious Europeans alike were embittered when India was made to pay the entire cost of the India Office building in Whitehall. They were further outraged when in 1867 it was made to pay the full costs of entertaining two thousand five hundred guests at a lavish ball honouring the Sultan of Turkey.

Economics aside, the British recognized a psychological and a moral commitment to India. Most British officers and administrators firmly believed themselves to be culturally, intellectually and morally superior to the races of India, with both a duty and a right to rule over them, thus

The homes of British officers could be quite lavish, particularly in the mid-nineteenth century. This is the home of Colonel D. Montgomerie, 7th (the Princess Royal's) Dragoon Guards, when he was Surveyor General of Madras. (National Army Museum)

bestowing upon them "the inestimable blessings of civilization." Many Britons had the comfortable feeling that something inherently superior in the British character, particularly in the breeding and education of British gentlemen, endowed them with a greater capacity to rule than it did those of other races or nationalities.

Colonel Sir Reginald Hennell, writing as late as 1924, little more than two decades before the creation of Pakistan and an independent India, said:

> The vast continent of India has been, from earliest times, the envy of the nations beyond its borders. For three thousand years, at least, it has not only suffered invasion after invasion . . . but has been the scene of perpetual internal warfare . . . religious fanaticism as well as plunder being the mainsprings of the strife, until at last it rests in peace and security under the beneficent rule of our King-Emperor George V and his Counsellors. . . .

Other dynasties have ruled for longer periods than that of Great
Britain, but not one of them has been able to confer so many
benefits on the inhabitants in so short a time.

Beliefs such as these bred that formidable British arrogance which Indians—among those of other races and
nations, it should be added—found so exasperating and
eventually intolerable. Many Britons made no attempt to
conceal their disdain for most of the native races of India,
a disdain the Mutiny exacerbated. Writing home on 16
December 1857, H. H. Stansfeld complained: "It is very dull
here, now and then a sepoy hung or blown away,* a cricket
match or two, and a little quail shooting. . . ."

Nearly twenty years later, in 1875–76, when the Prince
of Wales, the future King Edward VII, visited India, he was
appalled by the "rude and rough manner" in which the
Britons he met, particularly British officers, treated his
mother's Indian subjects. He found particularly offensive
their habit of referring to Indians, "many of them sprung
from great races, as 'niggers.' "

The British had not always been so overbearing. In the
seventeenth and eighteenth centuries when there were few
of them in India and they were not yet the grand sahibs
they later became, they appear to have been more civil. Cut
off from Britain by months of travel, they mixed freely with
Indians, learned their manners and ways, and the appropriate languages; there was then no place for racial prejudices.

British women—and the opening of the Suez Canal—have
been, with some justification, blamed for the change. In all
societies women have ever been the conservators of culture. When British women began to arrive in India in num-

---

* Atrocities and gratuitous cruelty were features of both sides. Captured
mutineers were often "blown from guns," i.e., strapped to a loaded
cannon in such a way that the body of the man was across the muzzle
of the gun when it was fired. It was widely believed that the Almighty
would then have difficulty assembling the parted portions of the body
in any afterlife.

British memsahibs tried to dress and to decorate their homes in the styles of Britain. In this sketch, only the punkah betrays the Indian setting. (India Office Library)

bers, they brought with them British attitudes, British fashions, and British morality; they were soon imposing their ideas, standards, and customs upon their new environment.

Early seventeenth-century pictures depict Englishmen in India dressed in Indian clothing, lolling comfortably on cushions and smoking hookahs. Among the outbuildings behind their houses were frequently found the *bibi khannas*, where the mistresses, widely regarded as the best of language teachers, lived. With the arrival of the memsahibs the sahibs exchanged their comfortable Indian dress for European clothes and smoked their tobacco European style; their mistresses and *bibi khannas* were swept away and the English Club and English marmalade appeared. Soon their households were deftly arranged as far as possible in the English style.

There were always more British men than women in India, so during the coolest season mothers brought their daughters out in the hope of making a good match. Such women were known collectively as "the Fishing Fleet." (G. F. Atkinson, *Curry & Rice,* 2nd ed. 1859)

The Suez Canal, which opened in 1869, shortened the distance between Britain and India by four thousand miles while it lengthened the social gulf between Britons and Indians immeasurably. British women in flocks came out to India for the "season," mamas bringing eligible daughters in the hope of finding suitable husbands for them among the bachelor officers and civil servants. British officers dubbed such visitors "the Fishing Fleet."

Social life, precedence and status assumed an enormous importance in the lives of Europeans. Although the British had come to India as merchants and it was merchants who founded the Indian Empire, by the mid-nineteenth century officers and government officials were disdainfully calling them "box wallahs,"* people concerned with boxes, bales and trade. Except for the few Indian princes who were allowed to provide tiger shoots and other such amusements, fraternization with Indians diminished almost to the vanishing point.

However white their skins and whatever their education, the offspring of European-Indian alliances were cast beyond the pale. These Anglo-Indians formed a caste of their own and eventually found their niche in the work world of the railway system, which was largely operated by them.

That the British made many needed improvements, that the Indian Army they created made India a safer place in which to live, that they provided an honest and intelligent judiciary and that they dug canals, built roads, strung telegraph and telephone lines, laid railway tracks, erected great dams and imposing buildings was, in the end, as nothing when weighed against their overbearing manner; their failure to take educated Hindus and Muslims into their homes and their clubs; their overt disdain for Indian religions, customs and manners; and their exclusion of Indians from the corridors of political power and from the commissioned ranks of the army.

Nevertheless, there always remained the assumption that one day India would take its place in the world as an independent nation. It was this assumption—that someday, not now, not tomorrow or in the near future, but *someday* Britain would return India to the Indians—which provided the moral basis for the British raj and sustained the British in their firm belief in their right to rule. Indeed, the notion that by setting standards—British standards—they were teaching the Indians how to govern themselves gave their rule a comfortable air of philanthropy. Only occasionally did Englishmen wince at the thought that they, representing the most democratic of governments, were denying the

---

* "Wallah" is a useful term applied to the person in charge of, or seller of, or responsible for, or expert at or associated with something. Thus rose wallah, competition wallah, machine gun wallah, et al.

political rights they most cherished to the hundreds of millions of Indians over whom they ruled. Even so, their illusions might have been maintained had not their self-image been marred by the extreme reluctance of British soldiers and administrators to place Indians in positions where they could learn the magic of governance.

When the Honourable East India Company's charter was renewed in 1833, it was announced that Indians were eligible for any appointment or employment; no one was to be barred because of his colour or creed. When the Company was abolished by the Queen's proclamation of 1858, the principle was reiterated, but opportunity to achieve an office of importance was severely circumscribed. Although appointments in the elite, justly acclaimed Indian Civil Service (ICS) were made on the basis of competitive examinations open to all, the examinations were held only in London and were so framed that the chance was remote indeed that any candidate not educated in a British public school could obtain sufficient marks. Although ICS eligibility rules were later modified and examinations could be taken in India, half of the ICS were still British when the raj ended.

In the Victorian Indian Army there were no vacancies open to Indians as officers in the combatant arms, for it was unthinkable that British officers, or even privates, should be asked to serve under Indians. In 1861, although Indians were appointed to a newly formed Legislative Council, their power was limited and executive control remained firmly in the hands of the Viceroy and his council. In 1904 the Viceroy, Lord Curzon, proudly pointed out that the King-Emperor's 230 million Indian subjects were ruled by 6,500 European and 22,000 Indian civil servants. However, he neglected to add that in the upper 5 percent of the Civil Service there were 1,200 Europeans and exactly 92 Indians.

The Mutiny swept away what little social intercourse was left between Briton and Indian. Friendliness and hospitality became unnaturally strained or nonexistent. The knowledge of ways of life, ways of thinking which come with familiar daily intercourse disappeared. Even in the army, distrust, however slight, distanced officers and their men in all but Gurkha regiments—and Gurkhas are not Indians.

In almost every way the Mutiny was a psychological watershed for the British in India, and indeed for British imperialism. Sir Lepel Henry Griffin, a high Indian government administrator, speaking fifty years afterwards, ventured that "Perhaps a more fortunate occurrence than the Indian Mutiny of 1857 never occurred in India." The Mutiny, he said,

> swept the Indian sky clear of many clouds. It disbanded a lazy, pampered army, which . . . had become impossible; it replaced an unprogressive, selfish and commercial system of administration by one liberal and enlightened. . . . Lastly, it taught India and the world that the English possessed a courage and national spirit which made light of disaster, which never counted whether the odds against them were two or ten to one; and which marched confident to victory, although the conditions of success appeared all but hopeless.

But the Mutiny left scars that did not easily heal. Lord Canning, the first Viceroy, tried to exercise a wise restraint on the passions of those soldiers—officers and other ranks alike—who cried aloud for vengeance, and he was called "Clemency Canning" and damned for his pains. Within the army and outside it, bitterness and a sense of betrayal remained lodged in British hearts.

4

First Wars and Troubles Under the Crown

O n India's North-West Frontier the British waged con- tinual warfare from the end of the Second Sikh War in 1849, when the Honourable East India Company first acquired its mountainous, ill-defined border with Afghan- istan, until British rule ended in 1947. Campaign followed campaign, some lasting only a few days and some many months, as the British tried to compel the unruly and ungovernable Pathan tribesmen in the hills to leave off raiding their neighbours on the plains and to stop slaugh- tering each other in long and bitter feuds. British might never succeeded in doing either.

Curiously, the tribesmen failed to take advantage of the revolt of the sepoys in Bengal in 1857–58; only one major disturbance occurred on the North-West Frontier during the Mutiny, and that was in the Yusafzai country west of Peshawar where the British maintained a fort at Mardan.

It was usually garrisoned by the Corps of Guides, one of the most famous units on the North-West Frontier, but in May 1857 the Guides were moved down to the Punjab to help quell the Mutiny. Their place was taken by the 55th Bengal Native Infantry, which at once mutinied, to the despair of its colonel who, in grief and chagrin over his regiment's behavior, shot himself.

A column was quickly organized under the redoubtable Lieutenant-Colonel John Nicholson, the "Lion of the Punjab," and it moved out from Peshawar to attack them. In a short, sharp campaign the mutineers were defeated: about one hundred were killed, another one hundred and fifty surrendered, and the remainder, about six hundred sepoys, fled to Swat. Those who surrendered were taken to Peshawar, where they were tried and sentenced to death. The young sepoys and those judged less culpable were reprieved, but forty were blown from guns. This awesome punishment had a salutary effect upon the Pathans, many of whom then hastened to enlist in the regiments being raised to replace the Bengali units that had mutinied or had been disarmed as suspect.

Most Pathan tribesmen recognized two major powers: the maliks (chiefs) and the mullahs (Islamic religious leaders). In Swat these were called the *Badshah* and the *Akhund*. Had these two united in welcoming the remnants of the 55th who retreated into their mountain fastness as well as the other Bengali mutineers who fled there, and had they seized the opportunity to proclaim a jihad, the British would have found the situation difficult indeed. But the land had been plunged into a political turmoil by the recent death of the Badshah, and many of the mutineers who had fled to Swat were escorted back across the Indus, where they were caught by the British and annihilated. Allowed to stay were those who joined forces with a peculiar sect known to the British as the Hindustani Fanatics. Centered in a village called Panjtar in an area known as Mangal Thana, they had teamed up with various local tribes and clans, notably the

Khudu Khels, and, according to Colonel Robert Warburton, the most knowledgeable man on the North-West Frontier, they had been joined by "all the Mullahs and disaffected rascals in the district."

A number of outrages were committed, notably an attack upon the Assistant Commissioner of Yusafzai. As soon as the Mutiny wound down and troops became available, a punitive force of 4,877 men of all ranks was collected and on 22 April 1858 Major-General Sidney J. Cotton (1792–1874) assembled them on the left bank of the Kabul River opposite Nowshera. Except for 260 bayonets from H.M. 96th Foot, the force was entirely Indian.

Cotton pushed his little army into Pathan territory in three columns and penetrated Mangal Thana. They destroyed crops, forts and villages (including the village of Panjtar), levied fines, and killed a few Hindustani Fanatics and their Pathan friends. After a fortnight of fighting, the Pathan tribes agreed to expel the Hindustani Fanatics and Cotton marched back to Nowshera. It was announced that "the objects for which the troops had taken the field being now fully accomplished," Cotton's force would be broken up and the troops returned to their cantonments. Eleven years later the government rewarded the survivors by granting them a clasp to their India General Service Medal.

This was the first time that the Enfield rifle had been used in the hills and it was reported that "its fire was most effective and made a great impression on the minds of the enemy." In all, Cotton lost six killed and twenty-nine wounded; the enemy lost sixty killed, including fifty Hindustani Fanatics, and an unknown number were wounded.

This little campaign was typical of the countless small expeditions on the North-West Frontier both before and after the Mutiny. Like most, it failed to solve anything permanently. Five years later the Hindustani Fanatics, still an irritant, provoked a similar expedition of about the same size under a doughty frontier fighter named Sir Neville Chamberlain (no relation to the late Prime Minister).

To avoid the heat of the day, troops often marched at night and early morning. (National Army Museum)

There were expeditions against the Wazirs in 1859, the Masuds in 1860, and the Black Mountain tribes in 1868. The latter transgressed when, encouraged by the Khan of Agror and other blackguards, they came out of their hills into British territory and fell upon a village called Oghi. The fate of the Empire did not depend upon retribution, but the Lieutenant-Governor of the Punjab thought so, for he declared that it was "absolutely necessary for the security of the frontier and the vindication of the British character that the clans engaged in this outrage should be suitably punished."

An expedition set forth; the Khan of Amb helped out; as usual, villages were burned, crops were laid waste, and a number of Pathans were killed. The attack on Oghi was thus avenged and the British character for ferocity was reaffirmed. The cost was trifling: five other ranks killed; one officer and twenty-eight other ranks wounded; and in the 6th Foot, marching from Rawalpindi to Abbottabad, thirty-eight men felled by the heat, eight of whom died.

Although in the twenty years following the Mutiny there was no major war, no major threat to the British Empire, the North-West Frontier was not the only scene of action. Numerous military expeditions were launched on India's North-East Frontier, where the British continually protested that they wished to be friends and good neighbours with the outlandish inhabitants of these remote states, but seemed not to know how to go about it. Relations with Sikkim provide a case in point.

The British started off well. After the Nepalese War of 1816–17, they restored to the Kingdom of Sikkim the Terai or submontane portion of the country, but in 1839 they reclaimed the Darjeeling area to use, it was said, as a sanatorium. One version, difficult to credit, claims that this beautiful land was "presented" to the British "out of friendship." However, the King was given an allowance of Rs. 3,000, later doubled. The British soon discovered that the area was ideal for growing opium poppies and tea leaves, both highly profitable, and only ten years after their occupation they found an excuse to go to war with their erstwhile friends.

Sikkim, a botanist's or a lepidopterist's paradise, is home to more than four thousand species of rhododendron and some three hundred species of butterflies. The noted British botanist Sir Joseph Hooker journeyed there in about 1850 and, being British, assumed he needed no one's permission to wander about the country, but the Sikkimese thought differently. They arrested him. This was excuse enough for a military expedition, and the British marched to Tumlong, then the capital. It was a short and lucrative war, ending with the British appropriation of a large area and relieving the King of many of his responsibilities, including control of his country's foreign affairs.

Because the King of Sikkim did not take kindly to British intervention or accept with the proper degree of gratitude his new, less onerous position, another expedition was sent forth in 1861 "to impose a treaty defining good relations"—a British concept he seemed not to have grasped satisfactorily and one that not even a British army marching over his land killing his subjects made clear to him. In desperation he petitioned Tibet to send troops to his aid, thus forcing the sirkar in 1888 to drive out the Tibetans. That done, a Resident was installed to "advise" the King, whose powers were reduced still further.

The Resident's high-handed interpretation of the word "advise" prompted the King to flee the country. He had hoped to reach Tibet, but he was arrested while passing through Nepal and turned over to the British, who kept him as a state prisoner until he died in 1914. In 1918 a handpicked King, one who understood what good relations with the British meant, was knighted and installed with somewhat increased authority.

Several expeditions were mounted against the Arbors, members of a large and warlike tribe on the North-East Frontier who held in subjection the more peaceable Miris. Described as "a sulky, intractable race . . . insolent and rude beyond all other tribes on this frontier," the Arbors ignored all friendly overtures, and when the British tried to tax the Miris, they were quick to respond with an offer to protect any of the tribe who wanted to escape their conquerors. In January 1858 they began a series of outrages. Punitive expeditions proved fruitless; after each murderous attack they melted into the fastness of their hills and jungles. At last the British discovered that bribery worked better than bullets. "Subsidies" were paid to the tribesmen contingent upon their good behavior and after 1863 they no longer presented serious problems.

The Lushais, another tribe on the North-East Frontier, who lived in the rugged, hilly area between south-western Bengal and Burma and made a habit of descending from their hills to raid the tea plantations, sometimes carrying off captives. Several halfhearted attempts were made to punish them, but they remained unrepentant and undiscouraged. A major campaign was mounted against them in 1871 when it was learned that they had captured Mary Winchester, a golden-haired little English girl, about five years old. The campaign was arduous and the mortality rate was high, diseases and accidents claiming more lives than were lost to the Lushais' primitive weapons. But little Mary was found. Smoking cheroots, in good health and spirits, and speaking only Lushai, she was the darling of her captors, far from the pathetic captive the soldiers had imagined. She had been spoiled outrageously—her guardians wept when she was taken from them and begged for a lock of her hair. Escorted back to India, it was learned that both her parents had died. Shipped off to relatives in Britain, she disappeared from history.

Between 1866 and 1887 eight expeditions were sent into the Naga Hills, but the pacification of the Nagas was not completed until 1892 (though it could be argued that they were never pacified, for they are still demanding a separate state, independent from India). In 1865–66 an expedition was sent to Bhutan for four months. In 1873, 1880, 1894, and 1896 violent disturbances had to be put down among the Moplahs on the Malabar Coast. In 1879–80 the Ramps in the Godagari Hills (now in Bangladesh) rebelled. In 1885, the Third Burma War saw the remainder of Burma annexed; and in 1892, an expedition was sent against the Kachins in the Burmese hills. The armies of the raj were never at rest.

At times the British authorities gave a helping hand to the military problems of friendly princes, some of whom lived to regret the loan. One such was the Gaekwar of Baroda who, in 1858, appealed to the Bombay government for help in controlling the criminal tribes—Mias, Mianas and

Troops were often used to search out bandit gangs (dacoits).
Here a naval captain, leading a party of soldiers and sailors,
questions a local official in Burma. (National Army Museum)

Waghers—living in Okhamandal, a 275-square-mile area
of his state lying in western Kathiawar.* Their stronghold
was a "bleak windswept promontory with very poor soil
and very uncertain rainfall." Unable to live by agriculture
they had turned to dacoitry—exacting money from pil-
grims and raiding their more prosperous neighbours.

The British were willing to oblige the Gaekwar, stipulat-
ing only that Okhamandal be placed under their political

---

* Kathiawar is a crowded peninsula (23,432 square miles) on the west
  coast of India. It is bounded on the east by Ahmadabad, to the south
  and west by the Arabian Sea, and to the north by the Ram of Cutch.
  Under the British raj it comprised two British agencies, 188 small
  princely states, and portions of Baroda.

Soldiers of the 2nd Goorkhas (Prince of Wales's Own) waiting to board a troopship in 1878. *(Illustrated London News)*

control until order could be restored. The Gaekwar agreed. When, a few years later, with the offending tribes more or less tamed, he asked that his district be returned, he was advised that the Waghers still appeared "incorrigible." Okhamandal was held by the British until 1917.

Some wars were remote from India. The Third China War, also known as the Arrow War, was a continuation of the series of opium wars provoked by differing opinions between the British and Chinese on matters of free trade, national sovereignty, public health, and whether right should always be on the side of the mightiest. In short, Britain indignantly resisted all efforts of the Chinese government to protect its subjects from the evils of opium-smoking by cutting off their main source of supply—the highly profitable opium trade with India.

When the Chinese confiscated chests of opium which British merchants had illegally imported from India, the merchants complained to their government, which agreed that such behavior was intolerable. Colonel Sir Reginald Hennell of the Mahratta Light Infantry has left a succinct description of what happened next:

> At last the Home Government determined to send an Ambassador to interview and remonstrate with the Emperor of China. On arrival at Pekin he was informed that he must "kow-tow" when he was admitted to the presence—that is, he must kneel down and make *obeisance*, as always insisted on at such interviews. This the Ambassador refused to do, as derogatory to the Royal Representative of Her Majesty the Queen of England, so he was ordered to leave immediately. This final action forced the English Government to declare war.

The British were further outraged when Chinese authorities boarded the schooner *Arrow* which had once been, but was no longer, registered in Hong Kong. Then the French, with their own axe to grind, discovered that a French priest had been murdered a few months earlier, giving them excuse enough to go to war with China at the same time.

The Arrow War is perhaps more confusing than most because it is difficult to sort out the players. On the British side were Admiral James Hope and General James Hope Grant, the latter a brave, likable soldier who, although he found it impossible to read a map and had the greatest difficulty issuing clear, unmuddled orders, was a splendid cellist. The Chinese were commanded by Sam Collinson— or so the English-speaking soldiers dubbed General San-ko-lin-sin. Most of the eleven thousand British troops were Pathans, Sikhs, Punjabis, Dogras and other Indians drawn from all three presidential armies; most of the enemy troops were Tartars and Mongols; Chinese helped both sides. One Chinese governor rented camp sites to the British; another sold them mules. For their part, the British dispatched an infantry battalion to Shanghai to help the Chinese governor there suppress a local rebellion. The British and French bickered, behaving more like rivals than allies. Whether the Union Jack or the tricolour flew on the highest flagpole appears to have been a matter of serious concern to both.

An Anglo-French force finally marched inland to the Chinese capital, and just as British guns were poised to open fire on Peking, the Chinese surrendered. Britain was given all that it asked for, including Kowloon on the mainland opposite Hong Kong and the additional treaty port of Tientsin. Sadly, the capitulation came too late to save the magnificent collection of buildings known as the Summer Palace. Thousands of manuscripts and objets d'art were wantonly destroyed as French and British troops looted and burned in the most outrageous act of vandalism in the nineteenth century.

Forces from India ventured ever farther afield, taking part in an expedition to Perak in Malaya (1875–76), to Aden (1865–66), and even to Malta and Cyprus (1878). The dispatch of six battalions of infantry, two regiments of cavalry and four companies of Sappers and Miners to Malta marked the first time that Indian troops served west of Suez. On hand in case of another war with Russia, they were pieces in the game that revolved around the "Eastern Question" and the slow crumbling of the Ottoman Empire.

In 1867–68 the land forces of India fought for the first time in Africa. King Theodore of Abyssinia had written a civil letter to Queen Victoria, but it appears to have languished unanswered in the drawer of a minister or bureaucrat. Theodore, unaccustomed to such uncivil behaviour, seized and threw into prison a few British subjects, thus bringing down upon his head the wrath of the Empire. An army was assembled in India under General Sir Robert Napier, Commander-in-Chief of the Bombay Army, and embarked for Abyssinia; its mission was to release the captives and to persuade the Abyssinian King, forcibly if necessary, to mend his ways.

Napier's expedition was a large-scale enterprise with 13,548 troops, 3,786 of whom were Europeans, accompanied by tens of thousands of mules, ponies, bullocks, donkeys and camels; there were even a few elephants. The future

A sowar in the Queen's Own Corps of Guides dressed in drill order. (National Army Museum)

Lord Roberts of Kandahar took part in the campaign, and so did Henry M. Stanley, who less than five years later found Livingstone in Central Africa. Roberts was there as a staff officer, Stanley as a war correspondent.

Napier and his men marched some five hundred miles into the Abyssinian highlands, suffering much from the extremes of climate and the difficulty of maintaining their long supply line to the distant coast, but they encountered little real opposition from King Theodore's forces, who had holed up in a great fortress at Magdala. All ended satisfactorily: the captives were released, Magdala was stormed, and Theodore shot and killed himself. Napier was rewarded with a peerage by the Queen and Parliament gave him its thanks and a much needed pension. (He was the father of fifteen children, nine sons and six daughters by two wives.)

This was the first major campaign in which some of the troops wore khaki, which had been officially introduced as approved working dress in 1861. Although approval was withdrawn in 1864, many troops, particularly those who had seen active service on the North-West Frontier, continued to dye their white drill uniforms with tea leaves or other substances. Khaki ("dusty") was said to have been invented by Lieutenant (later Lieutenant-General) Harry Lumsden when, in December 1846, he founded the Corps of Guides.

Not every conflict involved bloodshed; some of the most bitter were regimental brouhahas, unedifying internecine quarrels fomented by heat, boredom and the moral and social questions peculiar to the British Army in India. Usually such hubbubs went no further than cantonment gossips, but one such created an uproar that reverberated as far away as London.

CHAPTER
5

A "Moral and Social Question"

British regiments posted to India encountered problems, of course, in a new environment amid people whose habits were strange and exotic, but such problems were usually superficial, more easily overcome than one might imagine, for they fitted into a pattern of army life in India and there were always a few old India hands around to indoctrinate newcomers. Soldiers in British regiments mixed rarely with Indian sepoys, or with any Indians other than servants, merchants and artisans. For the most part officers stayed within their social and military sphere; other ranks followed the example of their officers, seldom straying from their social or military spheres. Indians of all classes were ignored. Many problems, whatever their nature, were internal, and almost all were usually kept within the regiment or battalion, certainly within the army itself. But one small internal disturbance ballooned to such an extent that it billowed out of the narrow regimental and army boundaries and into the pages of *The Times* at home. It was generally known as the Crawley Affair.

The 6th (Inniskilling) Regiment of Dragoons was a smart, fashionable regiment with a distinguished record. It had fought at Waterloo and in the recent Crimean War, where it had taken part in the charge of the Heavy Brigade at Balaclava, an action less well known but more successful than the charge of the Light Brigade. The Duke of Cambridge, Commander-in-Chief of the British Army, once said of the regiment that he knew it "by personal experience, to have been the equal of any in her Majesty's service." In England at the beginning of 1858 it numbered among its officers men of wealth and social position; three of its nine lieutenants were sons of peers. It was commanded by Lieutenant-Colonel Charles Cameron Shute, who had attended a public school (Winchester), and had purchased his commission and every step except one of his promotions. Shute had distinguished himself in the Crimea, where he had been awarded the French Legion of Honour and Turkish Medjidie (5th Class).

The character of the regiment, or at least the tone of the officers' mess, changed markedly when, later in the year, the Inniskillings were posted to India. Since the Mutiny was almost at an end and prospects of active service in a popular war seemed remote, many monied officers decided to forego the rigours of years of inactivity in an unhealthy climate and arranged to transfer to regiments staying comfortably at home. Young peers with ancient lineages uninterested in the "savage wars of peace" also preferred to stay behind. Such shifts were common practice and easily arranged. Their places were eagerly filled by poorer officers attracted by the higher standard of living they could enjoy in India. Some hoped for active service on the North-West Frontier and for early promotion. An officer who died on active service—and more officers did in India—was replaced by the senior officer in the next lower rank, who was not required to pay for his promotion, a custom that sometimes led reckless young officers to raise a toast to "a bloody campaign and a pestilential season."

Cavalry regiments, even the most elegant, usually contained two officers who were rankers: the riding master and the quartermaster. It was unusual for a fashionable regiment to have even one combatant officer who had risen from the ranks, but when the 6th Inniskillings arrived in India it had no fewer than three combatant officers who were rankers, including the senior captain, Archibald Weir, once the regimental sergeant-major, who had served in and survived the Crimean War. Although two of the rankers had recently been awarded the new Victoria Cross (instituted on 29 January 1856), Lieutenant-Colonel Shute was not pleased with his officers. His superior in India, General Sir Hugh Rose (later Baron Strathnairn of Strathnairn and Jhansi), said: "He entertained a mistaken idea that the credit of his regiment would be increased by its being composed of officers of birth or of a good social position."

For whatever reason, the officers' mess was soon in turmoil as its members bickered among themselves and quarrelled with higher authorities until four were severely reprimanded and all were punished by having their mess closed at eleven o'clock every evening. One of the worst offenders was an aristocrat who, unlike others, had remained with the regiment: the Hon. Charles Wemyss Thesiger, second son of Lord Chelmsford and an Etonian who had just purchased his captaincy. Conditions improved somewhat when he was given a staff assignment and sent off to the war in China, and when Lieutenant-Colonel Shute, perhaps despairing of making anything of a regiment with such a wretched group of officers, unexpectedly gave up his command and sailed for home.

After the departure of Shute and before the arrival of a new commanding officer from England, the regiment was commanded by Captain Weir, the former sergeant-major. He appears to have been an able but unpleasant man, and he not only kept the pot of turmoil boiling in the mess but went on to instigate his own quarrels with higher headquarters. Although General Sir Hugh Rose, who became

Commander-in-Chief, India, on 4 June 1860, had condemned the snobbery of Shute, he was himself a consummate snob and, like many officers, probably most, he disapproved of rankers. "Neither the officer so raised, nor the officers of *a superior class in life* with whom he associates, nor the soldiers he has to govern, are benefited by what is a disadvantageous anomaly, the transfer of a man of a very different, inferior and less educated class in life to one superior in all these respects," Rose said. He was soon complaining to the Duke of Cambridge about the temporary commander of the Inniskillings: "Captain Weir has too well succeeded in sowing a vast amount of dissension amongst the staff of the regiment to which he owes everything, and in which, from being an indifferent R.S.M. and a very moderate adjutant, he has risen from the ranks to be, in only six years, a captain without purchase."

What was needed in Shute's replacement was a man capable of dampening the prevailing snobbery, calming the ferment in the mess and inducing this prickly group of cavalry officers to work for the common good of the regiment; instead, on 25 April 1861, the regiment received Lieutenant-Colonel Thomas R. Crawley.

Crawley was a Sandhurst graduate and the son of an officer. He had served for nearly thirty years in British cavalry, but his only active service had been in the brief Second Sikh War of 1848–49. The Duke of Cambridge was to remark that he was "an officer not gifted with the special talent which unites with the firmness of command the tact which inspires confidence and creates good will." Crawley was an impatient man, quick to display an ugly temper; he used an aggressive arrogance, scowls, and a glowering eye to reinforce his authority. He soon alienated many of his officers, though he had his favourites.

From the beginning things went badly. The regiment was laying in the cantonment at Ahmednagar, and it took Crawley and his family a miserable sixteen hours to travel the sixty-five miles from Poona. They arrived, hot, dusty, and hungry, at about nine-thirty on the morning of 25 April 1861, and Crawley's first action was to order breakfast served in their quarters. When it failed to arrive, he fired off his batman to find out why. The breakfast had been ready for some time, he was told, but the distracted mess servants could not serve it because it was a rule that no silverware could be taken from the mess. Not until eleven o'clock, when an officer in neighbouring quarters came to the rescue with the offer of his own utensils, did the Crawleys at last sit down to eat. Not surprisingly, the Inniskilling officers learned quickly that their new colonel had a short fuse.

Serious trouble, as is not uncommon among congeries of men, seems first to have arisen over a woman: in this case the young (thirty-two years old in 1861) and charming wife of twenty-five-year-old Captain Richard William Renshaw, a newly joined officer who had his own reasons for wishing to leave England.

Crawley had been with his regiment less than three months when he was confronted with what came to be called "the regiment's moral and social question." Two of his officers, Surgeon Gavin Ainslie Turnbull and Captain Thomas Smales, the paymaster, called upon him with shocking news: Mrs. Renshaw was a divorcée. Her first husband had been a solicitor, whom she had married in 1850 when he was thirty-five and she twenty-one. Eight years later, in May 1858, he divorced her under the newly enacted Matrimonial Causes Act of 1857 when he discovered that she was having an affair with—more shocking news—none other than Cornet (as he then was) Richard Renshaw. A year later the two were married at St. James Church in Paddington, and in the spring of 1860 the Renshaws joined the 6th Inniskilling Dragoons in India.

Turnbull and Smales informed their colonel that they had discussed the matter with other married officers and that it was generally agreed they could no longer meet Mrs. Renshaw socially. Crawley, however, had taken a liking to Captain Renshaw, and Mrs. Crawley liked Mrs. Renshaw.

It was easy for him to decide that Turnbull and particularly Smales were troublemakers who had formed a cabal against him. His officers were soon sharply divided and quarrelling anew over this issue.

Crawley now began a series of petty persecutions and humiliations aimed at Smales, culminating in his arrest for disobedience when, in spite of Crawley's order, Smales refused to reopen the regimental pay office after hours to make a disbursement to Captain Renshaw. To Crawley's chagrin, his order proved to be illegal and the paymaster was released.

Unable to let the quarrel with his commanding officer die, Smales vindictively dispatched a letter directly to the Secretary of State for War in London charging Crawley with a number of irregularities, of which the most consequential was the allegation that he had signed as being present for several muster parades which, in fact, he had not attended.

Smales's letter was a violation of the regulation that all communications with higher authority must be sent through the commanding officer. He certainly knew this, but he was apparently willing to risk a reprimand in exchange for the chance to see Crawley relieved. When his first letter produced no response, he repeated his charges in a second, which he properly addressed to Crawley with the request that it be forwarded to higher authority. The consequence was unanticipated, at least by the paymaster: Crawley was not court-martialled; he was.

In the normal course of events, Smales's letter should have been examined by a Court of Inquiry at which he could have presented evidence to support his charges, but this was not to be. The regiment was then stationed at the large British cantonment at Mhow in Central India, commanded by Major-General Francis Turnley Farrell, a sixty-two-year-old officer with more than forty years service in the Indian Army who was described as "aged and infirm . . . mostly confined to his couch." Crawley consulted with Farrell and then forwarded the letter directly to Major-General Sir William Mansfield, Commander-in-Chief of the Bombay Army, accompanied by his vigorous denial of all the charges and the accusation that Smales had brought "a series of false charges" against his commanding officer. A supportive letter from Farrell recommended that Smales be arrested for insubordination.

Sir William Mansfield (later Lord Sandhurst) had been promoted major-general in the field for distinguished service during the Mutiny, but he had always hankered to be a banker and believed himself best fitted for high finance. He was not generally regarded as a popular officer and he was said to be "sometimes wanting in temper and judgment." His career in India was marred by a series of discreditable quarrels with other officers in which he more than once lashed out with wild accusations he could not substantiate.

Without bothering with a preliminary inquiry into the facts, Mansfield at once agreed that Smales be court-martialled for insubordination. Undoubtedly Mansfield's intention was to support the authority of the commanding officer of a famous cavalry regiment threatened by the accusations of a mere paymaster. Undoubtedly, too, Crawley's charge of a cabal against him raised thoughts of mutiny, a word which carried ominous overtones. To make sure that his own notions of justice would prevail, Mansfield appointed Crawley to be the prosecutor. This was neither the first nor the last time that Mansfield demonstrated his lack of any sense of justice and fair play.

On 1 April 1862 the court-martial of Captain Smales opened at Mhow. The president of the court was Lieutenant-Colonel William Payn, C.B., of the 72nd (Duke of Albany's Own Highlanders) Regiment of Foot, a veteran of both Sikh wars, the Crimea, expeditions on the North-West Frontier, and the Mutiny. Members of the court included four other lieutenant-colonels, a major and nine captains. The proceedings were long and often repetitious as Smales proved conclusively through the testimony of three officers—the regimental sergeant-major and two troop sergeants-major—that Crawley had indeed not been in attendance at the muster parade of 1 January 1862. Crawley did the best he could to discredit the witnesses, using his batman and a noncommissioned officer to threaten and to spy upon them; as a last resort he charged the noncommissioned officers with conspiracy and placed them under close arrest.

Although General Mansfield ordered Crawley to drop the charges against the sergeants-major—even he could see that Smales's discussion of the case with his witnesses hardly constituted conspiracy—he permitted the three to be kept under arrest and thereafter the sergeants-major were marched under guard to give their testimony. Throughout the trial the bias of the court towards Colonel Crawley was evident.

The circumstances surrounding the arrest and confinement of the senior noncommissioned officer, Regimental Sergeant-Major John Lilley, eventually cast Smales's case into obscurity and brought about the trial of Crawley himself.

The thirty-seven-year-old Sergeant-Major Lilley had enjoyed a successful, unblemished military career and he had led a happy life with his twenty-two-year-old wife and their two small children until tragedy struck. Within the space of a few short months his world collapsed around him: his children took sick and died; his wife fell gravely ill; and he was placed under close arrest.

Lilley and his family had occupied rather spacious quarters, but soon after his arrest they were moved into two cramped rooms. Through the hottest months of the Indian summer Sergeant-Major Lilley and his dying wife, Clarissa, were confined to these rooms. A guard was placed inside the house with orders to watch Lilley closely and to permit no communication with any other person. On 26 May 1862, before the trial was over, suddenly and unexpectedly Lilley fell sick and within a few hours died. After a post-mortem examination Surgeon Turnbull wrote:

> The excessive heat at this season of the year, the constitutional predisposition of the deceased to congestion, the peculiar and painful circumstances of his position, the serious illness of his wife, causing depression of spirits, together with bilious and nervous derangement induced by the sedentary life attendant upon close arrest in a man of the sergeant-major's active habits, probably acted as exciting causes to produce the complaint from which he died.

This was not a report pleasing to Colonel Crawley, who immediately set out to prove that Lilley was a drunkard and that his death was the result of over-indulgence, a task made difficult by the fact that no one had ever seen the sergeant-major drunk.

The record of the court-martial shows conclusively that Crawley lied when he certified that he was present for the muster parade. If, among others, the adjutant, the regimental sergeant-major and Captain Weir, who was in charge of the parade, did not see their colonel, he was certainly not there. However, the court regarded such facts as irrelevant. Crawley was not on trial, said the court; Smales was. On 7 June, after ten weeks, the court-martial ended: Smales was declared guilty and sentenced to be cashiered.

Smales and his family made their last farewells to friends and on 21 July left Mhow by public mail cart for Bombay, where they intended to take ship for England. It was a voyage they were not destined to make without considerable delays.

En route to Bombay, the mail cart was stopped and Smales was arrested on the charge of having absconded with £1,600. It was October before he was brought to court, and then a grand jury threw out the charge. Once again the Smales set off and this time reached Bombay and had actually boarded the SS *Malta* before he was again seized and hustled off to gaol. There he embarked upon a letter-writing campaign, firing off seven letters to the Adjutant-General at the Horse Guards and three to the War Office. When it was revealed that no misconduct had been, or could be, proven, he was ordered to be released. In early December, he managed at last to reach London.

Here he beseiged the Horse Guards and the War Office, demanding satisfaction and justice, but not until pieces of his story appeared in the press and questions were asked in the House of Commons was Smales, with great reluctance, granted a pardon. It was, however, a curious sort of pardon, for he continued to be treated as if he had been guilty. He was denied his back pay and no place was found for him in the army.

Smales himself excited little sympathy. It was the treatment meted Sergeant-Major Lilley and his wife which stirred the emotions of those at home. The newspapers seized upon their story and indignant readers discovered that the guard placed over Lilley was posted in such a position that he could, if he chose, peer through the dividing curtains of the room while Lilley tended his sick wife and, in particular, could look on while he applied ointment to her chest. That Clarissa Lilley had lived only six weeks after her husband's death made their story even more poignant.

It was generally felt that Crawley's conduct had been abominable and that he and his superior officers were being shielded. Provincial newspapers speculated on the effect the Crawley Affair would have on recruiting. As the Lincolnshire *Chronicle* put it, the army's method of administering justice would "inevitably tend to damage the popularity of the service among the class of people from which its rank and file are recruited." When the clamour became too great, Crawley was returned to England to answer charges that he had acted with "unnecessary and undue severity" in dealing with Sergeant-Major Lilley and that he had subjected Lilley and his wife "to great and grievous hardship and suffering." Witnesses—including twelve officers, sixty-one other ranks, three Indians and a woman—were brought from India, and Crawley's court-martial opened at the great military base at Aldershot on 17 November 1863.

The press now began to divide. *The Times,* which had been actively anti-Crawley in June, came down firmly on the side of the establishment in December, declaring that "a lot of false delicacy has been wasted" on Mrs. Lilley: "Privacy is a relative term; a sergeant's wife is not accustomed to the same sort of privacy as a fine lady, and to say that Mrs. Lilley's modesty was wantonly insulted because a sentry might have seen her lying in bed if he chose to look through the lining of a chick, or curtain, appears to us absurd."

On 24 December the court-martial board, doubtless eager to leave the court for Christmas, announced its verdict: Lieutenant-Colonel Crawley was acquitted of all charges. Furthermore, the court saw fit to criticize some of the defence witnesses, including Surgeon Turnbull and the regimental adjutant, for "the manner in which their evidence was given."

A public subscription to pay for Crawley's legal expenses raised £500 the first day. The Earl of Cardigan, leader of the disastrous charge of the Light Brigade at Balaclava, who had himself experienced difficulties with junior officers, contributed £100. Exonerated, Crawley returned to his command of the 6th Inniskilling Dragoons and ended his career as a major-general. He died in 1880 at the age of sixty-one.

Smales, eventually placed on half pay, gave up the fight to return to duty and emigrated to Australia, where his progeny still live. The quarrelsome Captain Thesiger returned from the war in China and a few years later commanded the regiment. Captain Weir left the army shortly after the court-martial at Aldershot; other officers involved in the turmoil removed to other regiments, including Captain Renshaw, who transferred to the 16th Lancers and served on for another dozen years, advancing only one more step, to major. Whether he remained happily married is unknown, but his name was still on the retired list a half century later.

In the closed world of the British Army in India passionate, emotion-packed little dramas such as those involving Renshaw, Weir, Thesiger, Crawley, Smales, Mansfield and Rose could be played out with almost no reference to the Indians among whom they lived. The only Indians involved in the Crawley Affair were a seller of spirits and his two assistants, Crawley's witnesses called to bolster his claim that Lilley was a drunkard.

CHAPTER

6

British Officers

The life of a British officer in India, whether in the British Army, the Indian Army, the Frontier Scouts or the Political Service, was at first changed little by the transfer of the sirkar to the Crown. His duties, pleasures and daily routine remained much the same. If he enjoyed an outdoor life, horses, sports, games of all sorts, occasional danger and trials of endurance, it was a good life indeed. For all officers, but particularly for subalterns, it was considerably enhanced by an independent income.

The lack of sufficient money was probably the greatest obstacle to happiness, and debt the major hazard to a military career. Credit was readily available, though often at extortionate rates. In England in the 1860s the pay of a second lieutenant was about £95 annually and his expected expenses were about £157. Although in India an officer's pay would usually carry him about 20 percent further than in Britain, few subalterns had the desire or the willpower to live on their wages, and in the most famous regiments an independent source of income was requisite.

Francis Yeats-Brown (author of *The Lives of a Bengal Lancer*) was only nineteen years old when he became a

An officer takes his ease on his veranda, tended by his servants. (G. F. Atkinson, *Curry & Rice*, 2nd ed., 1859)

"trusty and well-beloved servant of His Majesty King Edward VII" and sailed for India. There he was bedazzled by the goods and services available to him and the ease with which they could be purchased:

> I had only to shout *Quai Hai* [literally, "Is anyone there?" the expression used to call for a servant] to summon a slave, only to scrawl on a *chit* in order to obtain a set of furniture, a felt carpet from Kashmir, brass ornaments from Moradabad, silver for pocket-money, a horse, champagne, cigars, anything I wanted. It was a jolly life. . . .

Money bought wine in the mess, a brandy and soda at sundown, sporting guns, servants, polo ponies and their fodder. With sufficient rupees an officer could even support a wife, although a wife was generally regarded as a hin-

An officers' coffee party after parade. Present are officers from an irregular cavalry unit, a native infantry regiment, a regular cavalry regiment, and the horse artillery. (National Army Museum)

drance to a junior officer, however wealthy he might be, distracting him from the care of his men and horses, and allowing him less time for hunting, shooting and pigsticking. Money also enabled an officer to enjoy his ample leisure, for except on active service, work days for most regimental officers were usually limited to a few short hours, and leave time was generous.

Most young officers spent a great deal of time worrying about their finances and thinking about money, though they were universally contemptuous of civilians who did so. In letters home, in journals and memoirs there is one constant theme: lack of money and complaints about pay and allowances. It is impossible to relate rates of pay to present currencies, but to illustrate the differences in pay, in 1876 the commandant of a cavalry regiment, a lieutenant-colonel, received in pay and allowances Rs. 1,240, while his subalterns earned only Rs. 325. (A subedar-major would make only Rs. 125 and a naik Rs. 12.)

Although the sirkar instituted the fiction that all Indian Army officers were staff officers, an officer might supplement his income considerably if he could obtain a real staff appointment, which also offered more prestige and usually more absorbing work. A lieutenant could double his income if he obtained the adjutancy of his battalion.

An officer could always add to his income by becoming sufficiently proficient in languages to qualify as a translator. Thus a penniless but ambitious officer who studied languages and military administration, took an interest in discipline, and drank water with his meals might be able to live on his pay, but he was unlikely to be a popular addition to the mess.

Although Philip Mason, an authority on the Indian Army, denies that the officer corps in India formed a caste, he refers to it as an "Imperial class" because "it was not quite hereditary," but this is almost a difference without a distinction. Many of the officers' male relations were or had been officers. Their friends were other officers; their social life revolved around the mess. It was an existence that came close to being monastic. Absorbed in the life of their regiment, they formed their own rules of behaviour and notions of proper conduct. Not only Indians but all others so unfortunate as not to be born British were excluded from their social circle. Even among the British there were few civilians with whom officers cared to fraternize. Almost the sole exception were members of the Indian Civil Service (ICS) who, with the officer corps, represented official British society. No young officer had a "box wallah" for a friend, although there were tens of thousands of British young men working for commercial firms, in industry or on plantations.

Each regiment observed its own rules, spelled out to newly joined officers by the senior subaltern or the adjutant. Cus-

A young officer drew this picture in 1865 for those at home to illustrate "How my baggage travelled in India." (Windsor Castle. Royal Library. Her Majesty Queen Elizabeth II.)

toms, even modes of address, varied from regiment to regiment, although usually majors were addressed as "Major" and never by their surname; captains were addressed only by their surname. In no regiment did an officer ever offer to buy another officer of the same regiment a drink in the mess: the mess ante-room was their common living room.

A young officer was not expected to live up to the strict

One of a series of drawings by Captain George Franklin Atkinson of the Bengal Engineers illustrating cantonment life shortly after the Mutiny. They were published under the title "Curry & Rice." (G. F. Atkinson, *Curry & Rice*, 2nd ed. 1859).

code of the American West Point cadet who vows not to lie, cheat, steal or associate with those who do, but he was expected to show great physical courage and he could not be a cad or a bounder. Major-General Sir George Young-husband spoke with approval of the dressing down meted to one young officer at the viceregal lodge at Simla. Impatient for his drink to be served, he had cursed the kitmutgar (waiter) and unluckily was overheard by Lord William Beresford, then military secretary to the Viceroy, who minced no words: "That man is the Viceroy's private servant; this is the Viceroy's house and you come here as his guest. But it is clearly no place for you, and unless you are gone in five minutes I shall kick you out. And you will not come here again."

Most officers knew the manners of their class, for they came from vicarages and from families with military traditions. If a young man's father and grandfather had served in, say, the elite Skinner's Horse, his own chances of joining that distinguished regiment were excellent, for it was felt that he could be counted on to uphold his family's reputation and the reputation of the regiment. (Curiously, James Skinner, who founded what became the senior regiment of Indian cavalry, would not have been permitted to join it as a subaltern eighty years later, for Skinner was an Anglo-Indian, the son of a British officer and a Rajput girl.)

Members of elite regiments knew themselves to be better than the unfortunate officers of lesser regiments. Combatant officers looked down upon noncombatant officers. A subaltern in Probyn's Horse or the 2nd Gurkhas regarded himself as immensely superior to an officer of any grade in the Royal Ordnance Corps or the Royal Indian Army Service Corps, the initials of the latter being scornfully said to mean "Really I Am So Common." Philip Mason, who repeats Younghusband's story of the bounder in Simla, was never a regular officer himself, but he came from the "officer class," and he was "glad to note" that the offending officer was not a regimental officer. One cannot be sure, of course, what Lord William Beresford's action might have been had the offender been the second son of a marquis and a major in Probyn's Horse. Had he been asked, Lord William would doubtless have replied that such a situation could not possibly have occurred.

Very few non-Britons were ever allowed inside the inner circle of the officers' mess. Major Pierre Louis Cavagnari had an English mother but a French father, a general. Colonel Robert Warburton, one of the most effective political officers ever to serve on the North-West Frontier, had an Afghan mother. But she was a princess—or so it was believed.

An officer might cheat an American or an Indian, delay for years paying his tailor, snub a Jew, and be carried home dead drunk, but his behaviour could not stray from the standards of his regiment. Letters and diaries of officers of the raj sometimes exhibit truly extraordinary arrogance. In June 1915, when the Allies needed every man they could get and British and French politicians were eager for the Americans to enter the war, Captain Roly Grimshaw wrote scornfully of Yankee "dollar collectors" in his diaries: "The Yanks would be very useful belligerents. They could not, nor need they, actively participate in the fighting but they could supply ammunition free and place their destroyer flotilla at our disposal."

Disdain for Indians did not extend to those young princes who spoke proper English, played good polo and excellent cricket, and generously provided lavish entertainments and facilities for hunting, shooting or pigsticking, or to rajas and regents such as the westernized Sir Pertab Singh, who at the age of seventy led the Jodhpur Lancers to war in France in 1915. It has been said, with some truth, that the British in India knew only servants and maharajas, though most officers did get to know their peasant soldiers.

Wherever in the vast British Empire one might wander, British clubs were to be found, perhaps more in India than elsewhere. Most were for Europeans only, a place where Britons could be by themselves and relax the stiff upper lip. In many, such as the Yacht Club in Bombay, Indians were not allowed even as guests. Successful mixed clubs, such as the Willingdon Sports Club in Bombay, were rare indeed. Prior to 1939 the Dehra Dun Club had no restrictions, but only one Indian member. Others were proposed from time to time, but they were inevitably blackballed— by the Indian member, it was believed. The question of club membership for Indian officers came to a head with the Indianization of the army in the late twenties and thirties.

British subalterns destined for the Indian Army were not sent green to an Indian regiment but, whatever their arm or service, were posted for a year as extra officers on the Unattached List in a British infantry battalion serving in

India. Many Indian Army officers could look back with pleasure on their year with a British regiment, but this was not always the case. Regular officers were serene in their superiority and in at least one regiment the subalterns destined for the Indian Army were made to dine at a separate table in the mess.

During this first year the young officers were expected to become acclimatized and to pass at least the Lower Standard Urdu Examination. Urdu, the language of the army, is spoken in its purest form in the United Provinces; variations are found in adjacent provinces, but it was often unintelligible to those from distant or isolated areas. Nevertheless, officers and sometimes recruits themselves had to learn army Urdu. Few officers learned to speak it with any fluency until they joined their regiments and were required to work in the language. Gurkha officers had also to learn Gurkhali, the working language in Gurkha regiments. Invariably the officers came to speak in the uncultured accents of their peasant soldiers. Few could muster the proper grammar and intonations of the educated Indian classes.

In the course of their career officers were also expected to study for promotions. Further examinations were required for admission to the Staff College at Camberley. None of these examinations was easy and an officer had to devote considerable time to studying for them, but it was considered bad form to worry about them, and worse yet to be seen as a "mug," a man who "swotted" at his studies. Younghusband defined such a man as "a brother officer who neither rode nor shot nor played games, who drank water at Mess, went to bed early and swotted at algebra, fortifications or French." No regiment wanted a mug.

An officer who hoped to join one of the popular regiments—Gurkha, Indian cavalry, Frontier Force ("Piffers"), Baluch, et al.—had to be vetted. This was accomplished during a ten-day "casual leave," when he would be invited to spend a week with the regiment of his choice. His social status and antecedents would be known, but this was a time when the officers, particularly the subalterns among whom he would live, watched to see if he was the type who could "muck in" and turn his hand to any work, if he was good at polo or whatever sport the unit specialized in, and if he could hold his liquor on guest night in the mess.

A few officers obtained direct commissions, but most cavalry and infantry officers were educated at the Royal Military College, Sandhurst, and most artillery and engineer officers attended the Royal Military Academy, Woolwich, except for a fifty-two year period (1809–1861) when the Honourable East India Company operated its own military college (or "seminary") at Addiscombe, in north-east Surrey, producing about 2,000 infantry officers, 1,100 gunners, and 500 sappers. With the end of the East India Company, Addiscombe closed its doors. None of these schools provided other than military education; training lasted for varying periods at different times, but never exceeded two years. Unlike West Point or Saint-Cyr, graduates did not receive university degrees and few officers had ever attended a university.

Even before Sandhurst or Woolwich was founded, an enterprising officer named John Gaspard Le Marchant (born on the island of Guernsey in 1766) had persuaded the army to found the staff college which soon took root at Camberley. The course in advanced military administration and strategy was designed for field-grade officers and usually lasted a year. Officers who were successfully graduated had p.s.c. (passed Staff College) put beside their names on army lists. But in mid-century, and for some years after, the Staff College was not popular, and to have attended did not help an ambitious officer get on in his profession. Some of the more stylish regiments considered it smart never to have had an officer who had been graduated from Camberley. As late as 1879 only one officer of the Coldstream Guards had ever even applied. When Captain (later Field-Marshal) Edmund Allenby, 6th Inniskilling Dragoons, attended in

1896, he was the first from his regiment ever to do so. But by the last quarter of the nineteenth century, when it became obvious that those with p.s.c. attached to their names were obtaining the most prestigious appointments, there were more applicants than could be accepted. In 1886 six vacancies were reserved for Indians, but few were taken up. It was, of course, difficult for most Indian officers to find the money for the trip to England and even more difficult to handle the academic requirements. The expense of the voyage was a problem for many British officers as well; so in 1905, Lord Kitchener, then the Commander-in-Chief, India, instituted an Indian staff college, which two years later was firmly established at Quetta.

When Kitchener first proposed the Indian Staff College, there were objections on the part of those at the Horse Guards in London who feared that two schools of military thought might develop. Kitchener replied that the army had no school of thought. He would, he said, be pleased to examine evidence of any thought whatsoever on serious military subjects. As usual, he had his way.

Regimental officers were expected to devote a considerable amount of attention to the study of the men they commanded, to learn each man's name, his family background, his tribal customs, religious beliefs and his personal cares and concerns. Many, probably most, officers took a keen interest in their men, learning their habits and characters. Some learned several Oriental languages. General Francis Tuker was undoubtedly right when in 1950 he wrote that some British officers "knew the true India better than many of those Indians who spoke for her," for they played games with, drilled and fought beside the peasants and Indian yeomanry they recruited, and understood their cares and needs.

In the ninety years between the mutiny of the Bengal Army and the birth of an independent India and Pakistan, mutual trust and respect between British officers and their men increased enormously; the sepoy and sowar were never again serious threats to the raj. This trust and mutual respect made it more difficult for officers, particularly officers of the Indian Army, than for British politicians to understand why the raj could not go on forever.

Not every officer was conscientious, of course. In both the British and the Indian armies there were some, fortunately few, who knew only the names of their batman, their sergeant or havildar, and perhaps the battalion's sergeant-major or subedar-major. Colonel J. S. E. Western knew of a young subaltern in a British regiment in India who paid so little attention to his men that he knew the name of only one: Baxter, his former batman. In musketry training when the drill known as "control of fire" required an officer to call for an individual rifleman to fire, he invariably gave the command: "Baxter, fire!" Poor Baxter's life was a hell, for wherever he went—to the canteen, the barracks, the latrine, the playing field—men would call out: "Baxter, fire!" Harassed to desperation, he finally managed to obtain a transfer—out of India and back to the home depot of his regiment in England. As he reached the depot's barracks square, kit bag over his shoulder, prepared to take up a new life, every barracks window was thrown open and a hundred voices thundered: "Baxter, fire!"

Because it was felt that young women distracted young officers from their duties, sex, love, and particularly marriage, even if a subaltern could afford it, were discouraged. Captain Roly Grimshaw of the 34th Poona Horse, thirty-six years old and unmarried, expressed the views of many when he wrote in his diary (28 January 1915):

> Personally, I think the Indian Army is too much married both as regards British officers and Indians. I feel convinced that human nature must dictate terms of reasonable prudence when a man knows he has a wife and family dependent on him. It may be urged by some that the Indian has little regard for his wife and family, certainly far less regard than the average Englishman. I totally disagree. . . .

> I do not for a moment think that all married men . . . are guided by prudence and that all bachelors are reckless. I merely think that human nature being what it is, leads one to the assumption that there is a tendency on the part of a married man to be more prudent than a bachelor. I think that Indian units carry out their allotted tasks quite as well as British; but I think there is a tendency that, having done so, they stop at that and that they do not go out of their way, so to speak, to do more.

Although it was against King's (and Queen's) Regulations, some regiments required joining subalterns to sign legal papers promising to pay a sizable sum of money to the mess if they married before reaching the rank of captain or major. At balls they were expected to dance with the married women and leave the unmarried to the bachelor senior officers. The rule of thumb, in India as in England, was that subalterns must not marry; captains may marry; majors should marry; and colonels must marry.

Philandering was possible, of course, but in the tight little society where everybody knew everything, illicit sex was difficult and dangerous. Most hanky-panky occurred in the hot weather months when the wives of government officials and army officials fled to the cool hill stations.

Few, if any, Jewish officers were found in either the British or Indian armies; the officer corps as a whole was strongly anti-Semitic. Lord Baden-Powell, who had served as a soldier in Africa and India before founding the Boy Scouts,* spoke of "a prejudice against Jews not only among the officers, but also among the NCOs and men, which is a very important point in discipline," and confided that he could not blame younger officers, who "cannot help feeling that the average Jew who comes into the service does not do so for love of soldiering so much as to gain position in society. (Jews without money do not join the army). . . . "

---

* The Boy Scout movement was a rather snobbish affair in some parts of the British Empire. Indian lads were not permitted to join until well after World War I.

A Jew, he said, "is as a rule not an English gentleman and very often not even an English public school man—so he cannot well amalgamate."

Only a few British officers—Yeats-Brown and Richard Francis Burton being notable exceptions—took any serious interest in Indian religions, and, as far as is known, none was converted, but as Yeats-Brown wrote: "We were all a little mad in India, a little touched by a sun that over-ripens men's thoughts." For many officers, perhaps most, Islam was understandable; at least Muhammadans believed in only one god. Because it was the faith of their men, many tried to understand Hinduism, but most found it unappealing, and their wives generally regarded it as obscene at best. Still, pride in their men led some officers to adopt their religious prejudices, and there were instances where a commandant of a Hindu battalion would not allow organized games between his own men and those of a lower caste.

Officers in Gurkha and Indian regiments greatly enjoyed the ceremonies and celebrations of their men at *diwali*, *holi*, or *dashera*, and felt honoured to be invited to observe or participate in these rites; in many Hindu regiments the British officers would invite their Indian officers to their mess for a drink on Christmas Day. There were many holidays in the Indian Army, for all regiments celebrated all the religious holidays of their members.

Most regimental officers attended church every Sunday, usually Church of England, but few were deeply religious. Major H. M. Conran was an exception. He was surprised to find a few Christians among the Indians and he took a great interest in their prayer meetings. Twice he even disobeyed his commanding officer: once, when he "declined giving the use of government tents for the celebration of Roman Catholic worship," and again when he "refused the use of our guns for the native idolatrous festivals."

While most officers, if asked, would have said they were Christians, many adhered to a more pagan code, as did Roly

Grimshaw, who confessed in his diary: "My religion is my duty and vice versa, that is all." As he was about to go into action with his squadron in France for the first time, he added: "I only hope this 'philosophy' is sufficiently strong to carry me through the very great ordeal I am about to undergo. It's a big experiment, but so far I have never found any consolation or help from any religious doctrine." He did indeed endure the ordeal of Ypres in the winter of 1914 and was severely wounded in the chest just before Christmas; as he had expected, duty carried him through.

For Grimshaw as for others, whatever was demanded by chapel or church was perfunctorily rendered; his real religion was soldiering, the Queen's (or King's) Regulations his Bible, and his regiment or battalion his living temple.

7

Playing the Great Game

In 1877 Lord Lytton had been Viceroy for only a few months when he wrote to Lord Salisbury that "so far as India is concerned, no event would be more fortunate than a war with Russia next spring."

Russian domination of Central Asia and the threat that it might someday control Afghanistan had been a British bugbear since the Second Sikh War (1848–49) extended the frontier of British India westward against the mountains that formed the ill-defined boundary between India and Afghanistan. As the British were absorbing Indian states, so the Russians were conquering one by one the little khanates and primitive states in Central Asia that were the detritus of the Mongol Empire—Samarkand in 1868, Bokhara, Khiva and Kokand in 1868–75—drawing closer and closer to Afghanistan. Lord Salisbury spoke of the Russian advance over the steppes as "this Russian avalanche."

The passes through the mountains that divided British India from Afghanistan—Khyber, Kohat, Bolan, Gumal, etc.—were the traditional invasion routes into India from the west. Most of the subcontinent was protected by seas dominated by the Royal Navy; on the north-east, jungles formed an obstacle; on the north, the Himalayas rose. Until World War II, invaders came from the north-west.

In 1858 Peshawar, site of the main British base on the North-West Frontier, was a thousand miles from the nearest Russian outposts in Central Asia; by 1876 only four hundred miles separated them. As the two armies drew closer, fear of Russian intentions and capabilities grew. It was firmly believed that if Russia ever controlled Afghanistan, India would be in mortal danger.

To be the paramount influence in Afghanistan was the ardent desire of both nations. Both sides used spies, soldiers and diplomats in efforts to stalemate the other, but in the end it was Afghanistan, with its rugged warriors and wily amirs, that provided the bulwark which stopped the tide of invasion on both fronts. The cold war that resulted—called by the Russian statesman Count Karl Nesselrode (1780–1862) "a tournament of shadows" and by the British "the Great Game"—continued for more than a century without British and Russian armies ever engaging. (In *Kim*, Kipling's novel about the Great Game, the spy for the British, Hurree Babu, may have been based on an actual spy named Sarat Chandra Das.)

An earlier attempt by the British (First Afghan War, 1839–42) to establish their influence by bayonets had ended in disaster when, after less than three trouble-ridden years, a revolt forced the garrison of 4,500 British and Indian troops with some 12,000 families and camp followers to flee Afghanistan—or try to. Troops and followers marched out of Kabul on 6 January 1842; on 13 January, one lone European, Dr. William Brydon, exhausted, on a failing horse, reached the safety of the British fort at Jalalabad. He told a tale of slaughter, starvation and death from freezing in the deadly cold of the mountain passes, of false promises by Afghan leaders, of hostages taken and men and women captured and carried off. For many nights afterwards on the walls of Jalalabad fires were built and bugles sounded. Anxious eyes scanned the horizon. No other survivor arrived.

John Clark Marshman, writing a few years later, char-

PUNCH, OR THE LONDON CHARIVARI.—November 30, 1878.

"SAVE ME FROM MY FRIENDS!"

"IF AT THIS MOMENT IT HAS BEEN DECIDED TO INVADE THE AMEER'S TERRITORY, WE ARE ACTING IN PURSUANCE OF A POLICY WHICH IN IT INTENTION HAS BEEN UNIFORMLY *FRIENDLY* TO AFGHANISTAN."—*Times, Nov. 24.*

The British invasion of Afghanistan from India in 1878 was seen by *Punch* as part of the Great Game, with Afghanistan likely to be eaten by either the British lion or the Russian bear. (National Army Museum)

acterized the First Afghan War as one which "began in injustice and ended in the most signal disaster, and which stands forth in the history of British India as the most stupendous act of fatuity to be found in its pages . . . an expedition memorable in our Indian annals as having inflicted on us the most astounding disaster which had ever befallen our arms. . . ."

It is often said by those ignorant of history that wars accomplish nothing. But they do achieve something. That is why men engage in them so frequently. It is also said that wars teach lessons from which congeries of men can learn wisdom, but this is an ipse dixit.

In 1878, the British again invaded Afghanistan. Sher Ali,

the amir, had entertained a Russian delegation and had signed a treaty with Russia while refusing to receive a British agent, excuse enough for another war. Three British armies poured over the passes with such success that in May 1879 Yakub Khan, who succeeded his father as amir, reluctantly signed the Treaty of Gandamak, by which the Afghans agreed to accept a British Resident.

Major Sir Pierre Louis Cavagnari, a British political officer, was selected to be Britain's man in Kabul. The son of one of Napoleon's generals and an Englishwoman, he was a naturalized British subject and an officer in the Indian Army. Possessed of great energy, indomitable courage and a genial personality, Cavagnari had joined the Political Service and made a name for himself on the North-West Frontier. It was he who negotiated the Treaty of Gandamak. On his appointment he hastened to Kabul with a small escort of twenty-five sabres and fifty-two bayonets of the Guides under twenty-three-year-old Lieutenant Walter Hamilton, who had just won the Victoria Cross in the recent war.

Yakub Khan, whom Lord Lytton characterized as "a savage with a touch of insanity," gave Cavagnari and Hamilton such a friendly reception that on 2 September Cavagnari sent back a telegram ending with the words ALL WELL. It was his last dispatch. Six weeks later the two officers and all of the escort with the exception of two sepoys who managed to escape were murdered in Kabul by mutinous Afghan troops and a mob of tribesmen, an outrage that called for another invasion.

Not everyone in Britain agreed with what was called the "forward policy" in Afghanistan. Gladstone, campaigning in southern Scotland as the Liberal candidate for Midlothian, denounced it as immoral: "Remember the rights of the savage, as we call him. Remember that the happiness of his humble home, remember that the sanctity of life in the hill villages of Afghanistan, among the winter snows, is as inviolable in the eye of almighty God as can be your own."

His was not a picture that was recognizable to anyone who had lived on the Frontier, where the Afghan had seemed happiest when carving up his neighbour or turning loose his women armed with sharp knives to try the courage and endurance of wounded or captured soldiers.

Two armies were quickly assembled, a process made easier than in Mutiny days by the nine thousand miles of railway the British had laid down in the previous twenty years. The North Afghanistan Field Force was led by Major-General Frederick Roberts, and the South Afghanistan Field Force, somewhat larger, was under Lieutenant-General Sir Donald Stewart. Confident of success they crossed the border, and after several pitched battles the capital of Afghanistan was occupied by Roberts on 7 October 1879.

Roberts had been told: "It is not justice in the ordinary sense, but retribution that you have to administer on reaching Kabul. . . . Your object should be to strike terror, and to strike it swiftly and deeply." He obeyed. Eighty-nine Afghans who were believed to have been responsible for the murder of Cavagnari and his party were hanged with some ceremony facing the burned ruins of the Residency where the evil deed was done.

Yakub Khan was deposed and Abdur Rahman, a nephew of Sher Ali, was recognized as amir by the British and given a substantial subsidy; but the Afghans refused to admit that they had been subdued. Roberts's force was vigorously attacked at its encampment at Sherpur, outside Kabul, in December, though it managed to beat off the assailants and scatter them with a counterattack. Roberts was now safe, but he controlled only Kabul and the ground he stood on. He was surrounded by armed and unhappy Afghans who wanted nothing to do with an amir unable to conceal that he was a puppet whose strings were being pulled by the British.

In the south, another son of Sher Ali, Ayub Khan, who was Governor of Herat, speedily raised an army and prepared to depose his cousin and to make himself amir. From

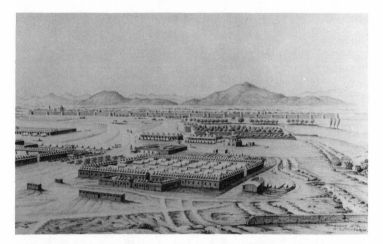

The British camp at Kandahar in 1879. (National Army Museum)

Herat with 7,000 foot-soldiers armed with British Enfield rifles, 1,000 cavalry, 3,000 irregular horsemen, and 30 guns, he advanced upon the British garrison at Kandahar, where Lieutenant-General James Primrose now commanded the South Afghanistan Field Force. On 27 July 1880 at Maiwand, about fifty miles northwest of Kandahar, Ayub Khan encountered a strong British brigade of about two thousand five hundred men under Brigadier-General George Reynolds Scott Burrows, who a few months earlier had been comfortably seated behind a desk as Deputy Quartermaster General of the Bombay Army.

The battle was fought on a hot, dusty open plain cut by dry watercourses. Fighting began in early morning and by one o'clock in the afternoon Burrows's brigade was in trouble. The Afghan artillery was well handled. Most of Ayub Khan's guns were 6-pounders, but three were modern, rifled 14-pounder Armstrong guns, heavier metal than anything Burrows possessed. The Afghan gunners had pushed their guns forward in bounds, taking advantage of every shred of concealment and cover. Some were sited to enfilade the British infantry and others to pound the British rear areas, which suffered almost as heavily as the firing line. So hot was their fire that bhistis refused to bring water to the sweating, thirsty men on the line; stretcher bearers could not be induced to leave the comparative safety of a ravine to bring in the increasing numbers of wounded; untrained recruits assigned to carry forward fresh supplies of ammunition balked and officers of both the 1st Bombay Native Infantry (Grenadiers) and Jacob's Horse took on the task. The brigade was almost surrounded.

As in most battles, there were cowards and there were heroes. Among the latter were a number of young sepoys in Jacob's Rifles who were led by a young, recently joined British subaltern. They had not eaten since the previous evening and had had little water. They did not know the unit on their right. In their front, flank and rear were hordes of hostile Afghans. There had been a comforting battery of British howitzers near them, but they had packed up and moved elsewhere, seemingly to the safety of the rear. It was an ordeal indeed for these young men, many merely boys, witness to the horror around them, caught in an action of which they understood little except their own peril; yet with rare courage they stood firm and did their duty.

By mid-afternoon ammunition for the British guns was almost exhausted and rifle ammunition was running low. The sepoys had difficulty protecting their blistering hands from the hot barrels. Ayub Khan chose the right moment for an all-out attack. His warriors were led by white-clad ghazis, men who welcomed a death on a battlefield fighting against infidels. They crashed through the British lines and set to work with their long Khyber knives. The sepoys broke; first a few and then in mobs, they ran for their lives. Not everyone fled, of course, and there were vigorous efforts by officers, British and Indian, to staunch the haemorrhage.

Burrows was finally able to begin a disorderly retreat because, although he was ignorant of it at the time, many

Afghans were held in check by an effective rear guard made up of the remnants of two companies of the 66th (Berkshire) Regiment of Foot, who, in spite of fearful losses, managed a slow retreat while beating back the pursuing Afghans. But at last, boxed in behind mud walls, only two young lieutenants and nine men—66th privates and Bombay sepoys—were left. They decided to die in the open. An Afghan officer later told of their end:

> Surrounded by the whole Afghan army, they fought on until only eleven men were left, inflicting enormous loss on their enemy. These men charged out . . . and died with their faces to their foe, fighting to the death. Such was the nature of their charge, and the grandeur of their bearing, that although the whole of the ghazis were assembled around them, no one dared to approach to cut them down. Thus standing in the open, back to back, firing steadily and truly, every shot telling, surrounded by thousands, these officers and men died; and it was not until the last man was shot down that the ghazis dared advance upon them. The conduct of these men was the admiration of all who witnessed it.

The end came just before sunset.

Present at this last stand was a small nondescript dog called Bobbie, whose master, a Sergeant Kelly of the 66th Foot, was among the dead. Although wounded, Bobbie hobbled through the Afghan horde and found his way back to his regiment at Kandahar. (Bobbie recovered from his wound and returned to England with the 66th. There he was presented with the Afghan Medal by Queen Victoria herself. Eighteen months after the battle he was run over and killed by a hansom cab. He can still be seen at the regimental museum of the Berkshires at Reading, for he was stuffed and now stands proudly in a glass case, his Afghan Medal suspended by a ribbon from his neck.) Captain William Hamilton M'Math's dog, Nellie, a great favourite in the 66th, was killed with her master in the action. The Afghans buried them together as a mark of contempt, but it was an insult lost on the British, who found the burial a tribute, touching and fitting.

Fortunately, when all resistance ended, most of the Afghans preferred to stay and loot the abandoned baggage rather than pursue the fleeing remnants of Burrows's brigade. Left behind with the baggage were the wounded, including those on doolies (stretchers) in the field hospital, abandoned when the hospital personnel fled.

Some soldiers of the 66th who tarried to loot their own officers' mess took the opportunity to get drunk. Lieutenant Arthur Mackworth Monteith sent sowars to collect horses and the drunken men were slung on them. They promptly fell off. Before they could be tied on, Monteith and his men were menaced by several hundred Afghan horsemen and were forced to flee, leaving a number of the drunks to the untender mercies of their foes, who liked to watch their enemies die as slowly and as painfully as possible.

Remnants of the brigade, exhausted from fear and fatigue and suffering from thirst, faced a long march across a desert. Some of the mounted men, able to range, managed to find water, but the infantry and the camp followers found little and fought among themselves for this. Bands of Afghans hung on their rear and the wretched, demoralized stragglers and followers were sniped at from every village.

First news of the disaster at Maiwand reached Kandahar at one-thirty in the morning of 28 July, when a jemadar of Sind Horse rode in with his troop and reported (wrongly) that General Burrows was dead and his force cut to pieces. Other stragglers found their way in throughout the night. At about 5:00 a.m. a small relief force was sent out under Brigadier-General Henry Francis Brooke, who described the returning survivors:

> I had never seen the retreat of a panic-stricken military force before, and I trust that I may never do so again, as it is too horrible for description, and this retreat excelled in terror any that I have ever heard of. All appearance of organization or

discipline gone; each man, whether European or native, was fighting, as it were, for his own life, careful of nothing but getting into safety. All were wearied and harassed, and many hardly able to move one foot before the other.

The gun carriages and wagons were loaded with sick, wounded and dead; the horses dying of thirst and exhaustion. Almost last of all came Brigadier-General Burrows. When he saw his friend Brooke, he broke down completely and could not speak. Brooke, shocked, made him dismount and gave him some whisky and water, then a bit of biscuit.

Amid the stumbling, demoralized soldiery and frightened followers who poured into Kandahar that afternoon was one small, perfectly disciplined and organized unit, the surviving half-company of low-caste Bombay Sappers and Miners under Lieutenant Thomas Rice Henn. Only twenty-one men were left standing out of forty-six, but outside the gate they paused to smarten themselves up, formed ranks, and marched in like the soldiers they were. In the heat and dust of battle and on the long, painful road back, they had behaved magnificently.

Burrows had suffered 44 percent casualties. Out of a total force of 2,565 officers and men, 962 were killed and 161 wounded survived. The Afghans took few prisoners. Casualties among the followers were uncounted. In 1880 this was a major defeat for a British force in Asia.

Few today have heard of the Battle of Maiwand, though readers of Sherlock Holmes may remember that Dr. Watson is said to have been present. It was also long remembered in the Royal Berkshire Regiment (as the 66th became soon after the battle), for although it is rare for a regiment in a defeat to be awarded a battle honour, the Berkshires proudly carried "Maiwand."* Unjust though it may be, it is also rare for Victoria Crosses to be awarded to defeated

---

* In today's British Army a battery of 29 Commando Light Regiment is the "Maiwand Battery" and celebrates "Maiwand Day" with a parade each year.

soldiers, but two were awarded for heroism during the terrible retreat from Maiwand, both to gunners: Sergeant Patrick Mullane and Gunner James Collis.*

With the return of the Maiwand survivors, General Primrose now had 3,250 effectives and 450 sick and wounded. Kandahar was a walled city with a perimeter that was 6,000 yards, enclosing an area too extensive for such a small force to defend. Most of the inhabitants of the town were at best unfriendly. Although there was a strong citadel, Primrose decided to defend the entire city. At the urging of Brooke and Burrows, all Pathan males of fighting age were expelled: twelve thousand left the city voluntarily and another seven hundred were forcibly ejected. Broken walls were repaired, gun emplacements were prepared and fields of fire cleared.

The Afghans, although they had won the day, had also suffered severe losses. Ayub Khan paused to allow his dead to be buried (most British corpses were left to rot on the ground), and his wounded to be carried off by relatives while the remainder of his army quarrelled over the division of the loot. Even so, by 5 August his advance guard had arrived before Kandahar and his main force came up two days later. The siege of Kandahar now began.

There was plenty of food in the city and good wells supplied water. As in most sieges, the investment was not complete; people managed to come in and go out. There were sorties and some bitter little battles, which created numerous casualties and accomplished nothing. Although in Kabul, Bombay, and London there was fear for Primrose and his

---

* Gunner Collis, twenty-four years old, won his medal for deliberately drawing fire on himself to save a load of wounded. He later left the army and joined the Bombay Police. Fifteen years after winning his cross, it was taken away from him, forfeited by Royal Warrant of 18 November 1895 because he was convicted of bigamy. He died in London in 1918. (Of the 1,346 Victoria crosses awarded to date, only eight have ever been forfeited, the last in 1908.)

Sergeant Mullane, a handsome twenty-eight-year-old Irishman, was a child of the army, born to a soldier father in Ahmednagar in the Deccan. He stayed in service until he retired as a regimental sergeant-major; he died in Sussex in 1919.

force, they were actually in little danger and help was on the way.

Just before the Battle of Maiwand, Lieutenant-General Sir Donald Stewart had arrived in Kabul and had assumed command from Roberts, who now wanted nothing more than to return to India and shake the dust of Afghanistan from his feet. Many of his troops had already begun the long march through the passes. Stewart had just written to his wife: "I can hardly believe that we are to get out of this country without trouble, and yet everything looks bright and promising at this moment." Then, by way of India, came the shocking news on 28 July of the disaster at Maiwand.

The evacuation was halted at once and the grumbling troops on the march, cursing in their various languages, were turned back to Kabul, where Roberts, on Stewart's orders, assembled a force of the best and fittest, about ten thousand men plus some eight thousand followers, and on 7 August led them out of Kabul to the relief of Kandahar.

The 320-mile march to Kandahar was indeed difficult. The days were blazing hot, the nights freezing, and food and water were in short supply, but they met no opposition and Roberts was able to average nearly thirteen miles a day. Although other units of the British Army had made more arduous and more hazardous marches, this expedition caught the popular fancy. Marching to rescue a besieged garrison and to avenge a humiliating defeat was stirring, of course, but perhaps it was the poetic alliteration of exotic names that caused Roberts's march from Kabul to Kandahar to thrill the Empire and to engender a wave of patriotic fervour that swept Roberts to the top of his profession and to a peerage.

At seven o'clock on the morning of 31 August Roberts reached Kandahar at the head of his little army and was wildly cheered by the defenders, who soon felt the full force of his wrath, for Roberts was outraged by "the demoralized condition of the greater part of the garrison." In his estimation they had been in no danger at all: "For British

While British soldiers were fighting the Dervishes in the Sudan, India's soldiers continued to do their bit on the Afghan Frontier. And in London's music halls in 1898 they sang such songs as this. (National Army Museum)

soldiers to have contemplated the possibility of Kandahar being taken by an Afghan army showed what a miserable state of depression and demoralization they were in." He was incensed that "they never even hoisted the Union Jack until the relieving force was close at hand." Only the Royal Artillery and the Bombay Sappers and Miners got good marks. It was perhaps thoughts of Maiwand and the Kandahar garrison which led Roberts ever after to think ill of the Bombay Army.

Roberts arrived at Kandahar with 940 men sick from bad food and lame from hard marching. He himself was suffering from a stomach complaint, but he signalled to India that "the troops from Kabul are in famous health and spirits." He lost no time seeking an engagement and on 1 September he attacked Ayub Khan, slaying or scattering his warriors, capturing his camp and all his artillery. His losses were 58 killed or mortally wounded and 192 wounded. Afghan casualties were estimated in the thousands.

Having slaughtered a great many Afghans and suffered substantial losses themselves from bullets, shells and diseases, Roberts's troops and the rescued forces returned from whence they came. The authorities did not even insist upon replacing Cavagnari with another Resident in Kabul. The British had for a second time been taught, as a hundred years later the Russians were to be taught, that although the Afghans can be defeated in open battle and cities can be captured, alien armies cannot hold the country or rule its turbulent peoples.

Fears of the Russians continued to haunt politicians and British generals who were concerned with India. In March 1890, Roberts, now Field Marshal Lord Roberts of Kandahar, wrote of his doubts about the ability of the Indian Army to face the Russian Army. Sepoys did well enough when faced with "badly armed, undisciplined Afghans and tribes which have but little cohesion amongst themselves," but how would they perform against well-armed, well-disciplined European troops?

I have no hesitation in stating that except Gurkhas, Dogras, Sikhs, the pick of the Punjabi Muhammadans, Hindustanis of the Jay and Ranghur castes (such as enlist in our cavalry) and certain classes of Pathans, there are no Native soldiers in our service whom we could venture in safety to place in the field against the Russians. . . . I should be sorry to find myself in front of a European foe unless my forces were composed of as many Europeans as Natives.

Fortunately for all concerned, the anticipated war between Russia and the British in India never occurred. The Great Game was never played to a bloody conclusion.

CHAPTER

8

The
Imperial Assemblage

O n 11 September 1876 a special gazette announced that on New Year's Day 1877 Queen Victoria would assume an additional title: Empress of India. After much discussion it was determined that the vernacular term for the Empress would be *Kaiser-i-Hind*, which had the advantage of meaning the same in Arabic and Sanskrit. In India Lord Lytton, the Viceroy, laid plans to celebrate the event at Delhi with an enormous viceregal durbar, or state levée, to be called an Imperial Assemblage.

Elaborate preparations began months ahead of time. Invitations were sent to the heads of all the princely states of India, of which there were more than five hundred, for this was perceived as an occasion to cement the loyalty of the princes to the Crown and to reward them for their support during the Mutiny. Each was advised that he could bring no more than five hundred retainers—plus servants, of course—and that he must come at his own expense. Only on the day of the proclamation would the princes be considered guests of the sirkar. One hundred gold commemorative medals (they were to cost no more than £20 each) were struck for the chief dignitaries; silver medals were struck for lesser lights.

The most important princes also were to be given banners of heavy Chinese satin emblazoned with spurious coats of arms with elephants and cows as supporters, mottoes in English, and crests with helms—significantly, no crest included a crown. (Rudyard Kipling's mother helped with the embroidery.) This provoked some sulking among those princes who were not on the list to receive banners. When the Khan of Khelat, ruler of about 72,000 square miles of a rugged mountain area in Baluchistan, demanded to know why he had been left out, he was diplomatically told that the banners were only given to the rulers of feudatory states, not to independent princes such as he. "I don't want to be an independent prince," he sulked, "and I do want to have my banner like all the rest."

Valentine ("Val") Prinsep, a Pre-Raphaelite painter with family connections in India, was commissioned—for £5,000 and expenses—to paint a picture of the event for presentation to Queen Victoria, the money to come from the princes. Each contributor was to have a recognizable portrait in the picture and was to receive a lithograph of the scene.

The Order of the Star of India was enlarged to include more princes, and a new order, the Order of the Indian Empire, was instituted. On the New Years Honour's List four maharajas were created Knight Grand Commanders of the Star of India; others were given lesser orders. In addition, several rajas were promoted to maharaja, and lesser chiefs were advanced to rajas. In all, more than two hundred Indians received higher titles.

Perhaps the most prized gift of all was an increase in the number of gun salutes allowed the most important princes. This had been formally set down and formed the basis for precedence, not only for the British but amongst the princes themselves (see Appendix B, p. 368). Lord Lytton wrote to Disraeli: "I believe that at the present moment an Indian

Maharaja would pay anything for an additional gun to his salute; and were we not such puritans, we might ere this have made all our railways with the resources thus obtained." Those raised to twenty-one guns were particularly delighted, for this was the same number accorded the Viceroy. They were to learn later that Lytton had raised the number of his own gun salutes to thirty-one.

Lytton also wished to offer the Indians something more substantial—an Indian Privy Council and an Indian peerage—but his plans were thwarted in London, where neither the government nor the press was enthusiastic about the durbar. *The Times* complained of the cost, pointing out that the Imperial Assemblage followed close upon a costly recent visit to India by the Prince of Wales, and reporting that the princes, too, were grumbling about their expenses, although the fact was that from the greatest maharaja to the smallest hill raja they had responded with enthusiasm; this was their kind of show. Even the Nizam of Hyderabad, ruling a country of more than eighty thousand square miles (larger than England and Ireland combined), and reputedly the richest man in the world, a prince who had never before attended a viceregal durbar, accepted eagerly.

On a plain four miles northeast of Delhi, beside the famous ridge where the British had confronted the mutineers in 1857, two thousand coolies laboured for weeks to create an enormous camp with separate areas for the Viceroy, the presidency governors, the commanders-in-chief, and the princes. In the Viceroy's camp his family, fifty-nine guests and staff were housed in a double row of tents forming an imposing street that ended at the great durbar tent and a huge iron structure painted red, white and blue, and open on one end. It housed the viceregal throne and a life-sized picture of the Queen-Empress. The artist Prinsep described the whole as "an Ossa of bad taste on the Pelion of shrieking colour." The Maharaja of Jaipur supplied the gas (made from castor oil) used in the lamps in the camp, as well as in the durbar tent's lamps of triple cast-iron designed by

Lockwood Kipling, father of Rudyard, now a ten-year-old schoolboy in England.

Among the assembled princes was one woman, the Begum of Bhopal, then aged thirty-seven, whom Edith, Countess of Lytton, huffily described as "a scruffy little woman with a wretched lolling husband," who "wears little shoes like galoshes." The British found much to laugh at. One raja boasted a corps of bagpipers dressed as Scots Highlanders, their knees covered with pink leggings to add authenticity. There was also a piper wearing an enormous yellow head-dress and a petticoat, and a musician sporting gilded armour. Another prince, too poor to aspire to a band, brought along an attendant who ground out "God Save the Queen" on a hand organ. In all some eight hundred titular princes and nobles were present, including some of the wilder sort such as the bannerless Khan of Khelat and his sirdars. Also in attendancce were ambassadors from a score of countries; the Imam of Muscat; journalists from fourteen European newspapers; and fifteen thousand Indian and British troops plus numbers of brightly clad soldiers of the princely states, accompanied by elephants in chain mail. The Gaekwar of Baroda's troops brought their cannons cast in silver and gold. In all, about a hundred thousand people camped on the plain. Most were already on hand on 23 December when the Viceroy arrived in state on an elephant preceded by three detachments of cavalry and a dozen trumpeters.

The Imperial Assemblage marked the first time that a female member of the Viceroy's family had ever appeared at a public function to which Indians were invited. Lytton hoped that the presence of Lady Lytton would "help to bridge over at least some portion of the inconvenient and deplorable gulf existing between English and native society," but it was not a popular innovation among the local Europeans. Most were shocked by the presence of the Viceroy's wife. They spoke of Lytton's term of office as the "Black Raj" and complained that social life was being corrupted.

Some 200 native princes and chiefs of various ranks met the
Prince of Wales on his arrival at Agra on 25 January 1876—the
two principal princes being the Maharao Raja of Bundi and the
Maharaja of Bikaner. When the Prince of Wales had passed
between the ranks of the princes, they formed up to make a
splendid elephant procession. *(Illustrated London News)*

Memsahibs sulked and, in spite of the trouble and expense
of having acquired new gowns, many refused to attend when
it was learned they were to appear with "dark gentlemen."

Lord Lytton, only son of Bulwer-Lytton, the novelist, was
not a popular Viceroy with the English-Indians. An eccentric who wrote poetry and loved finery, he was criticized
for his indolence and his failure to improve the tone of society in India. He raised a storm of controversy by suspend-
ing a magistrate who had fined a British planter a mere 30
rupees for killing his Indian coachman. Shortly after the
Imperial Assemblage he wrote to his friend, Lord George
Hamilton:

The fact is, the whole of Anglo-Indian society is mortally offended with the Prince of Wales for not having sufficiently appreciated its superiority to everything in creation. His visit has left a deep, rankling sore in the Anglo-Indian mind, which has got an idée fixe that I came out to India with secret instructions from his Royal Highness to snub and aggravate the whites, and pet and spoil the blacks.

Five days after his arrival at Delhi for the durbar the Viceroy held a levée attended by two thousand five hundred Indian and European gentlemen. The crush was so great that at one point the great durbar tent threatened to collapse. Val Prinsep, a witness to much that went on just behind the scenes and on the sidelines, was shocked by the behaviour of the young British officers:

> They made loud remarks about the rajas there present, and expressed a wish to cut their ears off to get their jewels—quite forgetting that many of the rajas understood English. This was, no doubt, the mere silly chaff of a lot of young fellows who were hot and uncomfortable, who kept up their spirits by *badinage*. But I doubt whether rajas understand chaff.

On 1 January 1877, the great day itself, every soldier in the Indian Army was given an extra day's pay and, with the exception of one Mogul prince whose power to do evil was still feared, an amnesty was granted to all those exiled for their part in the Mutiny. Some sixteen thousand prisoners were released and, contrary to popular British expectations and to the astonishment of all, there was, according to one source, "a general falling-off in petty crimes and offenses against discipline, which, to say the least, was unexpected and extraordinary."

Battalions of infantry and squadrons of cavalry graced the parade ground with their standards and guidons and drums, the totems of their trade, when Lord Lytton, wearing the long, light blue satin mantle and insignia of a Knight Grand Commander of the Most Exalted Order of the Star

Survivors of the Mutiny were presented to the Prince of Wales during his visit in 1876 by Dr. Joseph Fayrer, CSI, himself a surviving hero of the Siege of Lucknow. Native officers still in service are extending the hilt of their sword to be touched by the "Shahzadah." (Windsor Castle. Royal Library. Her Majesty Queen Elizabeth II.)

of India, mounted the throne as the representative of the Queen-Empress. An officer, said to be the tallest man in the army, dressed in a herald's tabard, read the proclamation in English. It was read again in Urdu. Then massed infantry fired a *feu-de-joie*—"furious joy," the soldiers called it. Begun by the right-hand man in the front rank firing his rifle into the air, followed almost instantly by the man on his left, it proceeded through every soldier in the line; when the last man of the line fired, the man behind him fired, followed by the men on his right. The effect was a rippling fire fading away into the distance and then moving back again. It was not a military rite admired by cavalrymen, particularly troopers and sowars on skittish mounts or subalterns on spirited chargers. According to Val Prinseps, the *feu-de-joie* "was splendidly executed and with excellent effect, for it made the rajahs jump, and raised quite a stampede among the elephants, who 'skedaddled' in all directions, and killed a few natives."

All in all the Imperial Assemblage was a magnificent spectacle, the most flamboyant pageant ever seen in India, and Lytton judged it a tremendous success. The only jarring note was sounded by the onset of an exceptionally severe famine which swept through the Madras and Bombay presidencies and the native states of Hyderabad and Mysore, an area of about 200,000 square miles containing nearly 40 million people. Food was plentiful elsewhere, but not enough transport was available to ship it, and even if transport had been found, the wretched people of the stricken areas were too poor to buy it. The notion that the government might use some of its wealth to provide free food to the starving people was, of course, not considered.

CHAPTER
9

Chota Sahib and
Burra Sahib

"Quite how or why we know not, but the fact has remained that for two centuries, with the exception of the madness of 1857, come weal come woe, come rain come shine, the sepoy has followed and trusted that unintelligible entity his sahib." So in 1911 wrote George MacMunn, a soldier who had seen much service. Although not quite true then or later, the statement was close enough. The Indian soldier, by and large, did indeed trust and obey his British masters, whether they were fresh-faced young chota (small) sahibs or grey-haired and distinguished burra (big) sahibs. The reasons are not readily apparent.

Soldiers, British and Indian, lived apart from the civilian population in cantonments, permanent military stations holding in separate sections the bungalows of the officers, the married British noncommissioned officers, and the barracks and quarters of other ranks, the whole kept neat by hundreds of Indian servants and workers. Usually on the edge of or a few miles outside of a major city, they were often adjacent to the civil lines, the areas where the

European civil servants lived and sometimes had their offices and courts. There, too, were the British churches and well-filled cemeteries, the clubs, the playing fields, the bank, expanses of lawn and gardens, and a shopping area (sadar bazaar) where European food and furnishings could be purchased.

There were first-, second- and third-class cantonments, depending upon the number and qualities of the amenities to be found; in each the interiors of the bungalows of officers and noncommissioned officers usually resembled those they had known in Britain. Only the swaying punkah, some wicker chairs perhaps, and the ubiquitous Indian servants gave them an unavoidable touch of the East. Although beautiful gardens could be made with local flowers and shrubs, wives struggled to grow English flowers. Their phlox and nasturtiums wilted quickly when the hot weather began, yet, as the wife of an officer in the 45th Rattray's Sikhs said, speaking of the period between the world wars: "You wanted to be surrounded by something that wasn't dust and dead leaves."

Two modern writers (Larry Collins and Dominique Lapierre) have called the cantonments "golden ghettos of British rule appended like foreign bodies to India's major cities." This is harsh, and certainly would not apply to most third-class cantonments; generally they were oases of European civilization implanted in the dusty, noisy, alien Asian turbulence that surrounded them.

Inside every cantonment there was an insistence that everything be done "properly." In his history of the Indian Army, Philip Mason wrote that it was by "doing things properly—more often at least than most Indians—that the British had established themselves in India and that so few ruled so many with so slight a use of force." This gives far too much credit to what was, after all, merely the observance of outdated etiquette, on a par with the demand for absolute precision in military drill and "a meticulous insistence on a knife-edge crease to khaki shorts." How-

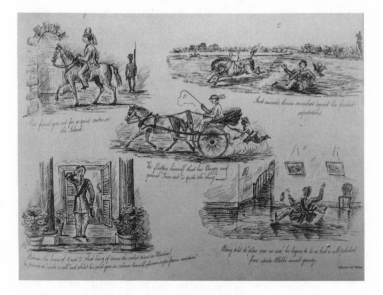

Caricatures of a subaltern's life in Madras in the 1860s.
(National Army Museum)

ever, doing things properly kept one British and gave men and women a comfortable sense of upholding standards. One of the most commonly used words among the English-Indians was *pukka* (or *pucka*), which came to stand for whatever was properly made or done, or was substantial and permanent: the way things *ought* to be.

Outside the barracks walls the bustling, pulsating bazaars and the noisome brothels flourished, magnets to the rank and file who, even so, were generally glad to return to the cleanliness, orderliness and familiarity of their cantonments.

Bachelor officers often clubbed together to rent a bungalow and often furnished it with rented European furniture. They usually shared servants: the *bhisti* (water carrier), *mehtar* (sweeper, who also cleaned the latrines), *chokidar* (watchman—usually a retired thief), and *mali* (gardener). Their personal soldier servants (called bearers) sometimes took turns as *kitmutgars* (waiters) at the mess.

Social life for the officers revolved endlessly around dances, dinner parties, amateur theatricals, card playing and particularly sport. It could be a trying life for their wives. Vere Ogilvie was the seventh generation of her family to live in India, but when in 1931 she married Captain (later Colonel) Christopher Birdwood of Probyn's Horse and lived in cantonments, she felt "a total loss of the quality of life." Army life, she said, was "excessively boring, trivial, claustrophobic, confined and totally male-oriented. The army wife was not expected to do anything or be anything except a decorative chattel or appendage of her husband. Nothing else was required of her whatsoever. She was not expected to be clever. It didn't even matter if she wasn't beautiful, so long as she looked reasonable and dressed reasonably and didn't let her husband down by making outrageous remarks at the dinner table."

Dinner parties were important. Officers' wives, particularly those of high-ranking officers, burra memsahibs, as well as aides-de-camp, when making seating arrangements for dinner parties to which civil servants were invited,

Dinner parties tended to be stilted, but there were always servants aplenty, including the punkah wallah, out of sight in this
sketch and out of sight to dinner guests. (India Office Library)

carefully consulted the government's *Warrant of Precedence*, a book which listed every rank of the army and every
government post of any importance in the order of their
social precedence.

Maud Diver, laying out the duties of a British wife in her
book *The Englishwoman in India* (1909), pontificated: "She
will be zealous in guarding her children from promiscuous
intimacy with the native servants. . . . The sooner after the
fifth year a child can leave India, the better for its future
welfare." European children, whose first memories were
most likely to be of their ayiah, were indeed often spoiled
by the servants. The children of officers usually retained
happy memories of their childhood before they were packed
off to Britain to be educated, and many children of British
other ranks, whose parents could not afford to send them
back to Britain, grew up happily in India and seem to have
adored it. "I grew up in bright sunshine," wrote the son of

An Indian cantonment. (India Office Library)

a British corporal, "I grew up with tremendous space, I grew up with animals, I grew up with excitement, I grew up believing that white people were superior."

A painful rite of passage for married officers and their wives was the departure of the children for Britain, particularly the first child, when the decision had to be made whether the wife and mother would return to stay as well. Maud Diver wrote: "Sooner or later the lurking shadow of separation takes definite shape; asserts itself as a harsh reality; a grim presence, whispering the inevitable question; which shall it be?" Husband or child? She could no longer have both. It was a separation of years. Some officers parted from their sons when they were five years old and did not see them again until they returned to India as subalterns to carry on the family traditions.

There are three seasons on the Indian plains: cold weather,

With a pretty woman, an elephant's howdah packed with good
things to eat and drink, riding horses, and plenty of servants,
one could enjoy a pleasant picnic in the country, weather per-
mitting. (National Army Museum)

hot weather, and monsoon rains. In March, when the cool
weather ended and the weather turned sticky hot, the women
and children with their ayiahs, along with the entire government of the presidencies, fled to the hill stations, leaving most of the officers and other ranks to swelter on the
plains below until, with the coming of the monsoons, soldiers ran naked from their barracks to greet the first rain.

There were numerous small hill stations but the most
important were Ootacamund (7,500 feet up in the Nilgiri
Hills between Madras and Bombay) in the south, and in
the north, Mussoorie, Darjeeling, Naini Tal and, above all,
Simla, crouching in the foothills of the Himalayas. Sol-

diers referred to Simla as the Viceroy's shooting box, Mount Olympus, or the Abode of the Little Tin Gods.

From 1863 until World War II, it was to Simla (1,170 miles from Calcutta, then the capital of Bengal) that the Governor-General (later, Viceroy), his council, the government of the Punjab, and all the presidency and provincial bureaucracies retired, and there, too, was the hot season headquarters of the Commander-in-Chief and the army. This great annual migration, lasting many days, usually began with long and tedious train rides, but even a chota sahib might have an entire carriage for his family and burra sahibs an entire train.

Simla, which for five or six months of every year became the capital of British India, was in many ways a curious place for the government to be and, because of its remoteness, an even stranger place for the Commander-in-Chief and the headquarters of the army. A small British enclave perched on a Himalayan ridge 6,600 to 8,000 feet above sea level, it was surrounded by princely states. The first British bungalow was built in 1819; by 1903 there were one thousand four hundred European houses scattered over the hillsides (although every year a few were swept away by landslides), and a Gothic-looking English church had been built, graced with frescoes around the chancel window designed by Rudyard Kipling's father. Numerous shops offered British goods, and visiting Europeans could put up comfortably at the Royal Hotel. A mall, a popular promenade for Europeans (forbidden to Indians before World War I), ran from end to end of the ridge. An Indian town clung to the lower slopes.

Simla's roads were too narrow for carriages or carts (even today they are too narrow for motor cars). Men rode about on horseback and women were carried in chairs or pulled in two-wheeled carts. On the north side of the ridge a wide valley held a racecourse and sports fields where gymkhanas were held and games were played. In the cool air men and women were able to "shake the plain's dust out of the

A memsahib with her child taking a tonga to Simla. (India Office Library)

brains" and to restore worn constitutions and frayed nerves. In large part it was the establishment of hill stations that induced British women to join their men in India, for it enabled them to keep their health. As one memsahib put it: "Like meat, we keep better here."

Simla was not easy to reach. Until 1903 the railway ended at the town of Kalka, forty-two miles away. The remainder of the trip had to be made in two-horse tongas (covered carts): an eight-hour journey. All of the household furnishings, government files, food and other supplies were carried up the steep ridge in bullock carts or on the backs of men.

Edith, Lady Lytton, wife of the Viceroy, complained: "The ladies are like that of any garrison town, Folkestone or Dover. The native servants *try* me very much, they smell so very strong when hot—like squashed bugs—but our own here have more on (red tunics with gold braid) and smell less strong." She found the lack of proper toilets and the necessity of using commodes another grievance, but otherwise noted with approval that "the ways are far more English than I have been used to."

Although women outnumbered men during the season at Simla, there were always enough soldiers around to add colour to the social scene. In addition to the Commander-in-Chief and his staff, odd officers came on leave or to convalesce, and the Viceroy's military secretary, an officer responsible for arranging levées, "drawing-rooms" and other social functions, was ever-present. According to Lord Lytton, "the social popularity of the Viceroy mainly depends upon that of the Military Secretary and it is essential that he should be a man of the world, with perfect tact, *savoir-faire*, and engaging manners."

Social life was so important a part of the Simla scene that it often seemed as if it was the sole occupation of government. Val Prinsep, the painter of the Imperial Assemblage, wrote:

> Simla is an English watering place gone mad. . . . Real sociability does not exist. People pair off immediately they arrive at a party. . . . Of course people gamble and do what they ought not. They do that everywhere. The play is very high, the whist execrable. All are bent on enjoying themselves, and champagne flows on every side. Every evening at eight the roads are full of *jampons** conveying the fair sex to the festivities.

In 1904 an article on hill stations appeared in *The Pioneer*, an English-language newspaper published in Allahabad:

> Nowhere possibly in the world are the passions of human nature laid so open for dissection as they are in remote hill stations on the slopes of the eternal abodes of snow. In the very small communities the round of gossip is incessant, probably inevi-

---

* *Jampon*—a kind of rickshaw said to have been invented by a man known only as "Public-Spirited Smith."

table. Resources there are none save such as are afforded by amusement committees. The men are deprived of sport, the women are overladen with calls and dressing and admiration ... with few housekeeping cares, with many luxuries, with a constant flow of amusements which few save in the richest society at home can attempt to enjoy incessantly ... there discontent breeds and jealousy and scandal dominate. The smallness of society, eddying round in such a tiny backwater, makes for stagnation.

William Russell, the famous war correspondent, was shocked, as had been the Prince of Wales and other European visitors, by the "wildness of spirit and lax notions of discipline and decency" exhibited by young officers, and he was particularly critical of those officers who abused Indians and spoke of their servants as "dogs of natives."

Few officers or their wives took any interest in the ancient culture of India. Its music, paintings, religions and mores were, as far as possible, ignored, and nowhere was this more evident than at Simla. Perhaps, as a writer for *Chambers's Journal* suggested in the 1880s, "the English in India are wise to surround themselves as far as they can with an English atmosphere and to defend themselves from the magic of the land by sport, games, clubs and the chatter of fresh-imported girls and by fairly regular attendance at church. They are probably following the instincts of self-preservation."

For many, Simla was synonymous with sex. Although other ranks made use of the many brothels and free-ranging Indian prostitutes, unmarried officers generally led a sexless life except, for a fortunate few, at the hill stations. Yeats-Brown wrote of his time in India as a young officer: "My life was as sexless as any monk's at this time; and in a sense I was only half alive, lacking the companionship of women. ... I do not know how far the discipline of the sex life is a good thing. But I know that a normal sex life is more necessary in a hot than a cold country."

Horse racing was a popular sport in India. In this scene, an Indian appears to be stealing the coat of a gentleman who is refreshing his horse with champagne. (G. F. Atkinson, *Curry & Rice*, 2nd ed. 1859)

It was difficult for officers, often stationed for long months in remote posts, to find women of their own race and class, for, as Brigadier R. C. B. Bristow pointed out: "Drawn to their own kind, the Britons in India seldom married outside their own race, and even without religious prohibitions were as exclusive as the caste Hindus and Muslims."

Many officers, when they attained their majority and returned to Britain on leave, hurriedly married. Others found wives among the young female relations of fellow officers or officials. Each year many of these, properly chaperoned, came out from England for a few months (which usually included the festive Christmas season) definitely looking for husbands. Known as the Fishing Fleet, their ideal was a

"Black Heart"—a very rich bachelor. Wise in the ways of the army, most avoided—or were steered away from—young and handsome but impecunious subalterns, who derisively called those who sailed home unmarried or unengaged "Returned Empty."

It was necessary that officers marry girls of the right sort and everyone, from the commanding officer's wife to the subalterns, took a keen interest in any courtship. One officer was known to have jilted the young woman he fancied because he was invariably greeted by fellow officers with groans of "Sam, you're not going to marry that girl!"

There was, of course, a considerable amount of philandering, particularly at the hill stations, though perhaps not as much as was imagined, for they were tight communities where all were watched and all were known. Too much attention to women was called "poodle-faking," and the colonels of some regiments banned some hill stations which were famous for their frivolity. Still, hill stations filled with bored wives whose husbands were sweating with their regiments on the plains below presented some officers on duty or leave there with a combination of desire and availability they found irresistible. Every season had its scandals, and it was said that some poodle-fakers came down from the hills fighting rearguard actions against enraged husbands.

Sir O'Moore Creagh, Commander-in-Chief, India, from 1909 to 1914, said of Simla: "Dinner parties, dances, and theatricals were of nightly occurrence, and in the afternoons there were race meetings, polo tournaments, dogshows, etc. without end. Stupid gossip or shop replaced intelligent conversation. . . . There was such extravagance that many . . . were either in debt or could only just scrape along."

Lord Lytton confessed that he was sorely tempted at Simla by the young, pretty and lively wives of two senior officials, but he feared the scandal that would have resulted. To his chagrin, both "consoled themselves" with his aides-de-camp.

According to Wilfrid Scawen Blunt, the poet, politician and traveller, who himself had an affair with one of them, "It was a regime which was compromising him [Lytton] without adequate return of amusement."

During the hot weather on the plains daring young officers would take out "B Class" young women, often quite beautiful but of a social class, usually Anglo-Indian, that made any thought of marriage unthinkable. When the cold weather returned and the social life of the regiment resumed, these hot weather partners were unceremoniously dumped.

The fringes of the Indian Empire saw no Fishing Fleets and there old customs lasted longer. In 1881 Colonel W. Monro, Deputy Commissioner of Bassein in Lower Burma, was denied promotion because he had a Burmese mistress, who had borne him numerous children. Monro protested to Charles Barnard, the Chief Commissioner, that his relationship had begun twenty years earlier when "things of this sort were looked at in a more venial light." Barnard conceded that the custom of native mistresses, once common in India, had lasted "a full generation" longer in Burma, but Monro was not promoted.

Thirteen years later the authorities were still fidgeting. In 1894 the Chief Commissioner in Burma opined in a confidential circular that a British officer with a Burmese mistress "not only degrades himself as an English gentleman, but lowers the prestige of the English name and largely destroys his own usefulness." However, a few years later Lord Curzon, then the Viceroy, was advised by his friend Lord George Hamilton that Burmese women were "engaging females, with a natural aptitude for the society of men, and I am afraid there always will be sexual relations existing between a certain number of Englishmen and their housekeepers in Burma."

Homosexuals were not unknown in either the British or the Indian armies, but seldom caused scandal. Former public school boys were not likely to be shocked by such proclivities and in some Indian regiments homosexuality among the other ranks was even more easily accepted. "The Wounded Heart," a popular Pushtu song, lamented: "There is a boy across the river with a bottom like a peach, but alas I cannot swim." It was the consequences of the heterosexual activities of the British other ranks that most concerned commanding officers.

10

Sex and the Other Ranks

M uch more is known of the sexual activities of other ranks than of officers. The principal reasons are to be found not in prudery or any prurient interest but in military efficiency. Troops unable to take the field because of disease were worse than useless and in the nineteenth century the most common diseases in the British Army were venereal. Commanders were therefore forced to take an interest in the sex life of their men.

Before the Mutiny it was generally assumed that at least 10 percent of the British soldiers in any unit at any one time would be in the hospital with a venereal disease. This was a conservative figure, for frequently the rate was much higher. In Indian regiments the rate was generally below 5 percent. An analysis made over a five-year period in the 1830s showed a rate of 32–45 percent among British other ranks and only 2–3 percent in Indian regiments. This anomaly was generally accounted for by pointing out that few British soldiers were permitted to marry, while many sepoys lived with their wives and families. Indians, however, had a different explanation: British soldiers were over-sexed and lustful.

In 1864 the government promulgated the Contagious Diseases and Cantonment Act of India, providing for the registration of prostitutes and for the inspection and control of brothels. Prostitutes were divided into two classes. First-class prostitutes were those frequented by Europeans, and only these were required to be registered and were subject to control by the cantonment authorities. Each first-class prostitute was supplied with a printed list of the rules and a ticket on which was recorded her monthly examination by the medical officer. Second-class prostitutes, whose customers were other Indians, remained unregulated.

In 1870 the Quartermaster General sent a series of circular memoranda to the general officers commanding divisions and districts, and in one of these he ordered: "Officers commanding troops on the line of march are directed to ensure the effective inspection of prostitutes attached to their regimental bazaars." However, a Royal Commission, meeting in London a few months later, shocked to learn that the army supplied Indian prostitutes to its British soldiers, piously concluded that "no considerations of health, economy or expediency can justify or excuse legal prostitution."

The members of the commission were particularly appalled by attitudes such as those expressed by Surgeon Alexander Clark Ross, an officer who had seen much service in China and had once been recommended for the Victoria Cross. Clark had suggested that prostitutes be included in the establishment of camp followers and assigned to units as they arrived in India. They should, he said, be housed in the regimental bazaar, medically examined, and supervised by a "matron appointed for the purpose." The revelation that Indian prostitutes were provided for British soldiers caused an uproar in England, where there was already considerable political opposition, in which Florence Nightingale played a prominent part, to the Contagious Diseases Act, a key feature of which was the compulsory examination of women in garrison towns who were merely suspected of carrying the disease.

Emphasis was almost always focused upon controlling the women, for as the Royal Commission explained in its report, "there is no comparison to be made between prostitutes and the men who consort with them. With the one sex the offense is committed as a matter of gain; with the other it is an irregular indulgence of a natural impulse." In spite of the high incidence of venereal diseases, genital examinations of soldiers were discontinued in 1857 because of their strong objections.

Although it was deemed essential to control the prostitutes frequented by soldiers, the most effective control seemed to be to legitimate prostitution, making it almost respectable. Well-regulated and inspected regimental brothels were demonstrably effective, but unless they were closely watched they could create small epidemics. In 1881, when the 51st Regiment (the King's Own Yorkshire Light Infantry) arrived at Rawalpindi after service in the Second Afghan War, it established a brothel in the bazaar under a local woman whose salary was paid from the Canteen Fund. A year later 13 noncommissioned officers, 5 buglers and 152 privates had contracted venereal diseases.

In the late 1880s the venereal rate began to rise at an alarming pace and the dilemma was deliberated at all official levels. In 1886 Dr. William James Moore, Surgeon-General in Bombay, gnawing on the problem, wrote a memorandum stating that "physiological instincts must be satisfied some way or other," and that British other ranks, coming from the lower reaches of society, could not be expected to "attain to the high moral standard required for suppression." There remained for them only masturbation, prostitution, or homosexuality. "The former," said Dr. Moore, "as is well known, leads to disorders of both body and mind," while prostitution exposed soldiers "to the fearful dangers of venereal." He found the third alternative too disgusting to discuss.

It was in 1886 too that General Sir Frederick (later Lord) Roberts, then Commander-in-Chief, India, writing to Lord Dufferin, the Viceroy, from Rawalpindi, noted that of 177 British other ranks in the hospital there, 101 were venereal-disease cases, and that this was not unusual. While admitting that "the subject is an unsavoury one," he asserted that "we cannot well shirk it." Soon after, on 17 June 1886, Major-General Edward F. Chapman, the Quartermaster General, wrote a memorandum he was later to regret. After noting the Commander-in-Chief's desire to check the spread of venereal diseases and the need to have prostitutes examined, he proceeded to discuss brothels in regimental bazaars. It was not only necessary to stock them with a sufficient number of women, he said, but commanders should as well "take care that they are sufficiently attractive."

Commanding officers fell on his advice and seem to have approached their recruiting of prostitutes energetically and with commendable professionalism, doing their best to see that enough prostitutes were available, that the facilities for their work were adequate, that they were well treated, and that when they were diseased, "every reasonable inducement" was offered to them to go into what were called "lock hospitals."*

A month after General Chapman's circular, Lieutenant-Colonel Frederick William Best Parry, commanding the 2nd Battalion of the Cheshire Regiment, wrote a "Requisition

---

* The term "lock hospital" is said to have been taken from the name of a London hospital founded in 1746 for treatment of venereal diseases of respectable wives who were the victims of their husbands' profligacy, although most of its patients came to be, in fact, prostitutes. Another, established in 1758, was designed for "repentant prostitutes," a place where those considered "morally insane" could be "brought to their senses" by education. At this same early period government hospitals for "diseased women" were established in India at Cawnpore, Berhampore, Dinapur and Fategarh. Women were often forbidden to leave until they were pronounced cured.

for extra attractive women for Regimental Bazar [sic] (soldiers)" to the cantonment magistrate in Ambala. Citing the memorandum of the Quartermaster General, he complained that he had only six women for four hundred men; he calculated that he needed six more. He ended his request with a plea: "Please send young and attractive women." The medical officer at Faizabad, also inspired by Chapman, requested that the prostitutes there be replaced by "others who are younger and better looking." Six months after General Chapman's circular memorandum, Dr. William Collis, Deputy Surgeon-General of the Peshawar District, reported happily that "efforts have been made and with some success to provide a more attractive lot of women."

Keeping clean, attractive whores in the regimental bazaar reduced cases of venereal disease drastically, but such a solution brought problems. However reasonably officers faced the situation and however energetically they set about to reduce the incidence of venereal disease, they had always to keep in mind a vocal corps of public opinion, both in India and in Britain, which resisted realistic measures for coping. The voices of protest reached a crescendo in 1887–88.

Most vocal of all was Mr. Alfred Dyer, a Quaker publisher and a reformer with an abiding interest in prostitutes. In 1887 he journeyed to India to see for himself what the army was up to and he found much to shock his sensibilities. Visiting the 4th Battalion of the Rifle Brigade on the march, he was scandalized to see pitched beside their camp thirteen tents occupied by their registered prostitutes, brought along on their move from Chakrata.

At Bareilly he was incensed to discover the temperance tent of the 2nd Battalion of the East Kent Regiment in an "obscure corner," while "the tents of the Government harlots confront the troops from morning to night, separated from their own tents only by a public thoroughfare, without any buildings or trees intervening." Delhi was, if anything, worse. There "the principal quarters of the women licensed to sin" were only eighty paces from the entrance to the Baptist chapel.

Poring over official reports on lock hospitals in Oudh and North-West Frontier Province, he came upon a proposal "to induce a greater number of prostitutes to reside in cantonments by making their residence there more attractive."

Bearing a wealth of such material, Dyer returned to England and published his findings in a series of articles in *The Sentinel*, a publication he owned. In the House of Commons James Stuart, a member who delighted in asking the government embarrassing questions, repeatedly raised inquiries based on Dyer's findings. In the House of Lords the Bishop of Lichfield followed suit.

By 1887 there were 361 admissions to hospital for sexually related diseases for every 1,000 British soldiers in India. In the following year, with the venereal rate rising to 370 per thousand, the Anglican bishops of India and Ceylon met and passed a resolution declaring it to be a "fundamental principle" that "the discouragement and repression of vice are of far higher importance than the diminution of suffering or other evils resulting from vice, and that consequently in all efforts to mitigate the physical effects of impiety no sanitary or material gain can justify measures which in their operation afford facilities or encouragement for vicious indulgence."

Not everyone agreed with these sentiments, certainly not soldiers, neither officers nor other ranks. Indeed, military authorities considered it dangerous to deny men sexual outlets. On this, Britons and Indians alike agreed. In 1888 *Almora Akhbar*, a Hindu weekly, said: "Not to provide women for European soldiers who are drunk and mad with lust would be like letting loose beasts of prey." British soldiers at home and abroad were generally considered to be filled with "beef, beer and lust." Beef was issued, beer was made available, and sexual outlets had somehow to be found.

But in Britain the clamour of the religious moralists grew

intense and could not be ignored. For a time, regulated military brothels were closed. General Chapman, called on to explain his circular memorandum, lamely replied that while the authorities strove "to mitigate the evils of prostitution," nothing they had done could "justly be interpreted as encouraging vice."

To find the facts, to determine the exact situation in India, the Women's Christian Temperance Union sent out two American women: Mrs. Elizabeth Wheeler Andrew, wife of a Methodist minister, and Dr. Kate Bushnell. The two women arrived in India in December 1891 and over the next three months they assiduously visited ten military installations, toured lock hospitals, inspected regimental brothels, interviewed prostitutes and examined official registers of prostitutes. They easily confirmed that the system had not changed.

The red-light district of each cantonment area—the *lal* (red) bazaar—they found was usually directly supervised by an elderly madam, politely called the matron. In Lucknow, they found the women housed in a large structure of fifty-five rooms opening onto two courtyards. The presiding matron was, in their words, "a fine looking woman, that is judging by the native type." Sex was remarkably cheap. The standard rate here and, it would seem, in all cantonments, was one rupee for a sergeant, eight annas for a corporal, six for a lance bombadier or lance corporal, and four for a private.

Indian men, they learned, were not allowed to enter the brothels (known as "rags") used by European soldiers. If they attempted to do so, military police threw them out. The garrison provost sergeant at Lucknow explained that "there is no order to that effect, but it is not right for natives to go where British soldiers go for their women." This never changed. Private Frank Richards, who served in India in the years just before World War I, wrote: "Our Regimental police relieved one another in patrolling the small street which the Rag was in. Natives who passed through were not allowed to stop and talk to the girls; if any of them did, the policeman would give him such a thrashing with his stick that he would remember it a long time."

The report of the Women's Christian Temperance Union kept the political pot boiling, and in April 1893 a departmental committee was appointed under the chairmanship of George Russell, Parliamentary Undersecretary for India. After reviewing the evidence collected by Andrew and Bushnell, interviewing missionaries, as well as Lord Roberts and other soldiers, the committee recommended that the government of India adopt new legislation to control prostitution and venereal disease. As a result, the Cantonments Act Amending Bill, designed to bring Indian law into conformity with the resolution of the House of Commons, became law in 1895.

The venereal rate for the army had by that time reached horrendous proportions. A comparison of the mean rate of venereal-disease admissions of soldiers in India for 1890–93 with admission rates elsewhere revealed that admissions in India were 438.1 per thousand, while for troops in Britain the rate was only 203.7. Even this was higher than that found in other European armies: the German Army recorded 77.3 per thousand and the French Army a mere 43.8.

By 1895 there were 536 admissions per thousand British soldiers in India. Some of these were readmissions, of course, but it would appear that at least half, and probably more than half, of the British soldiers in India had, or had once had, a venereal disease.

The authorities in India continued their efforts to explain why British soldiers needed Indian whores. In 1894 the Acting District Magistrate at Ahmadabad, pleading for the return of official brothels, wrote:

> Private soldiers are young men taken from the classes least habituated to exercise self-control—classes who in their natural state marry very early in life. You take such men, you do

not allow them to marry, you feed them well—better in most cases than they have been accustomed to be fed, and you give them a sufficient amount of physical work to put them in good condition and no more. It is asking too much to expect that a large majority of such men will exhibit the continence of the cloister.

By 1898, of 65,397 British troops serving in India, 24,286 were admitted to hospitals for some venereal disease and many, found to be hopeless cases, were invalided back to Britain. Kipling, siding with the soldiers, was outraged that the moral indignation of those whom the soldiers called the "shrieking sisterhood" should hamper military efficiency: "It was counted impious that bazaar prostitutes should be inspected; or that men should be taught elementary precautions in their dealing with them. This official virtue cost our Army in India nine thousand expensive white men a year laid up from venereal disease." It has indeed been reliably estimated that in the last two decades of the last century as many as ten thousand soldiers were sent back home as complete invalids due to venereal diseases.

In 1899 another Cantonments Act was passed, granting the military forces in India more leeway in their efforts to curb the spread of disease. Although it was bitterly attacked by the Women's Temperance Association, the British Committee Against Vice, and other pious or philanthropic organizations, the India Office this time refused to yield. The Army in India never again allowed home politics and British notions of morality to hamper the effectiveness of its troops.

When Lord Kitchener became Commander-in-Chief, India (1902–09), he took additional steps to make sure that officers and men paid attention to the consequences of venereal diseases. Kitchener, who never had or wanted to have sexual relations with any woman, must have been puzzled by the lure of the rag. Drink and idleness led men to impure thoughts, he said, and it was the duty of commanders to see that their men were kept busy and out of temptation.

He did not understand why men could not restrain themselves. "Every man can," he said, "by self-control, restrain the indulgence of these imprudent and reckless impulses that so often lead men astray." Having no knowledge at all of the slums where so many of his soldiers were bred, he tried to shame them: "What would your mothers, your sisters and your friends at home think of you?" With more success he appealed to their regimental pride and instituted a prize for the best battalion of infantry or regiment of cavalry in India. It was a much coveted award, but in order to win it, a unit had to have only a small number of men hospitalized for "actions within their own control." The award helped keep commanding officers acutely aware of their responsibilities in keeping their men free of venereal diseases.

As it was sometimes said that short service had brought into the army a large number of young men who were ignorant of the consequences of cohabiting with diseased women, Kitchener issued in 1903 a long memorandum on the subject for the edification of his soldiers. Syphilis contracted from "Asiatic women," he said, was far worse than that contracted in England: "It assumes a horrible loathsome form . . . the sufferer finds his hair falling off, his skin and the flesh of his body rot, and are eaten away by slow cancerous ulcerations, his nose falls off, and he eventually becomes blind . . . his throat is eaten away by foetid ulcerations which cause his breath to stink. In the hospitals, and among suicides, many such examples are found."

Whether such descriptions ever terrified a Tommy into abstinence, or the Kitchener prize ever inspired a lancer to resist a woman's wiles, or thoughts of his sister ever stifled a gunner's sexual proclivities is, of course, unknown, but the old army notion that the way to prevent disease was simply to see that as far as possible soldiers had their sex with registered and inspected prostitutes appeared to work best. As a result of strict controls imposed on cantonments, hospital admissions for venereal diseases fell dramatically from the high of 536 per thousand in 1895 to 67 per thousand in 1909.

In the late Edwardian era a military brothel at Agra was reserved for British soldiers. It was located in a narrow street in the bazaar about three quarters of a mile from the barracks and housed some thirty to forty Indian prostitutes between the ages of twelve and thirty, a number considered sufficient for the one thousand five hundred British troops that were normally garrisoned there. Private Frank Richards described it:

> Each girl lived in a separate shack of her own, which was made of plaster and mud with a hard baked mud floor. The only furniture was a native rope-bed with no bed clothes, a large earthenware vessel for holding water, and a small wash-hand bowl. . . . The Rag was opened from twelve noon to eleven at night, and for the whole of that time the girls who were not engaged would stand outside their shacks soliciting at the top of their voices and saying how scientific they were at their profession. . . . The girls who possessed punkahs considered themselves very up-to-date. . . . If a man wanted a gentle breeze during his short visit he would engage a punkah-boy outside the door, who charged one pice for the job. . . .
>
> Each girl had a couple of towels, Vaseline, Condy's fluid and soap; they were examined two or three times a week by one of the hospital-doctors, who fined them a rupee if they were short of any of the above requisites. There was also a small lavatory erected in the street, which had a supply of hot water.

Private Richards had a friend whose precautions included a careful examination of the girl of his choice with a powerful magnifying glass in "the professional manner of an old family doctor." In the brothel area of the bazaar, the girls would cry out to him: "Hullo, my spy-glass wallah!" Richards considered it unhealthy to abstain in a hot climate. "Venereal," he said, was usually caught from "sand rats." These were "native girls, who being in the last stages of the dread disease and rotten inside and out, only appeared after dark."

Although occasional protests about the use of official brothels for British troops in India continued, they could be generally ignored. Indian nationalists in the last days of the raj kept alive the concept of the lecherous British soldier. General Francis Tuker, lecturing on the role of the British Army in India, was exasperated to be so often asked "why it was that British troops were so sexual and so given to rape."

11

Sport

Officers and men spent far more time playing games and enjoying sport than in campaigning against the Queen-Empress's foes. Officers found in them a prophylactic against persistent and disturbing thoughts of sex, of loved ones at home in Britain, and of mounting debts. There was plenty of time. There was no work on Thursdays or Sundays. All Christian holidays were observed as well as Sikh, Muslim or Hindu festivals—and sometimes all of them. Officers were allowed one ten-day local leave and two months "privilege leave"—three months for those on the Frontier. After about three and a half years, when Urdu and other languages had been learned, an officer enjoyed six months, sometimes a year, of home leave.

Members of successful sports teams, officers and other ranks, enjoyed many extra holidays as they travelled about playing in tournaments. British officers in the Indian Army played games with their Indian other ranks within the regiment or battalion, but the number of British officers on any team was usually limited. Although mixed teams of officers and sepoys were the rule, not for nearly fifty years after the Mutiny were British Army teams allowed to compete with Indian Army teams. It was not to be admitted that Indian soldiers could beat British soldiers in anything as important as sports and games. A pretence was maintained that it would not be fair to pit strong young Britons against the slightly built natives. Eustace Miles, an amateur racquets and tennis champion at the turn of the century, expressed a common British attitude:

> We treat the natives under our power as they are. . . . We can express the best spirit of our Empire in those words: that we try to "play the game" with the natives; we do not try to play tricks with them or bully them, for that is not sportsmanlike; we give them a fair chance. Generally it should be a handicap game for we are bound to win if we play level and we generally do play level; but anyhow we do play them, and that is something.

That famous British public school exhortation: "Play up and play the game!"* implied a code of conduct to be fol-

---

* The public school notion of bravery and honour was well expressed in Sir Henry Newbolt's (1862–1938) poem *Vitai Lampada*, much read and often memorized by schoolboys. It begins on a cricket field and ends on a battlefield:

> There's a breathless hush in the close tonight—
>   Ten to make and the match to win—
> A bumping pitch and a blinding light,
>   An hour to play and the last man in.
> And it's not for the sake of a ribboned coat
>   Or the selfish hope of a season's fame,
> But his Captain's hand on his shoulder smote—
>   "Play up! play up! and play the game!"
>
> The sand of the desert is sodden red—
>   Red with the wreck of a square that broke—
> The gatling's jammed and the Colonel dead,
>   And the regiment blind with the dust and smoke:
> The river of death has brimmed its banks,
>   And England's far and honour a name.
>   ***
> This they all with a joyful mind
>   Bear through life like a torch in flame
> And, falling, fling to the host behind,
>   "Play up! play up! and play the game!"

lowed on and off the playing fields. It was the shibboleth of
a British gentleman, of the proper British officer. In World
War I young officers mangled by shellfire frequently mur-
mured something about playing the game, either as an
exhortation to their men or as last words to be passed back
to their public school headmaster. Sports and games set
the standards for living one's life.

The British attitude towards sport and war was perhaps
best expressed by A. B. Wylde in the late 1880s: "The
sportsman has had more to do in winning our battles for
us than anyone else, and what would have become of India
unless our officers . . . had been inured to field sports and
ready at any moment to take the opportunity when it offered
of going out to kill a man-eating tiger, a rogue elephant, or
any other dangerous beast."

In general, field hockey was the most popular army game
and it was played by all ranks. Rivalry was intense; spies
were sent to watch opposing teams and hours were spent
developing counter-strategies. Brigadier John Prendergast
remembered how in the inter-war years "the subject of
hockey dominated nearly all conversation *ad nauseam.*"

Polo, which the British press first referred to as "hockey
on ponies," was certainly the most expensive sport. In the
late Victorian era, it became almost an obsession, and many
regiments maintained a Polo Fund to which all officers
contributed whether they played or not. There were young
officers who sought to join certain regiments only because
of the reputations of their polo teams, while others, innocent of the fact that they were joining a polo-playing regiment, were warned that they had better learn to play.

In the 1920s when Lieutenant E. George Haynes joined
Skinner's Horse, he only managed to hit the ball once in
his first game and then he undercut it, causing it to strike
his commanding officer smartly in the small of the back.
To the colonel's roar of pain he managed to mumble a hur-
ried "Sorry, sir." That evening he was consoled by a fellow
officer in the mess. "At least the CO knew you hit the ball

once this afternoon," he said. "Not at all bad for a first effort."

Polo, a sport native to India, was seldom played in Central or Southern India, even by the Indians, during the early days of the raj and did not become popular among the British until the late 1860s. The first polo club in India was formed at Silchar, Assam, in 1859. The game was introduced into Britain in 1871 by the 9th Lancers and the 10th Hussars.

Because of the expense, polo was a sport only for the Indian aristocracy. The British, naturally, refined the rules of the game and codified them, but the rajas were not to be left out. Sawai Man Singh II, the westernized Maharaja of Jaipur, a keen player, collected a team of other young Indian aristocrats and with thirty-nine ponies, fifty-one syces (grooms), and a polo-stick maker sailed for England in April 1933. There he and his team won every cup in sight, establishing records which have never been equalled. In September they returned to India and never came back.

Cavalrymen had a distinct advantage in polo. On joining an Indian cavalry regiment, an officer was given a capital sum with which to provide himself with two chargers. Instead of regular mounts, the officers usually bought polo ponies and registered them as chargers, although in some regiments it was an unwritten law that at least one had to be heavy enough to be a legitimate charger. The army supplied forage and provided an officer with two syces. As officers on parade could not appear on small polo ponies, those without chargers rode ordinary troop horses.

All new troop horses were closely inspected as soon as they arrived from the remount depots with an eye for those which might be trained as polo ponies, a practice condoned under the convention that a good polo pony was naturally a good troop horse. Polo was strictly an officers' game. Sowars were not allowed to play, although the two best horsemen in each squadron were formed into a polo troop and these trained the ponies until they were fit to play fast chukkas. A keen player had the use of three or four of these specially trained horses in addition to perhaps four or more that he owned. Horses dominated the thinking of many officers, and although it was forbidden to talk "shop" in the mess, it was agreed that horses were not shop and horse-talk filled the ante-rooms of most messes, particularly those of cavalry regiments.

A subaltern who did not go out shooting—*shikar*, it was called—was considered deficient in important military virtues, so most acquired a shotgun and a sporting rifle. There was some justification for official encouragement; it gave a young officer a chance to rough it in the open, to develop his eye for terrain and cover, and to hone his skill in using a weapon. Then, too, the preparation for a shooting or hunting trip, with its calculations of needed supplies, number of servants, arrangements for transport, equipment to be carried, itinerary, and so forth, bore some relationship to military planning.

Game was plentiful before World War I. Sometimes as few as eight guns were known to bag more than a thousand ducks in a day. Although by the end of the 1930s most of India was largely "shot out," officers continued to hunt and shoot, and during World War I they even took their sporting weapons with them on campaigns. Skinner's Horse was in Persia (Iran) in 1942–43. That summer the temperatures averaged more than 100° F. and sometimes soared to 142°, while the winter was "the severest . . . ever known." Still, summer and winter, the eager sportsmen pursued their passion, shooting snipe, sisi, chikor, black and grey partridge, quail, imperial sand grouse, all forms of ducks and geese, bustard and pigeon in large numbers. Among small animals they slaughtered gazelles, wild pigs, ibexes, bears and mountain sheep.

There were no foxes in India, but a satisfactory imitation of fox hunting could be found in hunting the wily jackal. Many declared that jackals gave as good a run as a fox; some thought the jackal did rather better. At Quetta and

Jackal hunting replaced fox hunting in India, and a wide variety of dogs were pressed into service as hounds. (G. F. Atkinson, *Curry & Rice*, 2nd ed. 1859)

elsewhere, thoroughbred English foxhounds were imported. Most young women of the Fishing Fleet were ardent riders to hounds. One officer wrote: "They rode anything with four legs and fell into every river and had to be pulled out and generally added sparkle to our lives." On the North-West Frontier, Pathans on shaggy ponies sometimes joined the hunt, uninvited but getting into the spirit of the thing by crying out "Tally ho!" In the 1930s, when the RAF appeared on the Frontier, the aviators gained a deserved reputation as bad riders and a disgrace to any hunt they joined. Wing-Commander A. G. Trevenen James confessed that in jackal hunting, "the order of the field was the jackal first, closely pursued by the Air Force contingent, then came the hounds and the well-ordered rest of the hunt."

British other ranks used jackals for a different sport. Live jackals were purchased for about eight annas and then pitted against two or three fighting dogs in a closed room. Private Richards said that "ordinarily a jackal was a bit of a coward, but when he realized that there was no possible chance to escape . . . he would spring to a corner and turn like a flash to face the dogs. With arched back and bared fangs he looked a frightful creature. . . . He fought like a cornered rat. But the odds were against him; in ten or twenty minutes he was dead or shamming dead. . . ."

Indians would often come around the barracks carrying hares, wild cats or jackals in baskets on the ends of a bamboo pole balanced on their shoulder, offering them for a few annas to soldiers who owned greyhounds or other fast dogs. Private Richards complained that it was "difficult to keep a coursing-match private: by the time the hare was released all the dogs of the Battalion . . . would be on the spot and joining in the chase."

Most dangerous of any sport was pigsticking, the hunting of wild boar. Sergeant John Fraser wrote feelingly of the boar: "He is entirely without fear. . . . He alone goes down to the pool to drink without fear of other animals. He drinks without turning his head, except in curiosity. . . . Pigsticking was not for me, nor for any of the lesser fry."

Like polo, pigsticking was for officers only. It was an expensive sport, calling for troupes of beaters to drive the boar in the direction of the mounted hunters with their steel-tipped spears. It required good horsemanship, coolness in crisis, bravery and a fiery determination to succeed—all much admired qualities. Colonel Western spoke of it as "a cruel form of sport, though interesting and exciting." Officers practised by riding down and spearing the numerous pie dogs who roamed the regimental areas. Lord Baden-Powell, who strove to teach his Boy Scouts to be kind to animals, was as a young officer in India devoted to this cruellest and bloodiest of sports, even contending: "I really believe that the boar enjoys it too." Pigsticking, he said,

A popular but dangerous sport was pigsticking. This drawing was made in the 1870s. (National Army Museum)

was "invaluable to our prestige and supremacy in India . . . at once proving and preserving our rightful claim to superiority as a dominant race." Yeats-Brown said it "sweated the false civilization" out of him. It was widely believed that a vigorous day of pigsticking would even dispel dreams of soft women between clean white sheets.

The highest award for a pigsticker, the Grand National of the pigsticking world, was the Khadir (or Kadir) Cup, awarded yearly by the famous Meerut Tent Club, founded in 1866, to the man who achieved the most "first spears." The meet for it was held on the flat alluvial plain of the Ganges near Meerut during the cold weather, after the crops had been cut, when the land was mostly bare. Baden-Powell as a young officer won the Khadir in 1883 and six years later published a book on the sport entitled *Pigsticking or Hog Hunting*.

In March 1933 the trophy was won by Lieutenant Doug-

An offshoot of pig-sticking was the somewhat less dangerous sport of tent-pegging, where riders armed with lances tried to spear tent pegs driven into the ground while riding at speed. Depicted here is a disappointed Bengal Lancer who missed his peg. (National Army Museum)

las Gray of Skinner's Horse, who celebrated by giving a party in the mess to which pigsticking friends from other regiments were invited. Recently installed electric lights blazed, drinks flowed freely and someone suggested that Gray's horse, Granite, who had performed so nobly that day be brought in to share in the festivities. It seemed a good idea, so Granite was led in and served a bucket of champagne. A young subaltern from the 10th Hussars, carried away, shouted, "I can't win the Khadir Cup, but I will at least be able to say that I rode the horse that did," leaped on the horse's back and instantly crashed to the floor. The new electric ceiling fan had caught him a stunning blow on the head.

A by-product of pigsticking was the sport of tent-pegging, in which horsemen with lances rode at speed and attempted to stab and pick up wooden pegs driven into the ground. The pegs had to be placed at a slight slant away from the rider or the result could be a badly sprained wrist.

Tiger hunting was highly popular; every subaltern

dreamed of shooting one, but because it was outrageously expensive, most did not indulge in the sport unless a maharaja staged it or unless the government raised a hunt for a distinguished personage. Elephants bearing swaying howdahs and swarms of bearers and beaters were *de rigueur*. Conrad Corfield, who once served as adviser to the Maharaja of Rewa, remarked that there were "occasions when one felt the whole thing was so arranged that there was no sporting element in it." It was not unknown to place a tame tiger or an old toothless one in the path of a distinguished guest. Tigers shot by dignitaries were invariably larger than usual because in measuring them the tape was pressed down every four inches instead of taking the usual nose-to-tail measurements.

To lure the tiger, goats, bullocks or other domestic animals were usually tied overnight in likely spots to bellow or bleat; it was said of the unspeakable Maharaja Jay Singh of Alwar that he used children or aging widows.

Some lucky officers were able to hunt tigers with little expense and no ceremony. Man-eaters would sometimes terrorize villages and a British officer would be petitioned to shoot them. Richard Meinertzhagen claimed to have killed a man-eater in the Nilgiri Hills and to have so pleased the local chief that he sent him a beautiful girl of about fifteen with "a fair skin and lovely features." Meinertzhagen later wrote: "I am glad to say that my self-respect won a short sharp fight with animal instinct and I firmly said that she must go back to her father."

Falconry or hawking was the passion of some, particularly on the North-West Frontier, where a small species of bustard was hunted from horseback. Also hunted, using both hawks and greyhounds, were small, fleet-footed "ravine deer." The danger in this sport lay in racing at speed over unfamiliar ground while keeping one's eyes on the hawk. Colonel Western loved the sport and said, "I know no pleasanter way of passing the bright crisp days that constitute the cold weather."

A tiger hunt was de rigueur for visiting burra sahibs. The
Prince of Wales is here depicted being charged by a tiger on 28
February 1876. Such hunts were well arranged and it is highly
unlikely that the Prince was in any real danger. (Windsor
Castle. Royal Library. Her Majesty Queen Elizabeth II.)

The Maharaja of Jaipur (called "Jai" by his English
friends), who had taken the legendary polo team to Britain,
shared with British officers the intense love of the hunt,
and he declared the area for fifteen miles around his capital to be his private preserve. Only he, his friends and royal
relations were permitted to hunt there. When a peasant,
driving wild pigs from his field, accidentally killed one, the
master of the royal hunt, among other tortures, ordered
ground hot chillies pushed into his rectum.

It was a rare officer who had an aversion to blood sports,
but such existed. One, after shooting a brown bear, confessed: "I thought of all the little teddy bears that I'd ever
seen before and hated it." Claude Auchinleck, a burra sahib
indeed, a field marshal and the last British Commander-in-
Chief in India, had as a subaltern enjoyed shooting, but in
later life he became a conservationist and something of an

expert on Indian birds and foreswore the sport, refusing the many invitations from rajas he regularly received.

There were cycles of fashions in army sports. Cricket was popular in the late nineteenth century, but in the years just before World War I it was rarely played and cricket grounds were converted into badminton or lawn tennis courts. Soccer was popular, as was boxing, a crude version of which was sometimes compulsory in British regiments where a section of sixteen men were given gloves and lined up in two ranks. At the order: "Front ranks, about turn! Box!" they fell to.

Tug-of-war was popular in the late Victorian era, but a famous match held during an assault-at-arms at Peshawar put a damper on the sport. Two teams of Sikhs competed, the 14th Sikhs and the 29th Punjabis, and it took an hour and nine minutes for the 29th Punjabi team to haul the last man over the line, at which point both teams fell exhausted and had to be carried en masse to the hospital, where one man died. Most had strained their hearts and, as they had all been bare-footed, none had any skin left on the soles of his feet. Shortly after, orders were issued that army boots must be worn, but the sport's popularity waned.

At a few of the larger cantonments, such as the one at Agra, swimming baths were available for both officers and other ranks, a great boon during the hot weather, when drill could be carried out only in the early morning and games played only in the early evening. In most cantonments, in spite of sports and games, boredom stupefied soldiers for much of the year as through the heat of the long days they lay sweating in their barracks, gambling and cursing the punkah wallahs when they dozed.

As much time as possible was spent in the open, which was just as well, as sanitary conditions around the barracks were usually execrable. Florence Nightingale, who lived to the age of ninety (she died in 1910), took a particular interest in the army's sanitation problems. Although she never visited India, she is credited with doing much to improve the health of the soldiers there.

Like the officers, the other ranks had servants to do all of the most disagreeable chores. Indians swept and cleaned, washed clothes, cleaned equipment, shined boots and buttons, cleaned latrines, carried water, prepared meals, cut hair, and even came around with lanterns in the early morning and shaved the soldiers in their beds before reveille. So cheap were the services of these servants that there were few who did not employ them.

Towards the Indians, the British other ranks were as arrogant as their officers. Indians did not dare enter a barracks or a tent without removing their sandals and they were exposed to a continual stream of Hindustani curses, called crab-bat (Hindustani "karab-bat," meaning "bad language"), and were usually addressed as "niggers" or "black bastards" or "filthy pigs." It is not difficult to see why the British, in spite of their many virtues, were unloved.

CHAPTER

12

——————

Sepoy and Sowar

As Indian soldiers of the raj were usually illiterate, they have left little first-hand information about themselves. Of the many millions who served as sepoys and sowars during the two hundred years of the British military presence in India, only one man, Subedar Sita Ram Pande, ever wrote a book about his experiences—and that book, *From Sepoy to Subedar*, is suspect. The original manuscript, thought to have been written in Awadhi, or western Hindi, is lost and it is impossible to tell from the text in what regiments Sita Ram served. Nevertheless, many authorities have claimed the book to be genuine and its Urdu translation (made from an English translation), published in 1873, served for many years as a standard Urdu textbook. As such it was known, after about 1880, to every British officer who ever served in the Indian Army.

Subedar Sita Ram Pande, a Brahman of Oudh, enlisted in a regiment of Bengal Native Infantry as a sepoy in 1812 at the age of seventeen and saw service in the wars against the Gurkhas and Pindaris; he took part in the siege of Bhurtpore (Bharatpur), the First Afghan War, both Sikh wars, and the Indian Mutiny (in which he commanded the firing squad that executed his own son). He was wounded seven times, earned six medals, and was once captured and enslaved by Afghans. As was often the case in the pre-Mutiny army, by the time he reached the rank of subedar he was too debilitated by his long years of service and many wounds to perform his duties effectively. He retired on a pension in 1860 after forty-eight years of service.

Sita Ram Pande, naturally circumspect in his language, found no fault with the sirkar that paid his pension or the sahibs under whom he had served, and it must be assumed that many of his true feelings remained hidden. However, as is the way of old soldiers, he complained that the new army was not as good as the old army he had known; the new sahibs not as good as the old sahibs and their vernacular not as well spoken. He found strange and alarming the British admiration for brave enemies, "for is not a brave man the most dangerous enemy?" And he found the strictures against killing women and children incomprehensible—"Would I kill a serpent and leave the eggs?" He remembered bitterly that at Lucknow, although he was one of the heroes of the relieving force, he was still called a "damned black pig."

Young Indians enlisted for the same reasons young men enlist in other armies: delight in uniforms or the outdoor life; the need to earn a living; a yearning for fame or glory; a need to prove themselves men; the lure of following in the footsteps of friends or relations; or sometimes an impulse to spite or to escape from parents. In India there was the additional pull of caste and sons were often expected to become soldiers if their fathers and grandfathers had served, particularly if they were Rajputs, who claim descent from the original Ksatriyas and possess a strong martial spirit. For many, to become a soldier was almost a moral obligation.

Patriotism played no part. Indeed, until at least the turn of the century the notion of nationhood was nonexistent in the minds of most Indians. Recruits were, of course, made aware that they served a distant sovereign, but this carried little weight. In a sense, the Indian soldier was a mercenary in his own country, but he did not sell his sword to the highest bidder and as long as the British sirkar and its officers kept faith with him, he usually remained loyal to his alien masters.

Unable to imagine themselves serving under alien officers of a different race and colour, Britons sometimes wondered about the mystique of the Indian Army they had created. Most credited its success to their own superiority as leaders. Major George MacMunn, writing in 1911, mused:

> Some love of service, some power of the white man for attracting faithful service and admiration, must be the motive power that brings Hindu and Musalman, Afghan and Indian, Sikh and Gurkha, to an alien ruler and an alien race, to serve for small guerdon and smaller pension. For honour, no doubt, and hereditary love of the sword ... but there is more than this, and it would seem that so long as the British are worthy of it, so long as courage and justice and the strong arm keep up the confidence of a hundred races in our power ... so long will the soldier races of the East serve the Sirkar.

The average sepoy found it difficult to understand the upheavals that occurred from time to time when the army reorganized and the names and numbers of regiments changed. When he was Commander-in-Chief, India, General Sir O'Moore Creagh in 1912 wrote of the Indian soldier: "He enlists, not altogether without a feeling of loyalty, but mainly from the idea that he wishes to have a career in a regiment which he knows and which he, or may be his family, has had previous association. ... He cannot be expected to conform automatically to every passing wave of Government policy."

It was often difficult for politicians and bureaucrats to understand the deep effect which small changes could make in the life of the sepoy, changes that often went beyond the army, beyond the regiment and into the remote villages

A proud sowar of the
10th Bengal Lancers
about 1910. (National
Army Museum)

from whence the recruits had come, for sometimes strange
military castes developed.

Divinely ordered, pre-ordained, and fundamental to Hindu
social life were the four varnas: Brahman (priest), Ksatriya
(lord or warrior), Vaisya (merchant and trader), and Sudra
(serf). These were the four original castes from which the
immense number of subcastes sprang. Although usually
referred to simply as castes, these subcastes are not
immutable. They can and do change, disappear, and new
ones come into being; they are based on a wide variety of
factors, among them race, region and occupation. Soldiers
retiring to their villages might keep up military habits and
continue to wear their turbans in the style of their regi-

A sepoy in the 3rd
Beluch Regiment,
probably about the
turn of the century.
(National Army
Museum)

ment or cut their beards in the regimental way. As generations succeeded each other in the same regiment, such
fashions or mannerisms evolved into caste distinctions. It
was, then, no small matter if the regimental style or custom was changed.

In southern India a low-caste but proud people that came
to be known as Quinsaps was formed of families whose men
served in the Queen's Own Madras Sappers and Miners.
Sons enlisted in that corps only and their families gave their
daughters in marriage only to men who were serving or
had served in that distinguished unit. Sappers and Miners
were not officered by Indian Army officers but by volunteers from the Royal Engineers who served tours of duty in
India. They did more than simply dig trenches and mine,
for they included almost all of the skilled trades such as
blacksmiths, mechanics and surveyors.

In the Victorian era the use of medals to recognize gal-

Sappers and Miners hauling on a hawser for a swinging bridge. Guarding them are sowars from the 3rd Bengal Cavalry. (National Army Museum)

lantry in action or for war service became a standard feature of the reward system, but although sepoy and private, sowar and trooper, served as soldiers of the British sovereign, they were rewarded on different scales. Campaign medals and general service medals and clasps, issued in silver to British troops, were issued in bronze to Indian and Gurkha troops.

Because none of the medals for bravery awarded to British soldiers could be awarded to "native" soldiers until the late Edwardian period, the Indian Army developed its own set of gallantry medals. There were two: the Indian Distinguished Service Medal (IDSM) and the Indian Order of Merit (IOM); the latter carried a small stipend and was the more prestigious. Instituted in May 1837 by the Honourable East India Company, it laid claim to being the oldest official British gallantry award for general service. The medal was issued in three classes, gold for first class and silver for second and third class. A man had to earn a third-class medal before he could earn a second-class, and a second-class before he could earn the first-class. Thus, a soldier had to prove his bravery three times before being awarded the top medal. No official provision was made for further acts of valour. In 1911 when Gurkha and Indian soldiers became eligible for the Victoria Cross, the first class of the IOM was abolished.

The IDSM was not instituted until June 1907. The Royal Warrant stated that "Our Regular Indian Forces, including the Reserve of the Indian Army, Border Militia and Levies, and Military Police and Imperial Service Troops when employed under the Orders of Our Government" were eligible for the award, and in June 1917 eligibility was extended to noncombatants attached to the forces. The Gunga Dins could now get the medal.

All ranks complained that individual medals were almost never issued for the many campaigns on the North-West Frontier. Instead, all ranks were merely given a clasp stamped with the name of the campaign to be affixed to the ribbon of the Indian General Service Medal. For the Indian other ranks these "four anna clasps" were particularly unsatisfactory, for when off duty a soldier normally wore mufti, and he wore his medals without their ribbons on a cord around his neck.

Indian officers on retirement were occasionally given honorary commissions as lieutenants or captains. This was not only an honour, it doubled the officer's pension, which in 1900 was only about ten rupees per month. Sometimes pensions included *jagirs*, land grants entitling the pensioner to the revenue from a piece of land without conferring ownership.

Until almost the end of the nineteenth century no bar-

The 7th Bengal native infantry on parade, probably in the 1890s.
(National Army Museum)

racks were provided for Indian troops. On land set aside
for them they built huts, which were often firetraps. There
was seldom running water; drainage was usually poor; and
lack of adequate sanitary facilities often made the locations foul and pestilential. When barracks were finally constructed, they were not built on the dormitory system of
squad rooms, as were those built for European troops, but
were divided into cubicles housing two or three men.

Each recruit was given a uniform allowance (in 1876 this
amounted to Rs. 30 in the infantry) and a small sum (usually about Rs. 4) annually for upkeep. When the cost of lost
or ruined clothing—including sandals or light shoes, which
were worn by Indian troops until almost the end of the
nineteenth century—exceeded this amount, the soldier
himself had to pay for replacements, government penny-

pinching which sometimes created problems. Many a major review disintegrated when infantry, marching over wet ground behind cavalry, left their footwear in the churned-up mud. Sandals and shoes were too expensive to be abandoned and scores of soldiers breaking ranks to scramble after lost footwear destroyed every semblance of military order and discipline.

A soldier's pay was small, but his peace-time service was seldom arduous. Religious festivals and regimental holidays were many and the sirkar was generous with furloughs, particularly in the Bengal Army, where the average sepoy had two months leave each year and an additional six months after three years. Of course, it often took a soldier two or three weeks to reach his village if it was remote from his cantonment.

The communication problem in an army where the recruits spoke more than a dozen languages and dialects and the officers still another language had been solved by the Moguls when a camp language called Urdu had evolved. It was a mixture of Hindi and Persian with words from other languages added over time. Each Indian recruit and each British officer had to learn this language of the army, although this was not difficult for most Indians, as it resembled many Northern Indian tongues. Recruits often had to learn the language of the regiment in addition to Urdu when it differed from their mother tongue. Words of command, given in English, had to be learned as well. Drill books carried English on one page and the vernacular on the opposite.

During most of the Victorian era sick or injured Indian soldiers were treated only in regimental hospitals, often merely huts, tents or bungalows. Except for a doctor, an Indian assistant, and followers for the menial tasks, there was no medical establishment. Supplies were few; patients were expected to provide their own bedding and clothes. Food presented problems, particularly in regiments of mixed classes with differing diets, and usually a sick soldier had to rely upon his comrades to provide for him. When a doctor had done what he could, and the patient was still ill, he was sent home with orders to return if and when he recovered.

Regimental work days usually started early and in the hot weather ended before the midday heat. Little training could be accomplished in the hot season or during the monsoons. In the cavalry many of the available hours were spent exercising and grooming horses. Messing occupied much time, for each soldier prepared his own food.

What with the weather, the commensal restrictions of caste, the leave policies, language problems, and the need to provide for themselves necessities supplied by the governments of other armies, so little time was left for training that it is small wonder that it took a longer period of time to make an Indian into a soldier.

Much has been written about the ties between the Indian soldier and his British officer. Officers were indeed devoted to their men and often defended them or stayed with them rather than accept staff appointments, to the detriment of their careers. Stories of the devotion of sepoys to their officers are legion. Officers and men in their separate ways took care of each other, and it would be difficult to deny that, more frequently than in other armies, a special relationship existed.

When Lord Birdwood was a young subaltern on the North-West Frontier, he received a lesson in what this relationship meant. Bedded on the ground one cold and rainy night, he slept soundly and did not discover until morning that three of his men had covered him with their own blankets. "You are our sahib," one explained. "It is right that we take care of you." Indeed, this was so, for on the words and actions of this bright young officer depended their lives.

No VCO or noncommissioned officer could assume the authority of a British officer and, as time went on, the amount of responsibility given to VCOs decreased. Indian officers commanded platoons but not companies. Lord

Roberts, who spent forty years in India and laid some claim to knowing the Indian Army and the Indian soldier, said of them that if they were "brigaded with British troops I would be proud to lead them against any European enemy," but he was adamant in his belief that Indian officers would never be able to take the place of British officers: "Eastern races, however brave and accustomed to war, do not possess the qualities that go to make good leaders of men. . . . I have known many natives whose gallantry and devotion could not be surpassed, but I have never known one who would not have looked to the youngest British officer for support in time of difficulty and danger."

It was, however, British recruiting policies and methods which ensured that there would be few men in the ranks with the knowledge, initiative and leadership skills required of a commissioned officer, for the educated classes were deliberately excluded. The British favoured the recruitment of only those they classified as being members of a "martial race."

chapter 13

The
Martial Races of India

Prior to the Mutiny the Bengal Army recruited heavily from among high-caste Bengalis, particularly Brahmans. After the Mutiny many believed that the officers of the Bengal Army had paid too much attention to Hindu religious scruples and that the half-educated, urbanized Bengali Brahmans, considered too clever by half, had been overly represented and unreasonably pampered. It was said that "Bengal is a low-lying country inhabited by low, lying people."

The Indian Army under the Crown ceased to recruit such Bengalis until World War I, when one regiment only was raised—the 49th Bengalis, disbanded soon after war's end. The army also ceased to recruit low-caste Hindus. Between 1864 and 1884 nearly all the low-caste sepoys were mustered out and recruiting in their communities ended.

Eventually recruiting became limited almost exclusively to those of the so-called martial races, or, more correctly, martial classes. From the end of the Mutiny until the end of the British raj, most officers believed that certain classes of Indians made better soldiers than other classes, and this belief did much to form the character and characteristics of the Indian Army.

A modern writer, Dr. Jeffrey Greenhut, points out that "The Martial Race theory had an elegant symmetry. Indians who were intelligent and educated were defined as cowards, while those defined as brave were uneducated and backward." While no British officer of the raj would have put the matter so bluntly, such was indeed the effect. Greenhut maintains that this explained the British belief that only Britons could be pukka officers, for "only British gentlemen combined both the intelligence and courage for a man to become an officer."

Since the sepoys and sowars of the Madras and Bombay armies had remained loyal throughout the Mutiny, it might be thought that men from the south would be sought after, but this was not the case. Southerners were definitely the wrong type. George MacMunn thought that Southern India for too long a time had not experienced war, and he spoke of "the enervating effect on Asiatics of a few generations of peace." General Sir O'Moore Creagh considered southerners to be "timid both by religion and habit, servile to their superiors and tyrannical to their inferiors, and quite unwarlike."

General Roberts, too, had a low opinion of the races and tribes of Southern India, particularly the Madrasis. Regiments of the Madras Army fought under him during the Second Afghan War, and later he served four years (1881–85) as Commander-in-Chief of the Madras Army. Writing of that time, he said:

> Each cold season I made long tours in order to acquaint myself with the needs and capabilities of the men of the Madras Army. I tried hard to discover in them those fighting qualities which had distinguished their forefathers during the wars of the last and the beginning of the present century. But long years of peace, and the security and prosperity attending it, had evidently had upon them, as they always seem to have on Asiatics,

a softening and deteriorating effect; and I was forced to the conclusion that the ancient military spirit had died in them, as it had died in the ordinary Hindustani of Bengal and the Mahratta of Bombay, and that they could no longer with safety be pitted against warlike races, or employed outside the limits of southern India.

Between 1862 and 1864 twelve battalions of Madras infantry were disbanded. Roberts disbanded eight more.

Throughout Roberts's tenure as Commander-in-Chief, India (28 November 1885 to 8 April 1893), recruiting was almost exclusively in the northern part of the subcontinent, and in particular the Punjab and northwest. "Weaklings die in North India," wrote Yeats-Brown, "the survivors are a fine stock." The first step towards improving the quality of the army, said Roberts, was "to substitute men of the more warlike and hardy races for the Hindustani sepoys of Bengal, the Tamils and Telagus of Madras and the so-called Mahrattas of Bombay."

Southerners tended to be small and dark; the army developed a fancy for tall men with fair skins. A "cult of physique" or "grenadierism" developed as officers sought tall, broad-shouldered, light-skinned peasant types and mountain men from farms and villages, men who were physically tough, "plucky, hardy but shrewd," who were amenable to discipline and, although uneducated, were capable of learning the skills required of infantrymen and horse soldiers. As the hills bred many and fed few, recruits were usually plentiful.

Colonel J. S. E. Western, writing in 1922, spoke for many officers, probably most, when he said that "the non-fighting classes never have possessed the desirable virtue of courage." He was sure that "when the support now afforded to the educated, discontented, cowardly agitators who follow Mr. Gandhi is withdrawn," the non-martial classes would "again find themselves under the yoke of the more belligerent clans—and a good thing too."

George MacMunn, who became a general, was a firm believer in the martial classes doctrine and was perplexed by the differences he perceived: "It is extraordinary that the well-born race of the upper classes in Bengal should be hopeless poltroons, while it is absurd that the great, merry, powerful Kashmiri should have not an ounce of physical courage in his constitution, but it is so."

O'Moore Creagh believed that climate accounted for the superiority of northern men: "In the hot, flat regions . . . are found races, timid both by religion and habit, servile to their superiors, but tyrannical to their inferiors, and quite unwarlike. In other parts . . . where the weather is cold, the warlike minority is to be found. . . ."

Although India is a country with a staggering diversity of people, recruiting came to be limited to relatively few classes. By 1930, 30 percent of the Indian population formed the pool from which were drawn 87 percent of the soldiers. The most sought after Indians were the Sikhs from the Punjab, who formed the largest single class in the Indian Army. Most had remained loyal during the Mutiny and their physical characteristics were close to the popular ideal. Even though they represented less than 2 percent of the population—fewer than 5 million of the more than 300 million people in British India—they generally made up at least 20 percent of the Indian Army and an even higher percentage of those in the combatant arms. (Of the twenty-two Military Crosses awarded to Indian soldiers in World War I, fourteen were won by Sikhs.)

Most Sikhs come from that fertile area of northwest India called the Punjab, where Amritsar, the Sikhs' most holy city, home of their Golden Temple, is located. Yeats-Brown, writing of the Punjab during World War II, said: "Bracing cold in winter, staggering heat in summer, and a capricious rainfall that blesses the land or leaves it a desert; such are the conditions under which three-quarters of a million recruits are born and nurtured." During World War II 300,000 Sikhs served in the army, almost all in combatant arms.

Sikhs follow a monotheistic Hindu religion founded by their first guru, Nānak Chand, a weaver born near Lahore in 1469 who, after travelling widely and studying many religions, developed his own ideas, began to preach, acquired a following, and led a revolt against caste, idolatry, and the power and prestige of the Brahmans. He condemned child marriages, infanticide, and pilgrimages to shrines. He invited Hindus and Muslims alike to join his sect. In his lifetime he wrote part of what became the *Granth Sahib*, holy book of the Sikhs. Nine other gurus followed, the last being Guru Govind Singh (1666–1708), who was tortured to death by Muslims. Guru Govind Singh combined politics, religion and the cult of the warrior by establishing a religious and military fraternity known as the *Khalsa*, the Pure. (Sikhs like to drink but do not smoke, in contrast to orthodox Muslims, who smoke but do not drink.)

Although Guru Nānak Chand had welcomed Muslims to his ranks, Sikhs have never forgotten that it was Muslims who tortured to death Guru Govind Singh. Major-General S. Shahid Hamid wrote that "on the downfall of the Mogul Empire, the Sikhs butchered, bayoneted, strangled, shot down, hacked to pieces and burnt alive every Muslim they could find." They did the same again when the British raj dissolved in 1947.

Everyone agreed that although Sikhs were fine soldiers, they were difficult to command. Brigadier R. C. B. Bristow, a twentieth-century soldier who knew them well, wrote: "The Sikhs are the most militant and turbulent race in India." It would be difficult to dispute this characterization, but the Sikhs are not a race. Their common bond is their religion—the word *Sikh* means "disciple"—and the most distinguishing feature of Sikh males is their uncut beards, curled under their chins and brought up under their turbans. Their long hair *(kes)* constitutes one of the five K's which all good Sikhs possess. The other four, less visible but equally important, are distinctive undershorts *(kach)*, a steel or iron bracelet *(karra)* worn on the wrist to remind the wearer of his soldiers' creed, a dagger or sword *(kir-*

A sepoy of the 14th Sikhs in the field uniform of World War II. (National Army Museum)

pan), and tucked into the turban a wooden comb *(kanghi).* These he is permitted after a baptismal rite, *pahul* (or *paol*), involving water stirred with steel.

Nothing in the Sikh religion makes the turban one of the holy distinguishing marks, but it has come to be considered as such. When steel helmets were issued in World War I, the Sikhs refused to wear them. Even when reminded that Ranjit Singh, their great warrior hero, and many of his men wore steel caps, they refused—and they were humoured.

The British twice waged war against the Sikhs: in 1845–46 and 1848–49. Both were hard-fought affairs in which the Sikhs proved themselves brave and hardy adversaries and won the admiration of their foe. It has been said that it was the Indian Army of the British raj that kept Sikhism alive, helping its devotees preserve their martial traditions and customs and providing them with the stimulus of war without which the Sikh might long ago have lapsed into the ways of peaceful peasantry. There is some truth in this. Certainly the Sikhs occupied a special place in the Indian Army. Unless a man had been made a Sikh by being baptized by the *pahul*—and only then did he become a Sikh—he was not enlisted. On the march a copy of the *Granth Sahib* was carried at the head of the regiment and in camp it was carefully placed in a prominent position. Recruits swore their oath of loyalty on it.

Sikhs who grew lax in their religious observances were reprimanded by their British Church of England commanding officers. Yeats-Brown was adjutant of the 17th Cavalry when he was approached by his "woordy major" with a problem: one of the sowars wanted to become a Christian and couldn't the adjutant dissuade this misguided youth? Yeats-Brown sent the man off to the regimental horse farm, nearly a thousand miles away, to reconsider.

About two thirds of all Sikhs are Jats, and Jats were said to be the backbone of the Punjab. Not all Jats are Sikhs, however; some are Hindus or Muslims. Almost all are cultivators and many are landowners. Reputedly descended from Scythian ancestors, Jat characteristics were considered to be "stubbornness, tenacity, patience, devotion, courage, discipline and independence of spirit fitly reconciled." When the traditions of the Khalsa were added, one had the ideal Sikh sepoy.

Although one of the basic doctrines of Sikhism is the repudiation of caste, Sikhs of Rajput or Jat descent refused to eat or drink with Sikhs descended from menial Hindu castes and even though it was the much revered Guru Govind Singh who first admitted the Mazhabis (or Mazbhis or

Mazbis), a Hindu sweeper class, into the Khalsa, the Mazhabis found that the promised equality of all Sikhs was illusory. Not permitted to enlist in other Sikh regiments of infantry or cavalry, they were formed into pioneer regiments, where they performed creditably—indeed, often distinguishing themselves in action.

Sikhs were reputed to be broody and sulky, subject to fits of excitement and fanaticism, and intriguers who were overly fond of money, but despite these faults, their valour, loyalty, toughness, endurance, *élan* in battle, and their soldierly appearance made them valued by many officers above all other classes.

The largest group of Muslims to be taken into the army were from the Punjab. They were considered good all-round soldiers, the "backbone of the Indian Army," loyal to the sirkar and attached to their officers.

The shift in the composition of the Indian Army clearly illustrates the consequences of recruiting only the martial classes and can be seen in the statistics. The number of infantry battalions from the Punjab increased from twenty-eight in 1862, to thirty-one in 1885, and to fifty-seven in 1914. Gurkhas, who were mercenaries from certain tribes in eastern Nepal, were the most favoured of all recruits, in spite of their diminutive stature, and the increase in the number of Gurkha battalions was dramatic: from five in 1862 to twenty in 1914. These increases were accompanied by a decline in the number of battalions from southern India. Bombay and Madras, which had, respectively, thirty and forty battalions in 1862, were reduced to eighteen and eleven by 1911.

Also sought were Garhwalis from the foothills of the Himalayas west of Nepal, who resembled Gurkhas but were taller and slighter; they were believed to be a fusion of Aryan and Mongol races and were noted for their endurance of privation. Kumaonis, who also came from the Himalayan foothills, were readily accepted as recruits; they resembled

Garhwalis but were thought to "show more of the Mongol blood."

Among other classes considered martial were Baluchis, Dogras, Mers, Pathans and Rajputs. Many regiments not only restricted their recruiting to certain classes but narrowed their selections to include only particular clans, septs or tribes.

There existed, however, one southern India unit so outstanding that, even though it broke every fixed belief about the martial classes, its superiority could not be denied: the Madras Sappers and Miners were justly famous. Many of these soldiers were clever artisans and as a whole their intelligence was far above average. Furthermore, they did not object to being sent wherever they were needed, they ate what was given them, and they would turn their hands to whatever needed to be done. Although they came from classes generally despised by the army, the Madrasis in this unit—small, urban, educated, dark-skinned, low-caste southerners—were respected by all soldiers who came in contact with them. The Madras Sappers and Miners were never disbanded but by 1922 they were virtually the only Madrasis recruited.

(Although the use of the term "martial races" or "martial classes" is forbidden in the present Indian Army, the bulk of both the Indian and Pakistani armies are still drawn from these classes. The electoral system of modern India enables their representatives successfully to resist the broadening of recruitment, an aim of the government but considered a threat to the military castes for whom the profession of soldiering is considered a birthright.)

The non-martial, urban, educated Indian was not entirely divorced from army life. Because the peasant classes were largely illiterate, someone had to perform the Indian Army's clerical duties. It was here that the scorned *babu* (or *baboo*) functioned. A product of English educational methods in India, some had graduated from, or at least had attended, universities in Bombay or Calcutta, but they were universally considered, in the words of the *Hobson-Jobson*,* "a superficially cultivated, but too often effeminate, Bengali." Their so-called chi-chi English, much mocked, formed the subject of many jokes.

Because few government positions of any importance were open to them, many educated Indians became critics of the raj. Lord Lytton, when Viceroy, denied that they were in any way representative of Indian opinion: "The only political representatives of native opinion are the *Babus*, whom we have educated to write semi-seditious articles in the native Press, and who really represent nothing but the social anomaly of their own position."

Most commanding officers kept what was called an *Umedwar* (meaning "hopeful") book: a list of all the sons, brothers and cousins of men in the regiment or of influential men in the regiment's recruiting area. As these young men came of age they were given preference in filling vacancies. Commandants of famous regiments frequently needed to look no further for recruits. Often the list was unnecessary, for soldiers returning from furlough came back with a friend, a younger brother, or other relative or member of the same clan. Recruiting in this fashion remained in place for the duration of the raj.

If the *Umedwar* book or soldiers returning from furlough failed to produce a sufficient number of candidates or a new regiment was to be formed, recruiting parties, each under a havildar, or jemadar, or sometimes a British offi-

---

* *Hobson-Jobson* is a dictionary of Indian and other foreign words which were absorbed into the vocabularies of Europeans living in India. Many Indian words have been taken into the general vocabularies of English speakers: calico, chintz, khaki, bungalow, pajamas, veranda, curry, toddy, shawl, pagoda, typhoon, dingy, are a few. To help newcomers to India and others to understand, Colonel Henry Yule and Mr. A. C. Burnell in 1888 first published *Hobson-Jobson: A Glossary of Colloquial Anglo-Indian Words and Phrases, and of Kindred Terms, Etymological, Historical, Geographical and Discursive*. The book was many times revised and re-issued, the latest being published by Routledge & Kegan Paul in London in 1968.

cer, were sent to the regiment's recruiting grounds where sufficient suitable young men were found, passed by a doctor, attested by a magistrate at the nearest cantonment and dispatched to the regiment.

Prior to 1895 such were the sole recruiting efforts. Only when young men conforming physically to the regimental stereotypes were demanded were recruiting depots established in certain districts and recruiting put in the hands of "specially selected officers who understood Native character." Understanding the native character was important. British officers delved into the customs, religions, festivals, history, habits and characters of the men from the martial races. Much of their lore was embedded in a series of army handbooks, one on each major martial race, designed to help recruiters and newly assigned officers. Nearly all British officers in the Indian Army came to esteem themselves experts in the analysis and classification of types of people.

Understandably, many men from non-martial races hankered for the prestige, pay and pension of the soldier. Many claimed to come from a more acceptable tribe or clan than their own, and recruiting officers took elaborate precautions to make sure that a potential recruit was not lying. Unless a VCO could vouch for him, his claims were taken down and sent to civil authorities for corroboration.

By 1914 only twenty-four classes of men were recruited. World War I saw recruitment broadened to take in other classes and many were surprised by the showing of regiments recruited from non-martial classes. In Mesopotamia three regiments of Mahrattas—the 103rd, 110th and 117th— fought three successful engagements under horrendous conditions near Kut: in extreme heat, with only the water they carried in their canteens, they fought continuously for forty-eight hours. The 117th, which lost all of its British officers, fought on under its subedar-major. But nothing shook the fixed belief of officers in the cherished theory of the martial races.

Before World War II the unscheduled Hindu castes

(Untouchables) were not recruited; if any had dared apply, they would have been rejected out of hand. Three battalions of Mahars—short, sturdy and lithe Harijans from Mahratta country—were formed towards the end of the war, but they did not see action and their martial qualities were untested. Other southerners recruited during World War II performed creditably and Bengalis who were taken into signals and administrative services also did well.

Indian nationalists believed that the practice of limiting recruiting to the martial races was merely part of the British scheme to divide and rule, but the British belief in the martial races was real enough. Officers recruited from those classes because they genuinely believed that by doing so the army would be improved. Indeed, for small wars and frontier expeditions the Indian army of uneducated, loyal, strong-backed, peasant soldiers performed admirably.

14

The Frontiers

I n the last fifty years of the raj troops from India were sent to fight in China, Mesopotamia, France, East Africa, West Africa and North Africa, but never in South Africa. The Anglo-Boer War of 1899–1902 was regarded as a "white man's war," and neither black Africans nor Indians were used as combatants; yet only a dozen years later tens of thousands of Indian troops were sent to France to fight in what was most certainly a white man's war. So quickly can men's notions of what is fit and proper change.

In 1890–91 during a rebellion in the north-eastern state of Manipur, the British political agent and two other Britons were treacherously murdered. The two British officers on the scene panicked and it was left to Ethel St. Clair Grimwood, the young and beautiful widow of the murdered political agent, to lead them and their sepoys through the jungle, over a mountain and out of Manipur to safety. Mrs. Grimwood was awarded the Royal Red Cross Medal; the officers were cashiered. An expedition was launched against the Manipuris and the usurper responsible for the murders was duly hanged. Manipur then disappeared from the news of the world until World War II.

It was the North-West Frontier, with its turbulent tribes-men and its passes through which, traditionally, India's conquerors had always marched, that most troubled India's rulers. Fighting here was almost continuous, for campaigns were never conclusive, the tribes were numerous, the tribesmen prone to violence, and the border long.

After the withdrawal of Roberts and his forces from Afghanistan in 1880, the British wisely concluded that the country, difficult to invade, was impossible to hold—a lesson the Russians learned a century later. The boundary between British India and Afghanistan was clearly the Hindu Kush, that great mountain range sweeping down from the Himalayas in a south-westerly direction, and its offshoot, the Safed Koh range, but the British found a mountain range too inexact a boundary. In 1885 an Anglo-Russian boundary commission determined a portion of the Frontier, but not until 1893 was an agreement signed between the Government of India and the ruler of Afghanistan defining the boundary between the two countries. Over the next two years markers were placed along a thousand miles of the Frontier. This was the Durand Line, named after Colonel Sir Mortimer Durand of the Indian Army, who was primarily responsible for the agreement and for the placing of the markers.

Durand was one of those remarkable Europeans who were able to understand and make friends with primitive people. He believed in taking men as he found them and once remarked that "half of my most intimate friends are murderers." The Durand Line has been criticized as "illogical from the point of view of ethnology, of strategy, or geography." Indeed, it often divided tribes; its boundary stones were placed too far apart; and its twistings and turnings were, and are still, difficult to follow. But it was better than nothing, and the tribesmen living in the areas through which it passes knew little of nations and cared nothing for borders drawn on a map. Today, with little change, it divides Pakistan and Afghanistan.

Neither Britain nor Afghanistan ever attempted to rule or even to maintain law and order in their respective border areas. Along the British side of the Durand Line, stretching from Chitral to Baluchistan, there ran a belt of independent tribal territory, ten to a hundred miles wide and about four hundred miles long, encompassing lands without laws or police in which every man was armed and a law unto himself. The social order, such as existed, consisted of families, clans and tribes held together by tribal meetings, *jirgas*, at which tribal leaders *(maliks)* and elders attempted, not always successfully, to use their influence. Occasionally a malik or a mullah (religious leader) would for a time hold sway over some tribes, but usually each Pathan male regarded himself as the equal of any other man.

The line separating tribal territory from British-administered territory was termed the "administrative border." Throughout the entire area lived the Pathans, a Pushtu-speaking people. Those who inhabited the administered areas were known as cis-border Pathans; those in tribal lands were called trans-border Pathans.

The British held the half-dozen key passes through the mountains in the tribal areas, but in most of the territory between the administrative border and the Durand Line they were content to permit the trans-border Pathans to murder, rob and torture each other at their pleasure—which they did. Arable land amid the rocks was too scant to support the tribal populations and the Pathan temperament made the tribesmen at best indifferent farmers and herdsmen. Forays into the plains had for centuries fortified their economies; they naturally failed to understand British objections simply because their raiding grounds had been made administrated areas.

In their attempts to keep the Pathans pacified the British tried flattery, threats, bribes and, when necessary (which was often), punitive raids. Tribes which behaved themselves were given substantial subsidies; their old men were paid as *khassadars*, ostensibly to guard the roads but actually to provide an occupation that precluded robbing travellers; young men were paid to build or maintain roads, chop firewood and erect government structures such as small forts. None of these expedients were ever known to work for long. Carrying on the family feud, responding to a fanatic mullah's cries for a jihad against the infidels, or raiding across the border had stronger appeals than following a plough, tending a flock, or swinging a pick on the sirkar's roads. Without the excitement of feuds, raids and jihads, life might have been boring on the rocky slopes.

A report on the Pathans made in 1855 by the secretary to the Chief Commissioner of the Punjab deserves to be quoted at some length:

> Now these tribes are savages—noble savages, perhaps—and not without some tincture of virtue and generosity, but still absolute barbarians nevertheless. . . . They have nominally a religion . . . [but] in their eyes the one great commandment is blood for blood, and fire and sword for all infidels. . . . They are superstitious and priest-ridden. But the priests *(mullahs)* are as ignorant as they are bigoted, and use their influence simply for preaching crusades against unbelievers, and inculcate the doctrine of rapine and bloodshed against the defenceless people of the plain. . . . They are avaricious. . . . They are thievish and predatory to the last degree. The Pathan mother often prays that her son will be a successful robber. They are utterly faithless. . . . Every tribe and section of a tribe has its internecine wars, every family its hereditary blood-feuds. . . . Every person counts up his murders. . . . Reckless of the lives of others, they are not sparing of their own. . . . They possess gallantry and courage themselves and admire such qualities in others. . . . They are too fickle and excitable to be industrious in agriculture or anything else. . . . They will take military service and, though impatient of discipline, will prove faithful, unless excited by fanaticism. Such briefly is their character.

Such being their character, what has been their conduct towards us? They have kept up old quarrels, or picked new ones with our subjects in the plains and valleys near the fron-

tier . . . they have plundered and burned our villages and slain
our subjects; they have committed minor robberies and isolated murders without number; they have often levied black-
mail from our villages. . . . When inclined for cruel sport, they
sally forth to rob and murder, and occasionally take prisoners
into captivity for ransom. They have fired upon our own troops
and even killed our officers in our own territories. They have
given an asylum to every malcontent or proclaimed criminal
who can escape from British justice. They traverse at will our
territories, enter our villages, trade in our markets; but few
British subjects, and no servant of the British Government,
would dare to enter their country on any account whatever.

Such was the attitude toward the Pathan at the beginning
of the rule of the Crown in India. It did not change markedly in the next ninety years, and neither did the character
of the Pathan.

The British vainly studied in detail Pathan habits, customs, language, government, religion, family relationships
and genealogies (see Chart 2). Over the years they developed a kind of love-hate relationship. Colonel Buster Goodwin, who served for twenty years on the North-West
Frontier, once said: "Our dealings with the Pathans was a
gentleman's game, you know. No matter how poor a Pathan
was, he may meet the King of England or the Viceroy of
India, but he'd look him straight in the eye and shake hands
with him as if to say that I'm as good a man as you are."
And they were not, after all, without honour. They lived by
the code known as *pukhtunwali*, which decreed that fugi-
tives must be given refuge and protection; any insult to a
person, his family or his clan must be avenged; and, most
important of all, hospitality must be offered at all times,
even to a deadly foe.

When Lord Kitchener became Commander-in-Chief, India,
British battalions of infantry took tours of duty on the North-
West Frontier, and were rotated so that practically every
British battalion that served in India had some frontier
experience. Usually this was the only warfare men would

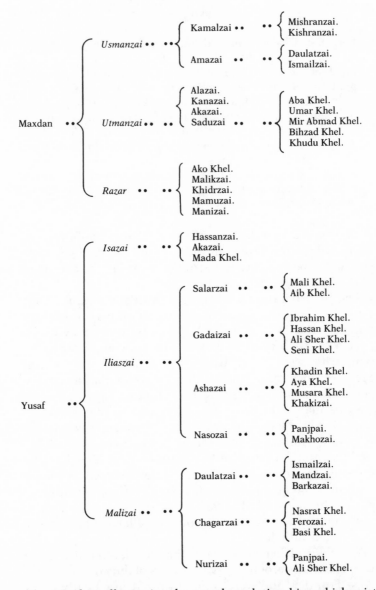

Chart 2: Chart illustrating the complex relationships which exist in every Pathan tribe. This shows the various clans, septs and extended families among the Yusafzai Pathans.

see. It was, said one British officer, "a form of soldiering enjoyed, on the whole, by all ranks, spiced as it was with the ever-present element of a chance encounter, and a climate of ever varying degree from 125° in the shade during the hot weather at Tank to the snow-bound winter of Razmak."

The Frontier held dangers other than the Pathans. Lieutenant J. S. E. Western of the 1st Punjab Cavalry at Dehra Ghazi Khan (popularly known as Dehra Ghastly) wrote feelingly of the "poisonous creepy-crawleys of the most repulsive kind," including "nasty venomous scorpions and huge spiders called 'jerrymungulums' whose bite . . . caused . . . the victim to bleed at the ears."

Selected Gurkha and Indian battalions also served on the Frontier, but they were rotated less often. Some, permanently stationed close to the border, were part of the Punjab Field Force (known as "Piffers"). Political officers posted among the Pathans were able to call upon their own little private armies, made up of tribesmen and led by specially selected British officers. Such forces, known collectively as Frontier Scouts, were variously named South Waziristan Militia (later Scouts), Kurram Militia, Tochi Scouts, Gilgit Scouts, Zhob Militia, and, perhaps most famous of all, the Khyber Rifles.

These units gave a young Pathan an alternative to building roads, ploughing fields or making forays into the plains. He could join the British effort to control his fellow tribesmen. It had its appeal. A scout was given a good rifle, the most prized of possessions on the Frontier. He was clothed and fed and earned cash, always scarce; he could live in the hills he loved, for scouts stayed permanently in their own area, and he usually found enough excitement to satisfy him. Tribesmen with the worst reputations—Mahsuds, Afridis, Mohmands, Wazirs, Orakzais, Yusafzais—often made the best soldiers.

The British eventually developed a system on the Frontier not unlike that used by the Romans: lightly armed militia and local auxiliaries (Frontier Scouts) were used as a first line of defence, with the heavy legions (brigades of infantry and regiments of cavalry) in camps well behind the frontiers but close enough to support them if necessary. Roads were pushed through tribal territories and forts built to protect them. Like the Germanic tribes facing the expanding Roman Empire, the Pathans came to regard roads as the greatest threat to their freedom.

To defend the roads that led through the few passes, the British relied upon the Frontier Scouts, who occupied small, often isolated forts from which, under the policy and direction of the local political officers, they enforced communal justice, holding an entire village or clan responsible for outrages committed by a few or even by an individual, punishing offences at times by burning villages or taking hostages, often by levying fines payable in numbers of rifles. Only when outbreaks were too extensive to be contained by the scouts was the army called in to fight the lashkars (tribal bands) and to lay waste large tracts of tribal land, burn villages, cut down fruit trees, and destroy crops and stored grain.

Whether the tribes were peaceful or restless often depended upon the skills of the political officers, men who lived among them as representative of the sirkar. Many were seconded from the Indian Army although they could also be selected from the Indian Civil Service. All were required to be good linguists and were expected to be skilled diplomatists, knowledgeable about the ways of primitive men and particularly the mores of the tribes among whom they worked.

The political officer moved in an unbureaucratic world of few files where his own personality counted far more than his ability to write minutes and memos. Ian Copland, speaking of those men selected to deal with rulers of princely states, described at the same time political officers everywhere when he said: "To win the confidence of the chiefs . . . personal contact was essential. And the men who did best at this game were invariably those with the most magnetic personalities: extroverts and sporting types, sensitive to the cultural milieu of the courts but strong-willed enough to resist the temptations inherent in this environment." *The Times of India* (7 July 1893) remarked that "a complete Political Agent should before all things possess a mind polished by social intercourse rather than that crowded with fusty learning." Bookish types were eschewed.

Army officers did not universally admire the political officers, for they were often inclined to identify with *their* own tribe, even at times remarking after a battle, "Our chaps fought well today," meaning *their* Afridis or Masuds, sentiments which the officers who had led the fight against them often had difficulty appreciating.

Political officers (called District Commissioners in cis-Frontier areas and Political Agents in tribal territory) reported to a Chief Commissioner (called Governor after 1932) of the cis-Frontier Districts, who was also Agent to the Governor-General in his relations with the trans-Frontier tribes. A grand personage, he lived at Peshawar, "the premier Frontier station in India," which housed a substantial army garrison.

Among the most famous political officers, and certainly one of the best, was Robert Warburton. Like Colonel James Skinner, founder of Skinner's Horse, Colonel Warburton was that rara avis, a socially acceptable half-caste. He grew up speaking not only English and Pushtu but also Persian, which was the language of the most cultured Afghans. He was a man universally liked by the most snobbish Englishmen as well as the fiercest tribesmen. Posted among the Afridis, who were specially noted for their bravery, their perfidy, and their cruelty, he never carried a weapon and was never harmed. Furthermore, he permitted no violence in his camp and feuding families could meet there in safety. Four or five years was considered the longest a political officer could stand the strain, but Warburton was seventeen years on the Frontier.

As long as he was at his post, the Khyber was safe. To protect the Pass he formed the Khyber Rifles in 1879 and he placed in command an Afghan of high character, constant loyalty and great ability, Major Sardar Mohammed Aslam. The unit, consisting mostly of local Afridis, was first called the Khyber Jezailchis because it was equipped with primitive local muskets known as *jezails*, but it soon acquired Snider Rifles and with them the name by which it became famous.

Even though members of the Khyber Rifles, like other Frontier Scouts, were not required to serve outside their own area, they volunteered to serve in the 1888 and 1891 punitive expeditions in the Black Mountains, where they fought in all major actions and distinguished themselves, earning a reputation for bravery and endurance.

Over the years, Warburton, with an eye to the future, continually begged the sirkar to send him suitable officers to serve as his second-in-command and as second to Mohammed Aslam, but this was never done. Mohammed served as commandant of the Rifles until an advanced age before retiring. When Warburton himself retired, the Afridis promptly revolted and all that he had accomplished was swept away on a tide of religious fanaticism which probably only he could have prevented. He was recalled, but it was too late.

The trouble began in Swat, where one of the many "mad mullahs" raised a jihad. Other mullahs joined in. A political officer and his escort were attacked in the Tochi Valley, and on 26 July 1897 there was an attack on the garrison in the Malakand Pass. In early August Sir Bindon Blood, an experienced frontier fighter, took command at Malakand and led a successful punitive expedition in Upper Swat, an expedition recorded by young Lieutenant Winston Churchill. By the end of August the entire Frontier was aflame. The blackest day in the history of the raj on the North-West Frontier was 25 August 1897, when the British lost the Khyber.

The authorities, who had undervalued the skills of Warburton, never completely understood what had happened
and how they themselves had contributed to the tragedy.
The official history spoke of "that sudden and, at the time,
almost unaccountable display of hostility toward the British Government." By the end of the summer three field forces
had swung into action: in Swat, in the Tochi Valley, and
against the Mohmands. More troops were called up to punish the Afridis and the Orakzais, who had committed the
most egregious outrages.

South-west of the Peshawar Valley lay a large chunk of
tribal territory, unmapped and unknown to the British,
called the Tirah. The northern section was the summer home
of the Afridis; the Orakzais claimed the southern part. Into
this tribal haven the British launched a major punitive
expedition led by Sir William Lockhart, one of the best and
most experienced frontier fighters.

Some forty-four thousand troops took part in the Tirah
campaign (1897–98), a larger army than had been sent to
the Crimea. About sixty thousand transport animals were
assembled: camels, bullocks, donkeys, mules and elephants. George MacMunn described the army on the march:

> The roads in every direction were full of gathering troops,
> Highland regiments, Gurkhas, Sikh corps . . . long lines of Indian
> cavalry, their lances standing high above the acrid dust that
> they stirred. By the side of the roads strings of camels padded
> on beside the troops, the jinkety-jink of the mountain guns, the
> skirling of the pipes . . . all contributed to the wild excitement
> and romance of the scene.

Although the campaign was launched at the beginning of
the cold weather and each man was issued a warm coat, no
tents were taken and even officers' baggage was limited to
twenty-six pounds each. It was thought that snow would
not fall for another seven or eight weeks, time enough for
the work ahead. And so it proved, but barely.

Foul weather, wet and cold, rough terrain, and the hos-

A scene from the Tirah campaign of 1897–98. (National Army Museum)

tility of every inhabitant of the area made the campaign an arduous one. In spite of the numbers of troops involved, the campaign is remembered, if at all, only for the charge of the Gordon Highlanders on 20 October 1897 at Dargai where Piper George Findlater won the Victoria Cross. Wounded in both legs and unable to walk, he propped himself against a rock and under heavy fire from the heights above continued to play "Cock o' the North" to the charging Gordons.

Dargai was the only stand-up, set piece battle, but the Pathans, individually and in small groups, pressed heavily on the rear guard, sniping and falling upon supply columns and foraging parties.

The heart of Tirah was the Maidan Valley, fifteen miles long and seven or eight miles wide, fertile, populous and prosperous. Into this lovely valley Lockhart's army descended, sowing fire and destruction. Fruit trees were felled, stores of grain and crops were burned. Lionel James, a Reuter's correspondent with the expedition, wrote of the scene at night: "The camp was ringed by a wall of fire—

byres, outhouses, homesteads, and fortresses one mass of rolling flame, until the very camp was almost as light as day."

Because the Pathans swarmed around the expedition like angry hornets, the withdrawal from the Tirah when the destruction was completed had all the hallmarks of a defeated, retreating army. The troops were "drawn, pinched, dishevelled and thoroughly worn." This was the first and last army to enter the Tirah.

There were larger expeditions—to the Bazar Valley and to the Black Mountains—and smaller expeditions elsewhere. In March, the Khyber Pass was retaken. Eventually the Afridis caved in and agreed to pay the levied fines, but they remained hostile and nine years later the sirkar had to admit that "their attitude towards Government is much the same as it was prior to 1897."

Queen Victoria drew the right conclusions, as she so often did. She wrote severely to Lord Elgin, then Viceroy: "The Queen cannot help fearing that there was a want of preparation, of watchfulness, and of knowledge of what the wild tribes were planning, which ought not to have been." True enough. It was a state of affairs never experienced when Warburton was on the Frontier.

15

Kitchener and Curzon

Lord Curzon (1859–1925), eldest son of the fourth Lord
Scarsdale, was undoubtedly the most intellectual
Viceroy in the history of the raj. He possessed an exceptionally keen brain and, in spite of almost constant pain from
curvature of the spine, boundless energy. Before the age of
forty he had been raised to the peerage, married an attractive American heiress, and been appointed Viceroy of India.
His term as Viceroy, from 1899 to 1905, the longest of any
Viceroy, has been called the high noon of the raj. He had
prepared himself for his high office by extensive travel
through India, including its North-West Frontier, and he
had even crossed into Afghanistan to confer with its ruler.
He not only had a clear-eyed view of India's problems, he
had developed imaginative solutions for many of them.

Curzon hoped one day to become Prime Minister, but his
career in India and in Britain was wrecked on what was,
au fond, scarcely more than an administrative detail. In
spite of having bred some of the greatest intellects in history, the British have always distrusted intellectuals. Curzon was thought by many to be too clever by half. When he
was a student at Oxford another undergraduate wrote:

My name is George Nathaniel Curzon.
I am a most superior person.
My cheek is pink, my hair is sleek,
I dine at Blenheim once a week.

The doggerel clung to him and haunted him all his life.

Curzon arrived in Bombay on 3 January 1899 and at once announced his intention to "hold the scales even" in dispensing justice among the many races in India. When he learned that a Scots Fusilier who had bludgeoned to death a punkah coolie because he had not fanned him energetically enough had been acquitted by a court-martial, he vowed: "I mean, as far as one man can do it, to efface this stain while I am here." Soon after, action followed rhetoric in the "Rangoon Incident."

A group of drunken soldiers from the 1st West Kent Regiment, stationed in Rangoon, staggered from an illegal bar and seized a young Burmese woman who was on her way home. Dragging her to an open area, they raped her in turn. Her screams brought other Burmese to the scene and the rapists were identified, but the Burmese witnesses, all of whom had been threatened, declined to testify at the court-martial and the soldiers were acquitted. Officers in Rangoon were inclined to make light of the matter and the civil authorities seemed not to care.

Curzon was outraged and heads rolled. The colonel was relieved of his command, several other officers were censored, the sergeant-major was reduced to the ranks, the culprits were dishonourably discharged and the entire battalion was posted to Aden, the hottest, most uncomfortable military post in the British Empire. Furthermore, Curzon issued an Order in Council expressing his "profound sense of horror and outrage."

In a letter to the Undersecretary at the India Office in London he wrote: "Hitherto I have not met one soldier in India who is on my side. The majority of them openly denounce me, and unblushingly proclaim the law of license.

I do not suppose that any Viceroy has ever had to bear the brunt of such a campaign of malice and slander. . . ."

The Rangoon Incident occurred during a kind of interregnum at the headquarters of the Indian Army. Sir William Lockhart, who died on 18 March 1900 after serving less than eighteen months in office, was to have been replaced as Commander-in-Chief, India, by Lord Kitchener, popularly known as "K," then serving as Governor-General of the Sudan, which he had recently conquered, wresting it from the Mahdist Dervishes. However, the Anglo-Boer War broke out in South Africa before he could take up his post in India and he was dispatched to fight the Boers. His seat was kept warm for him by the senior officer in India, Sir Arthur Power Palmer, an Indian Army officer who had served in many campaigns but had had little administrative experience. Not until 28 November 1902 was Kitchener able to assume command in India. A few months before that date another sordid incident occurred.

The 9th (or Queen's Royal) Lancers was one of the oldest and most distinguished regiments in the British Army. It came into being in 1715 during the Jacobite Rising and had fought in Buenos Aires in 1806, Walcheren in 1807, and for three years (1811–13) on the Iberian Peninsula under Wellington, but it had earned most of its laurels in India and Afghanistan, fighting in both Sikh wars, the Mutiny, and the Second Afghan War. On 9 April 1902 it returned to Sialkot in India from the war in South Africa and the troopers celebrated with a party, which they shared with a battalion of the Black Watch. Two lancers, doubtless drunk, fell upon and battered severely an Indian cook whom they felt should have provided them with women. The cook died nine days later and a court of enquiry predictably failed to identify the killers. A week later a second Indian was murdered and the local inhabitants were convinced that the deed had been done by 9th Lancers. With no faith in military justice, a kinsman of one of the victims appealed directly to the Viceroy.

Curzon was outraged by the army's callousness. He ordered an extensive investigation, and when the murderers were still not identified, he decided to punish the entire regiment. Officers on leave and other ranks on furlough were recalled; no more leave was to be given for six months; and extra sentry duties were ordered. "I will not be party to any of the scandalous hushing up of bad cases," Curzon declared, "or to the theory that a white man may kick or batter a black man to death with immunity because he is only a 'damned nigger.' "

The 9th Lancers, the army, and indeed the entire European population in India were enraged. In clubs and army messes Curzon was cursed as a "nigger-lover." Even distant London was not immune. During a debate on the Indian budget in the House of Commons, Colonel the Hon. Heneage Legge, who had served in the 9th Lancers in the Afghan War and had later commanded the regiment, rose indignantly to protest the collective punishment.

In addition to his interference in what most considered to be strictly the affairs of the military, Curzon instituted a number of reforms that rocked the bureaucracies. One of the most unsettling was the creation of a North-West Frontier Province with a Chief Commissioner directly responsible to the Government of India rather than to the Lieutenant-Governor of the Punjab, a step he took without even bothering to inform Mackworth Young, the Lieutenant-Governor of the Punjab.

Curzon was soon confronted with the animosity he had aroused. He had taken enormous pains to hold a grand durbar in Delhi on 1–9 January 1903 to celebrate the coronation of King Edward VII as Emperor of India. Its splendour rivalled that of Lord Lytton's Imperial Assemblage of 1877 and wits referred to it as the Curzonisation. Representing the King in India was his brother, the Duke of Connaught. Before a vast and brilliant assembly attended by more than a hundred Indian princes, the Nizam of Hyderabad was made a GCB; Lord George Hamilton (Secretary of State for

The visiting Duke of Connaught and the Viceroy, leaving Delhi
by train, bid good-bye to Indian rajahs and chiefs in 1903. The
Viceroy, Lord Curzon, is wearing a political officer's costume;
the Duke, seen shaking hands, is in the uniform of a British field
marshal. This sketch was made by Melton Prior (1845–1910),
one of the most famous war artists of the Victorian era. He had
just arrived in India to cover the Delhi Durbar from Somaliland,
where he had sketched the British campaign. (Windsor Castle.
Royal Library. Her Majesty Queen Elizabeth II.)

India) and the Rajah of Cochin were made GCSI; the rajahs
of Travancore and Nabha became GCIE; and eight other
princes were knighted.* To celebrate the occasion, 16,188
prisoners were set loose upon the populace and about 600
surviving veterans of the Mutiny were honoured.

Taking part in the ceremonies were thousands of troops,
including the 9th Lancers. Kitchener, who had arrived in

---

* GCB—Knight Grand Cross of the Most Honourable Order of the Bath.
  GCSI—Knight Grand Commander of the Most Exalted Order of the
  Star of India.
  GCIE—Knight Grand Commander of the Most Eminent Order of the
  Indian Empire.

India only a few weeks earlier, wisely suggested that the 9th Lancers be left out of the show, but Curzon insisted that he wanted "all the cavalrymen I can get"—he only had 35,000. He ought to have heeded Kitchener's advice, for when the 9th Lancers rode past in review, the crowd gave a mighty roar of welcome; even Curzon's guests from England applauded. Unmoved, Curzon sat on his horse, fully aware of the implications of the cheers. "I do not suppose," he said later, "that anybody in that vast crowd was less disturbed than myself." He was thinking, he said, that the ranks of that regiment riding past him held two murderers, and he felt "a certain gloomy pride in having dared to do the right."

Kitchener had little to do with the durbar except to sit his black charger at the head of his troops. His tunic covered with medals and stars, his head adorned with a plumed Wolseley helmet, he made an imposing figure, a hero known to all for his successes in the Sudan and South Africa. Mortimer Menpes, the artist who had come to India to paint pictures of the great occasion, was doubtless correct when he wrote: "It was impossible that the thought should not enter the head of everyone with the smallest imagination that the man who now fulfilled the role of C-in-C was destined one day to sit in the seat of the Viceroy." Kitchener thought so himself, and when in August Curzon's term as Viceroy was extended, he was furious. Curzon, aware of his sentiments, wrote to Hamilton: "I suspect he is one of the keenest wishers of my retirement. . . ." The careers of both men would have been considerably enhanced had Curzon retired on schedule.

The tall, stern-faced Kitchener was the picture of the simple, honest soldier, but he was a complex man indeed, and not always an honest one. Perhaps no man in modern times better fitted Gibbon's description of Septimus Severus, for, like him, Kitchener was a man whose ambition "was never diverted from its steady course by the allurements of pleasure, the apprehension of danger, or the feelings of humanity." He courted the influential, curried favour with the powerful and, it was said, "his charm was never wasted on underdogs." He had a well-earned reputation for ruthlessness and a less well known but soon to be demonstrated talent for intrigue.

Curzon had looked forward to Kitchener's arrival and he was eager for him to carry out army reforms, but he was soon to complain that "it was harder to govern Kitchener than to govern India." Kitchener was also eager to institute reforms, but they were not all of the kind that Curzon had in mind. Kitchener was a man who neither brooked restraint nor accepted advice, and he wanted full and complete control of the Indian Army, even though the organization of the Government of India made the assumption of such power impossible.

The Government of India was a cabinet form of government composed of the Viceroy (who retained the title of Governor-General) and a small council. Although in the order of precedence the Commander-in-Chief ranked second only to the Viceroy, a military member of the council was in charge of what was called the Military Department, which was responsible for military administration, medical stores, supply, transportation, clothing, remounts, military works and military finance. The military member also gave the Viceroy his advice on any proposal submitted by the Commander-in-Chief.

This peculiar system of "dual control" had worked well in the days when the Commander-in-Chief was commanding the East India Company's army in the field and communications were poor. He could march off to war and leave behind the military member to keep his army supplied with necessities and to give military advice to the Viceroy. Kitchener was not the first Commander-in-Chief to object to the system, but he was the first and only one effectively to do anything about changing it. It was particularly irksome to him that his proposals and plans were commented on by an officer considerably his junior, for Kitchener was a full general and the military member a mere major-general. He set about to destroy the Military Department and to depose the military member.

Curzon strenuously objected. Kitchener, he said, was proposing a "military despotism" which would "dethrone the Government of India from their constitutional control of the Indian Army." In spite of their differences, during the first year and a half of Kitchener's appointment he and Curzon remained on good terms, at least outwardly, but in a series of letters to powerful people in England, he laid the foundation for a campaign against Curzon. To Lord Roberts, now the Commander-in-Chief of the British Army, Kitchener wrote that he found his position "galling," and he complained continually of the Military Department, which he damned as inefficient, and of Sir Edmund Elles, the military member, whom he called "narrow-minded and bigoted." Roberts, who had had no trouble working under the system when he himself was Commander-in-Chief, India, was unsympathetic.

Undeterred, Kitchener called on other friends in London who were willing quietly and diligently to help him, among them the private secretary to the Secretary of State for War and Lady Salisbury,* the wife of the Undersecretary of State for Foreign Affairs and the first cousin of A. J. Balfour, the Prime Minister. To make sure that his campaign proceeded with professional acuity, he dispatched two loyal members of his staff to London to further his interests.

In the summer of 1904, while Curzon was absent in England where his wife was seriously ill, Kitchener opened his campaign in earnest by pressuring Lord Ampthill, the acting Viceroy, to transfer the responsibility for supply and transportation from the Military Department to his control.

In a letter to St. John Broderick, the Secretary of State

---

* She was Lady Cranborne until August 1903, when her husband became the fourth Marquis of Salisbury on the death of his father.

for India, the beleaguered Ampthill wrote that "Lord Kitchener is desperately keen on the subject. He refers to it on every possible and impossible occasion, and he even dragged it in the other day on some papers relating to the diseases of camels." Finally Kitchener threatened to resign, and although he had frequently resorted to this expedient, Broderick panicked.

On 1 January 1905 Kitchener set forth his arguments in a lengthy memorandum in which he complained that the Commander-in-Chief could not

> issue orders for the movement of troops or introduce any but trifling improvements in any of these matters without the previous sanction of the Military Member . . . [who] has power to interfere with the decisions of the C-in-C or prevent his wishes being carried out even in questions of discipline and training. . . . In war, the present system must break down; and, unless it is deliberately intended to court disaster, divided counsels, divided authority and divided responsibility must be abolished.

From the first almost to the last Curzon regarded the matter as a "constitutional position of the Government of India," an internal matter to be settled by the Government of India. He was naïve. In a letter to Broderick he wrote, "I do not quite understand what is at issue." Others saw sooner than he that this was a clash of personalities. Ever-busy Kitchener carried on a voluminous correspondence with influential people in London and fired off telegrams in code to his staff officers, who developed an efficient intelligence-collecting organization. He even mounted an effective press campaign, a tactic which would never have occurred to the aristocratic Curzon.

Broderick, tending more and more to favour Kitchener, now set up a commission, chaired by himself, to investigate the function of the Military Department and to determine who could, or should, advise the government on military matters. Curzon, whose relations with Broderick had badly deteriorated, professed himself unable to understand why Broderick was heading a commission to advise himself. General Sir George White and Field-Marshal Lord Roberts, the only two members of the commission who had themselves been Commanders-in-Chief, India, and whose views ought to have carried great weight, were the only members who did not agree with Kitchener. They were ignored.

When Curzon returned to India he carried out his own formal investigation, which concluded that yielding to Kitchener's demand would concentrate too much power in the hands of one person, the Commander-in-Chief. Curzon's council concurred. Kitchener did not bother to argue his point, for he knew, as Curzon did not, that the matter would be decided in London. As he foresaw, London ignored the advice of the Governor-General in council and the Cabinet followed the recommendation of Broderick's commission; Kitchener prevailed. All departments except Finance and Stores were to be handed over to him; he was to be the sole adviser to the Viceroy on military matters. Kitchener's aides in London learned of the decision at once and telegraphed him the news; Curzon did not learn of his humiliating defeat until nearly three weeks later. He was shocked by the decision, as well he might be, for he had assumed that the views of his own government were being seriously considered and would carry the most weight.

For several days he postponed meeting with Kitchener while he tried to compose himself and decide what course he should take. There then occurred a Sunday meeting, the results of which surprised everyone. According to Kitchener, Curzon broke down in tears, but this seems unlikely. However, to everyone's astonishment, Curzon persuaded Kitchener to agree to certain face-saving modifications of the Cabinet's decision, most important of all, to agree that the Viceroy would receive "a second military opinion" from an official now to be called the military supply member, who would be of major-general rank. This time it was Curzon who threatened to resign. Kitchener explained his concessions by asserting that it was necessary to agree to a watered-down version of his scheme because he felt it necessary to "let him [Curzon] down easy." Broderick, considerably embarrassed by what appeared to be Kitchener's volte-face, was forced to agree to the modifications.

Just when all the dust seemed to have settled, it was stirred up once more by an official of the Indian Post Office who offered to supply Curzon with copies of all Kitchener's private telegraphic messages. There was nothing illegal about this; the Viceroy did, in fact, legally possess the power to see private telegrams. When Kitchener learned of the offer, he panicked. He need not have, for Curzon, whose behaviour throughout had been as honourable as Kitchener's had been disreputable, refused to look at them.

General Sir Edmund Elles, a pawn in this great clash of political powers and monumental egos, resigned. Curzon wanted to replace him with Major-General Sir Edmund Barrow, a capable man of independent mind, a distinguished soldier who had served in the Second Afghan War, the Egyptian Campaign of 1882 as DAQMG, on the North-West Frontier as AAG, and as Deputy Secretary of the Military Department. Kitchener protested that Barrow was too good a man for the job and declared that he wanted him for his own chief-of-staff. In Barrow's place he suggested Major-General Charles Egerton, a brave but elderly general of no administrative experience. Curzon, laughing, suggested that Egerton be Kitchener's chief-of-staff. Nettled, Kitchener blurted, "Oh no, I don't want a duffer."

Curzon formally recommended to Broderick the appointment of Barrow, but it was effectively sabotaged by Kitchener's friends at the War Office. At this slap in the face Curzon offered his resignation and, to his astonishment and chagrin, it was quickly accepted. It had never occurred to him that the Cabinet would prefer his resignation to that of Kitchener.

Although Curzon's resignation was effective 22 August

1905, he stayed on in India to receive the Prince and Princess of Wales, who arrived on 9 November. Nine days later he left India, an angry, bitter man. His place was taken by Lord Minto, a man with no desire to cross swords with the redoubtable Kitchener.

In a paper he wrote later, Curzon contended that the home government had "thrust aside as valueless the reasoned arguments and the earnest representations of the entire Government of India, and have ordered a revolutionary change in the Indian constitution in deference to the views of a single soldier who had been in India only two years, who had never served in India before, and who was not in touch with the Native Army." All this was true, but irrelevant. Kitchener the war hero, popular with the people and the press, was a political asset; Curzon, the aloof intellectual, was not.

When Curzon left India, Kitchener tried, unsuccessfully, to alter records so that Curzon's actions would appear unjustifiable and his own warranted, but the facts gradually leaked to the press and Curzon, who as Viceroy had so often been unpopular, became a hero, at least in the eyes of the English-Indians, while Kitchener and Broderick were roundly condemned in every responsible newspaper in India. Kitchener tried in vain to silence the flood of criticism. Satisfying as this must have been to Curzon, the damage was done. In England he faced a political future which now appeared bleak. He received no public recognition for his work in India and it was eleven years before he returned to the main political stage. Ironically, on the day after his arrival home the Balfour government fell and Broderick, his nemesis, was out of office.

Kitchener's term, due to expire in November of 1907, was extended in March of that year for an additional two years, giving him seven years in all as Commander-in-Chief in India, years in which for the most part he had his own way and he made changes that were happier than those which forced Curzon's resignation. He improved training and in

1905 founded a staff college at Deolali, moved the following year to Quetta. He provided the Indian Army with modern arms and equipment, notably the .303 magazine rifle and a new mountain gun. He promoted sports, provided better rations and encouraged the establishment of regimental clubs and institutes. To make his army more self-sufficient, he built arsenals and took steps to organize it to fight a modern war.

Rejecting the notion that the purpose of the Indian Army was to hold India against the Indians, Kitchener laid down four interlocking basic principles:

1. The chief role of the army in India was to defend the North-West Frontier, guarding India from invasion from Russia through Afghanistan. The Great Game was still being played.
2. The army's organization, training and deployment should be the same in peace and war.
3. Internal security was a secondary role for the army.
4. All troops must be trained to fight on the North-West Frontier.

Complaining that the army was scattered "all higgledy-piggledy over the country, without any system or reason whatever," he set forth his plans for its reorganization in two memoranda. The first, issued in November 1903, was entitled "The Re-Organisation and Re-Distribution of the Army in India"; the second, issued soon after in January 1904, was labeled "The Preparation of the Army in India for War." Roberts's reforms were as nothing compared to the shake-up given by Kitchener.

The bulk of the army was formed into nine divisions grouped in two commands, each deployed on an axis parallel to the Frontier. Divisional areas remained fixed, but units rotated between divisions after several years duty so that each regiment and battalion acquired experience on the Frontier. The old regimental designations of Madras,

Bombay and Bengal, left over from presidency days, were dropped from regimental titles. Except for the Gurkhas, all regiments were renumbered in a single sequence for each arm. The Punjab Frontier Force was disbanded as a separate organization and incorporated into the Indian Army, although regiments were allowed to keep "Frontier Force" as part of their titles. Burma was separated from the Madras Command and made into a separate Burma Command. The Hyderabad Contingent (four regiments of cavalry and six battalions of infantry) was broken up and delocalised. Many small posts were abandoned.

Kitchener cast the theory of the martial classes in bronze when he decreed the "complete elimination of units raised from unwarlike races" and the raising of new regiments "from amongst hardier populations."

One of the most important military innovations was not Kitchener's creation but Curzon's. Urged by Queen Victoria to find a way of "providing somehow increased opportunities for the military aspirations of Indian gentlemen and princes," he conceived in 1901 the notion of establishing an Imperial Cadet Corps with schools at Meerut and Dera Dun to train Indian officers both for the Indian Army and for those armies of princely states which could be used as imperial service troops. Admission was limited to the sons of princes and nobles. The course lasted two or three years and in 1905 those who were graduated received a special commission in "His Majesty's Native Indian Land Forces." Although the graduates could not command British troops and in the Indian Army could not rise above the level of squadron or company officer, it was the first small step towards the "Indianisation" of the Indian Army officer corps.

The school was not without its special problems. Some cadets arrived with swarms of servants and few had ever before been subject to discipline. Curzon sent one young prince known to be a homosexual to the school in the hope that he would acquire some self-discipline, but then wor-

ried that he might corrupt other cadets. A list was compiled of young princes he suspected were homosexuals, some
of whom, it was believed, had fallen under "sodomistic
influences" at Mayo College, an imitation British public
school near Ajmer where many young princes and nobles
were sent to be educated. Curzon himself believed that
Indian marriage customs were to blame for the prevalence
of homosexuality among the Indian nobility. In a letter to
Lord George Hamilton, he wrote: "I attribute it largely to
early marriage. A boy gets tired of his wife, or of women,
at an early age, and wants the stimulation of some more
novel or exciting sensation."

The Imperial Cadet Corps was not popular with British
officers, who did not look forward to a day when their closed
world would be open to Indians, however highborn. The
Indians who received such commissions were not entirely
happy either, for their status was clearly inferior to that of
officers who held the King's Commission.

It was during the Kitchener-Curzon era that the first
serious rumblings of discontent from nationalists were
heard. The Indian National Congress, founded in 1885, was
not initially anti-British and the government viewed it with
benign goodwill. Its founder was an Englishman, Allan
Octavian Hume (1829–1912), a retired member of the Indian
Civil Service. At the 17th session of the Congress in December 1901, Indian leaders expressed their "appreciation" to
the government for the founding of the Imperial Cadet Corps,
calling it a progressive step. A mere two years later Gopāl
Krishna Gokhale, the East Indian professor and leader of
the moderate nationalists who became president of the
Congress in 1905, railed against Indian exclusion from "all
voluntary participation in the responsibilities of national
defence," and denounced the British Army, which he said
was "maintained in India for Imperial purposes."

Kitchener, who entertained no fears of another serious
mutiny but suspected sedition, wrote in a letter to Lady
Salisbury (6 June 1907): "The principal agitators are the

more or less educated lawyer class. They . . . are doing all they can to get at the loyalty of the Army. They preach another mutiny, to drive us out of the country." But for the moment the army and the raj were safe. Gandhi was still in South Africa, Nehru was in England, Jinnah was a mere judge, and Independence was nothing more than a small black cloud on the horizon of British imperialism.

Before he left India, Kitchener was treated to a round of farewell parties. At one, a dinner held at the United Service Club in Simla on 20 August 1909, replying to a tribute from Lord Minto, he read a lengthy speech written by a member of his staff, unaware that it freely incorporated substantial portions of a speech given some years before by Curzon, a plagiarism spotted and gleefully reported by the press.

K's place as Commander-in-Chief was taken by Sir O'Moore Creagh, V.C., who quickly became known as "No More K." A soldier with little administrative ability, he instituted few reforms. He was succeeded in March 1914 by Sir Beauchamp Duff, a former aide of Kitchener's who, as Barrow wrote to Curzon, had "never commanded a Regiment, a Brigade, a Division or an Army." Lovat Fraser, writing in *The Times of India*, called him an "office clerk" and in a letter to Curzon wrote: "I don't often venture on prophecy, but I firmly believe that the terrible mistake of appointing two unsuitable C-in-Cs in succession will have disastrous effects." Creagh or Duff would have been putty in Kitchener's hands had Kitchener, as he fully expected, become Viceroy, and he would then have been a virtual dictator. Since not Kitchener but Lord Minto became Viceroy, India—with Duff as Commander-in-Chief—was left to meet the military needs of a nation involved in a world war with the system largely created by and for Kitchener. Neither Duff nor the system proved a success.

16

Indian Princes and Their Armies

Although in nineteenth-century maps India was commonly coloured British red or pink, nearly a third of the subcontinent, about 600,000 square miles containing a fifth of the people, was never under direct British rule. The disintegration of the Mogul Empire left hundreds of crumbs in the form of more or less sovereign small states scattered about the subcontinent. The British conquered most of the large martial states, but by the middle of the nineteenth century there were still nearly six hundred extant ministates. Most were tiny, measuring only a few square miles, but a few, such as Hyderabad, and Jammu and Kashmir, were half again as large as England, or nearly twice the size of Pennsylvania. After the Crown took control of British India, no further attempts were made to subdue Indian states. There was no need to do so. Britain was content to be the paramount power and to serve as the fount of honours. The princes were lavished with medals, decorations, titles and privileges.

In the Proclamation of 1858, when the Crown took over

the responsibilities of the East India Company, Queen Victoria specifically stated:

> We desire no extension of our present territorial possessions; and while we will permit no aggression upon our dominions and our rights, to be attempted with impunity, we shall sanction no encroachment on those of others.
>
> We shall respect the rights, dignity and honour of native princes as our own; and we desire that they, as well as our own subjects, should enjoy that prosperity and social advancement which can only be secured by internal peace and good government.

Under the Crown the princely states were divided into three classes according to their size, wealth and power. The 118 First Class states were known as "salute states" because their rulers were entitled to gun salutes. When General Lord Wavell was Viceroy (1943–47), he mastered the names of the five most important states—Hyderabad, Kashmir, Mysore, Gwalior and Baroda (all entitled to twenty-one-gun salutes)—by keeping in mind that Hot Kippers Make Good Breakfasts. Rulers entitled to thirteen or more gun salutes were styled maharajas. The title "His Highness" was originally given only to those seventy-three rulers who were entitled to eleven or more blasts of the cannons; however, this caused so much ill-feeling that the limitation was eventually reduced to take in nine-gun rulers. (A few rajahs were honoured with personal gun salutes, but such honours were not necessarily extended to their successors. See Appendix B.)

First Class states enjoyed complete legislative and administrative independence within their own borders, at least in theory. Second Class states enjoyed partial executive independence and criminal and civil jurisdiction under British supervision. The great majority of the states, more than four hundred, fell into the Third Class, which enjoyed no legislative rights at all. Rulers of Second Class and Third Class states were not entitled to gun salutes.

Many of the perquisites of European royalty were forbidden the Indian princes. They could not call their realms "kingdoms" or refer to themselves as "kings" or their status as "royal." They were forbidden to refer to their *gadi* (cushion) as a throne—they assumed the gadi, not the throne—and they were not permitted to use letterheads with "arched crowns" (as opposed to "open crowns"). When, in 1925, Maharaja Tukoji Rao Holkar of Indore introduced a new letterhead with the prohibited arched crowns, the act was regarded as a serious infringement upon the rights and privileges of the King-Emperor.

Indian rulers were autocrats with a bewildering variety of titles. The word *raj* means "rule" or "reign," and the most common title was rajah (ruler) or maharaja (great ruler), but the ruler of Hyderabad was styled Nizam, and the chiefs of other states were, to name a few, Khan, Rao, Mir, Tham, Nono, Gaekwar, Jam, Peshwa, Thakore. Some titles, such as the Nawab of Amb, the Wali of Swat, the Jam Sahib of Nawanagar* or the Nono of Spitti, struck English ears as amusing, but they were real enough to their holders.

Taken as a whole, the princes were a spirited lot, adding glamour and colour to a land of mud hovels and grinding poverty. As Kipling remarked, "Providence created the Maharajas to offer mankind a spectacle," and this they did.

The princes were, of course, anathema to the nationalists, a species of politician which scarcely existed before the twentieth century, before the British permitted Indians to educate themselves in Western ways and taught them about John Locke, Jeremy Bentham, John Stuart Mill, Wil-

---

* "Jam" was the oldest of Indian titles, dating back to the days of the Moguls. The best known jam in the eyes of the Western world was the Jam Sahib of Nawanagar, K. S. Ranjitsinhji (1872–1933), popularly known as "Ranji," one of the most famous cricketers in the history of the game. He was champion batsman for All England in 1896 and 1900, and was with the famous All England XI in Australia in 1897–98. In 1900 he achieved a season aggregate of 3,065 runs with a highest score of 275.

liam Blackstone, the meaning of democracy and how to belabour British bureaucrats with their own principles. Mohandas Gandhi, although himself a son of the prime minister of the princely state of Porbandar (642 square miles), said of the princely states: "The existence of this gigantic autocracy is the greatest disproof of British democracy and is a credit neither to the princes nor to the unhappy people who have to live under this undiluted autocracy."

But the unhappy people seemed for the most part rather to like their atavistic princes. On the whole, princely taxes were lighter than those of the sirkar; it was cheaper to keep a prince in luxury than to support a legion of bureaucrats. In all the years of the British raj the princes' subjects showed not the slightest inclination to rebel against even the worst of their rulers in spite of the best efforts of the nationalist leaders.

The natures and qualities of the princes—often called feudatory chiefs by the British—varied widely from humane to cruel, from intelligent to idiotic, from virtuous to corrupt. Many were attentive to their duties and ran model states; others devoted themselves to frivolity and spent much of their time junketing about Europe. By the 1890s many of the princes or their sons had become highly anglicized, a credit in large part to the influence of indomitable English nannies, many of whom were imported to reign in princely nurseries. Unfortunately anglicization did not always produce the desired character. In some cases it served to sharpen old vices and to add a few new ones.

Lord Curzon had just arrived in India when, at Gwalior in December 1899, he made an effort to invigorate the princes by lecturing them on "where their duties lay." In so doing he created an uproar that reverberated back to Britain.

Upbraiding the assembled princes as if they were a pack of errant schoolboys hauled on the carpet by their headmaster, he warned them: "The Native Chief has become an integral factor in the Imperial organisation of India. . . . He cannot therefore remain a frivolous or irresponsible despot. His figure should not merely be known on the polo-ground, or on the race course, or in the European hotel. These may be his relaxations . . . but his real works, his princely duty lies among his own people. By this standard shall I, at any rate, judge him." In conclusion he informed them that "the desire of a Prince to visit Europe can only be gratified by formal permission from the Government of India," i.e., himself.

Well pleased with his speech, which he considered an example of his ideal of "plain speaking combined with perfect courtesy," Curzon arranged that its main points be incorporated into a formal document and published in the *Government Gazette.* The response was vehement and immediate. Curzon was astonished by the uproar he created, in Britain as well as in India. His American wife, Mary, explained to a friend: "What George has not realized is that the people at home thought he had taken on too much power in the matter of the Maharajas. The people of England look upon it as if an edict were published saying Dukes must not go to Monte Carlo to gamble."

There was, in fact, some precedent for such high-handedness. In 1897, when Lord Elgin was Viceroy, he had refused to allow the young Raja of Pudukkottai to attend the Queen's Jubilee in London because he was "addicted to amusements" and would "probably get into mischief." What kind of mischief? "We specially fear his marrying a European woman."

Indian princes visiting Europe, particularly England, were welcomed in exalted social circles, as most of the officials who ruled over them in India were not. The marriages which sometimes resulted were seen as a threat to the social distance which English-Indians believed essential between themselves and those they ruled.

Not all of the beautiful young women whom the rajas encountered in Europe were from noble families. British officialdom in India was shocked when in 1893 the Maharaja of Patiala married a Miss Florry Bryan over the vehement objections of Viceroy Lord Lansdowne. There was another brouhaha in 1910 when Maharaja Jagatjit Singh of Kapurthala married Anita Delgrada, a Spanish dancer. Even as late as 1943, in the middle of World War II, the marriage of Maharaja Yeshwant Rao Holkar of Indore to an American provoked correspondence which created six thick files in the India Office, much of it deliberating how his wife was to be addressed.

Britain wished to control three main areas of government in the princely states: the military establishment, communications, and foreign policy. To assure compliance with its wishes, every state of any importance accommodated in its court a British Resident; political officers supervised smaller states. All such officials were expected to exert their "moral influence" on the princes, who would then, the home government confidently expected, "yield a ready deference to the views of the British Representative." Some did.

Quentin Crewe, in his fine biography of the last Maharaja of Jaipur, succinctly summed up the British attitude: "What the British liked to see in a princely state was a pliant Maharaja, a soundly run government and a placid, old-fashioned peasantry with no knowledge of any other kind of existence."

Political officers could be intrusive, often imposing their own notions of propriety upon the princes. The Maharawal of Dungarpur, who ascended the gadi as a small boy in the 1920s, was married when he was eleven, but was forbidden by his political officer to sleep with his wife until he was nineteen—and he complied.

Although political officers tried not to interfere with the internal affairs of a state, efforts were made to curtail the excesses of sadistic rulers with unhinged minds. However, mere insanity was not seen as cause enough for rejection. In 1866 the Raja of Akalkot, who was certifiably insane, was not deposed, but in 1869 Porbandar was reduced from a Second Class to a Third Class state when its ruler cut off the ears and nose of a courtier who was alleged to have corrupted his son by leading him to drink.

It was recognized that the Resident often needed a big club. Princes who seriously misbehaved could be deposed. In Baroda, the Gaekwar was permitted to execute prisoners by standing elephants on their heads, but in 1875, when the Gaekwar, Malhar Rao, attempted to serve arsenic-laced sherbet to Lieutenant-Colonel Robert Phayre, C.B., the British Resident, he was deposed.

The Maharaja Jay Singh of Alwar, a ruler whom one British political officer described as "sinister beyond belief," was a notorious pederast. He was also a handsome, clever, erudite and urbane man who loved fast Hispano-Suiza motor cars and in time came to believe that he was the reincarnation of Rama. He was deposed by the British in 1933, not because he mismanaged his state or debauched small boys, but because after a chukka of polo in which his pony had stumbled and thrown him, he drenched the unfortunate creature with gasoline and set it afire. The British maintained their standards.*

Before 1885 the sirkar was content merely to regulate the size of princely armies and to provide advisers. Almost every state of any consequence had its own army—even the Raja of little Lunawada (388 square miles) boasted a squad or two of Rajput infantry. As foreign mercenaries were less likely to become embroiled in court intrigues, princes seldom recruited their own subjects. Princely troops were often very irregular indeed. They were usually badly trained and poorly armed; their pay was often uncertain and they frequently presented a rag-tag appearance. Included in the state army of Jaipur were 6,000 infantry, 1,000 cavalry, and

---

* To the regret of scandal-loving historians, nearly all of the secret dossiers which the British political officers had carefully compiled on the foibles and excesses of the princes were destroyed when India became independent in 1947.

somewhere between 3,000 and 6,000 irregular Nagas, a peculiar body of semi-religious devotees of a saint called Dadu Dayal. In 1868, Colonel James Croft Brooke wrote: "The Nagas are a body of religious mendicants who are trustworthy and true to the State. . . . They are armed with matchlocks, and will not undergo any discipline."

There were, however, exceptions. Certainly one of the best managed and best armed of the princely states was Gwalior, which the British had beaten into submission in a brief, two-battle war in 1853. In the 1860s Gwalior, although not the largest state, had one of the most efficient armies that included 5,000 infantry, 6,000 cavalry, 600 artillerymen and 163 serviceable guns.

When in March 1885 a Russian force attacked and routed an Afghan force at Penjdeh, a village on the ill-defined Afghan-Turcoman frontier, the British were so alarmed that for several weeks Britain and Russia seemed on the verge of war. The Army in India was soon on the move towards the North-West Frontier and many princes, following the spontaneous, generous—the British even called it "patriotic"—example of the Nizam of Hyderabad, offered large sums of money for the war chest. The "Penjdeh Incident" ended with a compromise, but the princes' generosity prompted the authorities to consider whether some military muscle from the princely states would not be even more useful than cash, and it was suggested that a portion of the armies of the larger princely states be trained and equipped to take their place in the line should their services be needed. The sirkar agreed to update arms and equipment and to provide officers to train and supervise, an offer most of the principal states were happy to accept. The troops so designated were known as Imperial Service Troops. Thus for a relatively small cost the sirkar was able to add some twenty thousand troops to its order of battle.

An inspector-general of Imperial Service Troops was appointed and the states were formed into groups, each with its own inspecting officer and assistants, whose duties were to train the troops to a reasonably high standard of efficiency and to advise the durbars (governments of the princely states) on military matters. Inspectors and their assistants, although military officers, were not responsible to the Commander-in-Chief, but to the Political Department.

The sirkar wrought a notable change by decreeing that Imperial Service Troops must not be foreign mercenaries but subjects of the rulers. Certain exceptions were allowed, notably in Jammu and Kashmir, where it was the custom for Gurkhas to serve in considerable numbers. The British, who had long used Gurkhas themselves, could hardly find reasons for denying the services of these hardy hillmen to the princely states.

Beginning in about 1895, Imperial Service Troops took part in numerous frontier expeditions; they subsequently served in both world wars, and participated in expeditions to China and Somaliland. Even so, the British, still haunted by the Mutiny, harboured lingering suspicions and fears. Kashmir alone was permitted Imperial Service artillery: two batteries of 2.5-inch mountain guns were allowed, principally for the defence of the Gilgit Frontier, although one battery performed creditably in the Tirah campaign.

By 1914 the Imperial Service Troops totalled 22,479 officers and other ranks from twenty-nine princely states and included, in addition to infantry and the Kashmiri mountain batteries, eleven regiments of cavalry plus eight under-strength squadrons; four companies of Sappers and Miners; a mule and pony transport corps with 1,650 army carts; two camel transport corps with 1,200 camels; a Camel Corps (500 mounted infantry); and some odds and ends. After World War I the numbers of Imperial Service Troops increased, and by 1923 they had risen to 27,030.

In many states the rulers appointed themselves commanders. The Maharaja of Bikaner named himself colonel-in-chief of his Imperial Service Troops, which included the famous and flashy Bikaner Camel Corps that had helped

A sowar of the 25th
Punjab Cavalry
mounted on a camel,
about 1895. (National
Army Museum)

the British chase the Mad Mullah in Somaliland and had
fought well in Palestine during World War I. Elsewhere sons
or relatives of the ruler took command. All the officers were
scions of the nobility; many had been trained in the Imperial Cadet Corps or at the Indian Military Academy, Dehra
Dun.

By World War I the British had succeeded in binding the
princes ineluctably to them and the princes had indeed come
to consider themselves an integral part of the British
Empire—just as a dozen years earlier Curzon had told them
they should be. When war was declared, the Maharaja of
Rewa sent a telegram to the Viceroy: "What orders of the
King-Emperor for me and my troops?" The Gaekwar of
Baroda, a twenty-one-gun state, placed the entire resources
of his state at the disposal of the King-Emperor, as did the
ruler of Suket, a tiny, non-salute state in the Punjab with
fewer than 55,000 inhabitants.

In all, eighteen rulers put themselves at the head of their own troops or offered themselves for military duty and served in one theatre or another. Eight rulers donated their private airplanes to the Indian Air Force. The actions of the rajas attracted more newspaper attention than the hundreds of thousands of ordinary Indians who volunteered.

One of the firmest believers and staunchest defenders of King and Empire was Sir Pertab (or Pratap) Singh, the Rajput regent of the state of Jodhpur in Rajasthan and the most famous of the Indian commanders of Imperial Service Troops. Born in 1885, the third son of the Maharaja of Jodhpur, he was said to have been fearless as a child and he grew up with the sole desire to be a soldier. He served in the Tirah campaign, where he was wounded, but concealed his wound until threatened with blood poisoning.

Sir Pertab endeared himself to British officers by daring to lose caste through a generous gesture. In 1907, when a young British officer died at the Jodhpur Court, only three men, all Christian British officials, could be found to carry the coffin. Sir Pertab volunteered to be the fourth. When Brahman priests later confronted him and warned that he would lose caste by touching the coffin of a Christian and must therefore go through a purification ceremony, he replied that he would do nothing of the sort, that both he and the deceased belonged to the highest caste of all: that of a soldier. In World War I, at the age of seventy he led the Rajput Horse to France, where, he said, he hoped to lead a cavalry charge that would be a "death ride." He believed that "a soldier's death wherever won was the best and greatest gift of life."

However, the opportunity to die in a cavalry charge failed to present itself and Sir Pertab survived to instruct and admonish the Prince of Wales. In 1921 the future Edward VIII visited India and went pigsticking with the old gentleman, who was an expert. Overconfident and careless, the young prince made a dangerous blunder, and Sir Pertab minced no words. "I know you are the Prince of Wales," he said, "and you know that you are the Prince of Wales, but the *pig* doesn't know you are the Prince of Wales."

Sir Pertab, at seventy, was the oldest prince to serve in World War I. His two sons also served, as did his great nephew, Sumer Singh, who was only seventeen and the youngest of the princes. The Jam Sahib of Nawanagar, the famous cricketer, also served, as did several members of his family. His nephew was adjutant of the Jodhpur Lancers and was killed in France. Rama Jodha Jang Bahadur of Nepal, who was under no obligation whatsoever to serve the British, won the Military Cross as a second lieutenant at Ypres in 1915.

Not all of the princes or their noble kinsmen who volunteered for service in the war were permitted to serve with troops in the trenches of Flanders or Mesopotamia. Most were given appointments on the staffs of senior generals. Maharaja Kumar Gopal Saran Narain Singh of Tikari served as a lieutenant at Haig's headquarters, delivering dispatches at breakneck speeds on his motorcycle and demonstrating his marksmanship in the trenches with his Westley-Richards .475 high-velocity double-barrelled tiger gun, until the Germans protested that the latter was a contravention of the Geneva Convention.*

The Imperial Service Troops performed with mixed results in the Great War, though they had their share of casualties. Out of 26,099 combatants sent from the princely states for field service, 2,754 were killed or wounded. They won 572 awards, and, though none gained a Victoria Cross, four Imperial Service Troops officers earned Military Crosses. Except for the Gurkhas in the Kashmiri contingent, they performed poorly in East Africa, fleeing at the first shot at

---

* It was not, in fact, a contravention of either of the Geneva Conventions then in force to use such a weapon. Neither convention placed any prohibition or restriction on the means or methods of waging war. However, the prince was probably using soft-nosed, expanding slugs, which were outlawed by a convention of the First Hague Peace Conference of 1899, a convention to which Great Britain reluctantly acceded in 1907.

An Indian lancer in France in 1915. (National Army Museum)

the Battle of Tanga. Elsewhere, however, some gave praise-
worthy performances: the Bikaner Camel Corps did well,
and the Maharaja of Jodhpur's Lancers led the charge that
took Haifa from the Turks in Allenby's Palestinian campaign.

After World War I the numbers of Imperial Service Troops
were increased and by 1923 numbered 27,030, but in still
another overhaul of the Indian Army, a committee of princes
and political officers evolved a new scheme whereby all of
the princely armies, except irregular forces such as the Nagas
of Jaipur, would be reshaped and redesignated Indian State
Forces. The armies of the princely states were classified into

three categories: Class A troops were those organized, armed, equipped and trained as corresponding units in the Indian Army; Class B units did not follow the organization of the Indian Army and were less well armed and equipped; Class C units were militia formations which were not permanently embodied and whose standard of training and level of armament was lower than that for Class B units. Initially the sirkar provided free weapons to Class A and B units, and many states joined the scheme. In 1931 arms were no longer passed out free and efforts to upgrade units from Class B to Class A were discontinued.

The rulers of the princely states could, of course, assign whatever ranks they pleased to their officers. In the Jammu and Kashmir Army, the lowest commissioned rank was major prior to 1928, when captains and lieutenants were added and the hitherto popular rank of general was abolished. In the early 1930s steps were taken to improve the quality of the officer corps and ten places were reserved for selected State Forces cadets at the Indian Military Academy, Dehra Dun. On the eve of World War II the Indian State Forces numbered between fifty and sixty thousand men.

The three brigades in the Jammu and Kashmir forces (mostly Dogras, with numbers of Jats, Gurkhas, Muslims and Sikhs) were considered excellent. The cavalry in Hyderabad was good, but its infantry was rated poor. The units in Patiala and Bhopal were rated fair. Some of the State Forces in the smaller states were of questionable value. They sported splendid uniforms and were suitable for ceremonial purposes but little else. Lack of good officers and insufficient training made them unfit for battle.

In 1932 the Maharaja of Jaipur, who had spent a year at Woolwich, raised a regiment of seven hundred officers and men which he moulded into an imitation of the British foot guards. A former Coldstream Guards sergeant was imported to drill them and they were outfitted with uniforms resembling British Guards except for their headgear. Turbans replaced the familiar bearskins. Every sepoy was a Rajput and at least six feet tall. In the officers' mess the only toast drunk was to Matsya, the first avatar of the god Vishnu.

A special and peculiar relationship existed between the British and the army of the Nizam of Hyderabad. It began in 1766 when the East India Company signed a treaty with the Nizam promising to respect and defend the integrity of Hyderabad and providing for the establishment of a British officered military force to be paid for out of the revenues of a part of the Nizam's state known as "the Berars." When this force, which came to be known as the Hyderabad Contingent, proved too expensive, costing more than the Berars could provide, the Nizam got out from under by assigning to the East India Company the government, but not the sovereignty, of the Berars, a distinction the British chose to ignore. In spite of frequent requests the territory was never returned; the British, ostensibly to protect the Nizam and his state, retained a firm control of both the Berars and the Hyderabad Contingent.

Among the rulers who stood by the British in World War I was the Begum of Bhopal, ruler of the one principality whose evolution and development had been directed by a succession of forceful, intelligent and independent-minded women. Like most Muslims, she must have had her crisis of conscience when Turkey entered the war on the side of Germany, yet she remained loyal. In a manifesto addressed to her people, she urged them and all Muslims to remain faithful to the sirkar and she staunchly offered her own services in defence of the King-Emperor and his Empire.

Not every prince was converted into an ally. Maharana Fateh Singh of Mewar disdained British honours and was one of the few princes who refused to support the war effort in World War I. Yet at the end of the war the British conferred upon him the splendid and coveted GCIE (Knight Grand Commander of the Most Eminent Order of the Indian

Empire). When it was presented to him, he disdainfully ordered that it be put on his horse. Later, when he was asked by one more daring than most what service he had performed to merit such a distinction, he answered: "While the British were away fighting the war in Europe, I didn't take over in Delhi."

chapter 17

The Singapore Mutiny

In 1914, although unprepared to fight a European war, Indian soldiers had no objection to fighting Germans. The only difficulty in sending troops overseas was a minor matter: the fear on the part of some Hindus of losing caste by "crossing the black water." But this was a venial offense which could be absolved by purification ceremonies on the soldiers' return. It was Britain's declaration of war on Turkey on 5 November 1914 and in particular the Sultan's declaration of a jihad against the Triple Entente eleven days later that created crises of conscience among many Muslim soldiers, for the Turkish Sultan, Mehmed V, was still the revered Calif of Islam. Matters were exacerbated when Turks spread the word that Kaiser Wilhelm had been converted to Islam.

Not all Muslims were prepared to believe in a converted Kaiser, but many had qualms about making war on their Turkish co-religionists. Although in the early months of the war the British made a conscious effort not to send Indian Muslims to Egypt, the Sudan, or Mesopotamia, almost every unit scheduled for service overseas had to deal with the rumour that Muslims were being sent to fight Muslims on the side of the unbelievers. General Herbert Vaughn Cox, commanding the 29th Indian Brigade, which landed at Suvla Bay at Gallipoli on 1 May 1915, refused responsibility for the loyalty of his two battalions of Punjabi Muslims, and in consequence they were used only for supply and communications work on the beaches and they gave no trouble. On the North-West Frontier, the British were fortunate to have another remarkable chief commissioner. Sir George Roos-Keppel was a formidable character who had earned the confidence and trust of the Pathans. It was in large part thanks to him that during the difficult war years the Frontier remained relatively quiet. Only once did rumours of being sent to fight co-religionists trigger an emeute, and this took place not in India or in Mesopotamia but in, of all places, Singapore.

The British had grown careless. Had they been more careful, more conscious of the feelings and fears of their Muslim sepoys, the unfortunate affair at Singapore would not have taken such a serious turn and presented such a formidable danger.

Monday, 15 February 1915, was New Year's Day in the Chinese lunar calendar and in Singapore it was a public holiday. Brigadier-General Dudley Howard Ridout, age forty-nine, commanding the troops in the Straits Settlements, was suffering from a bout of malaria, but he dragged himself from his bed and rode to Alexandra Barracks, five miles south-west of the city, to hold a pre-embarkation inspection of the 5th Indian Light Infantry, the only battalion of regular infantry on the island. The SS *Fiji*, a troopship anchored in the Singapore Roads, waited to carry the regiment to Hong Kong.

The 5th Indian Light Infantry, a single-battalion regiment and one of the few single-class regiments, was composed of Muslims recruited from the cis-Jammu and trans-Jammu region of the Punjab and from Hindustan. It had served ten months in Singapore and to all outward appearances was a smart, well-disciplined unit. Ridout gave the men a few words of praise and wished them luck in their new posting. There is some dispute as to whether or not Brigadier-General Ridout or Lieutenant-Colonel Edward Victor Martin, commanding the 5th Light Infantry, told the troops where they were going, but if either did, he was not believed. In the event, the regiment never reached China.

By 3:00 p.m. Ridout was back in his quarters and back in bed when he was roused by a telephone call from Martin, who reported that half of his regiment (about four hundred men) had mutinied and that two of his officers had been murdered.

In spite of his fever, Ridout acted with vigour. He hastily dressed and called up all the support he could muster, but he had at his disposal only a handful of troops: some gunners from the Royal Garrison Artillery, a mule battery of the Malay Guides (mostly Sikhs despite their name), a detachment of the Johore State Forces, some local European volunteers (many of them elderly), and some unarmed Sikhs who were in transit to Weihaiwei (then a British enclave in China).

There were, however, other sources of help. A former sergeant-major had the presence of mind to alert the captain of HMS *Cadmus*, a Royal Navy survey ship with a complement of ninety which was then in the harbour, and he at once dispatched an armed shore party. The Japanese Consul rounded up 190 Japanese civilians who were quickly enrolled as special constables and issued rifles.

While her husband was calling up help, Mrs. Ridout worked furiously with the recalcitrant Singapore telephone system to alert the guards at the internment camp at nearby Tanglin. Captain Lionel Plomer Ball of the 5th Light Infantry tried desperately to rouse the civil police—Malays, Chinese and Indians under mostly British officers. Neither the internment camp nor the police were reached in time. The inspector-general of police later complained that he was not informed until 4:45 p.m., "otherwise some lives might have been saved."

Happily, there was no panic. Most of Singapore's residents, European and Asian, remained ignorant of the crisis, for the mutineers' gunfire was mistaken for the exploding firecrackers of the Chinese celebrating their new year.

The mutiny was not a well-organized affair. Although two VCOs and several noncommissioned officers were among the instigators, no one took command. Sikhs in the mule battery of the Malay Guides joined the mutineers, but it seems never to occurred to any of them to shell Singapore. The Sikhs simply walked away from their guns and the sepoys did not know how to work them. It was just as well, for as the *Straits Times* said later (15 May): "If one single capable leader had appeared among the mutineers, they could have marched into Singapore and have done pretty much as they pleased, for the island was deplorably unprepared for such an event." It was true. Had they been well led and resolute, the mutineers could have taken possession of one of Great Britain's most important naval bases.

The principal instigators easily agreed on their first objective. In the packing up preparatory to breaking station, the regiment's 300,000 rounds of ammunition were being loaded onto lorries to be turned in at the ordnance depot. On a signal from a sentry who fired into the fatigue party, mutineers from A and B Companies opened fire. One soldier in the fatigue party was wounded. The rest fled.

The mutineers now had all the ammunition they needed, but they seemed unclear or divided about their next step and the ringleaders were unable to exercise united control. With no one in overall command, they split into groups. One of these, without any clear plan, simply wandered about, killing almost every Briton they found. They found seven. One was young Mrs. Gordon Woolcombe, whom a friend described as "such a pretty girl." She had married only a few days before. Her body was found lying across that of her husband: she had apparently flung herself upon him in a vain attempt to save his life.

An eccentric Englishman named Gibson was encountered by the mutineers as he was walking along a road talking to himself. Deciding that he was mad—and thus perhaps holy—they allowed him to pass unharmed. Britons were their prey, but cosmopolitan Singapore contained scores of nationalities. Every European was stopped and asked, "Are you Inglees?" Those who answered yes were shot out of hand. One man escaped when he indignantly exclaimed, "No! I'm Irish."

In general, women were not molested. Mrs. D. Marshall, who saw sepoys with fixed bayonets standing in the road, walked up to one and asked what was happening. She was merely told: "Go away. A war is on."

Horror stories of the Mutiny of 1857 were recalled by every Briton in Singapore as word of the uprising spread. Mrs. F. L. Tomlin, wife of the manager of a mercantile firm, when ordered by her husband to dress quickly and prepare to leave, wondered if she should take her jewellery, but, as she later recalled, she "somehow felt how silly I was to worry about it when our lives were at stake. The Indian Mutiny flashed into my mind, also the fact that we had no white troops."

The authorities wasted no time in declaring martial law; immediate steps were taken to save the European population. Cars were requisitioned and dispatched to the suburbs to bring in women and children, who were installed first at Government House and, when it was filled, in various hotels; later they were put aboard ships in the harbour.

The largest body of mutineers, about a hundred men, marched to the internment camp at Tanglin, only two miles from their barracks, where they caught the guards, mostly local volunteers, completely by surprise. Lieutenant J. H. Love-Montgomerie, the guard commander, was mortally wounded while talking on the telephone with Mrs. Ridout, who had finally managed to get through to him. She heard with horror the shot that killed him and the thump as he fell. Also killed were the camp commander, two volunteer

British officers, four noncommissioned officers, four privates, a Malay officer, two Malay soldiers, and, accidentally, a German prisoner of war. Three British volunteers
were wounded.

Cheering, the mutineers threw open the gates and poured
into the camp, jubilantly shaking hands with the dazed
prisoners. The German and Austrian internees, mostly Singapore businessmen, were horrified by the sudden violence
and would have nothing to do with them. Instead, as soon
as they had rallied from the shock, they set about tending
the wounded. A group of German sailors who had been
working assiduously on an escape tunnel decided that it
would be somehow dishonourable to take advantage of this
opportunity simply to walk away. As one said later: "War
was war, but this was mutiny, and we wanted nothing to
do with it."

Not until later in the day did seventeen Germans leave,
taking their possessions with them. Four were later recap-
tured, but the rest managed to make their way to the Kar-
imoen Islands in the neutral Netherlands East Indies, where
one of them sent a cheeky telegram to the Governor of Singapore: "Arrived safely." Eight managed eventually to reach
Germany, including Oberleutenant sur Zee Julius Lauterbach, who before his capture had been navigator on the
famous German raider *Emden.*

The mutineers were astonished by the refusal of the Germans to join them, especially when they repeated what they
themselves had been led to believe: that a Turkish warship
would come to pick them up. They were also puzzled to see
the internees caring for the British wounded. Bewildered,
they wandered around the camp without an idea of what
to do next. Some finally turned towards Singapore; others,
suddenly aware that the world outside their barracks was
not as they had imagined, fled north into Malaya and sought
refuge in the Johore jungles.

The only other sizable group of mutineers prepared an
ambush just outside Singapore, but when a truck loaded

with sailors off HMS *Cadmus* roared down the road, a Maxim machine gun mounted on its roof, they assumed it had come from the warship they were expecting. Dashing out from their hiding places they ran towards the truck cheering. One called as he ran, "Are you Germans?"

"No, you bastard, we are not!" yelled a stoker, and shot him in the shoulder. The Maxim quickly accounted for three killed and a number wounded; the remainder fled back towards Alexandra Barracks.

Lieutenant-Colonel Martin barricaded himself in his bungalow. With him were Major and Mrs. William L. Cotton, Captain Lionel Ball, and a handful of British volunteers. Also present were a few loyal sepoys whom a distrustful Martin had foolishly disarmed. The bungalow, a substantial stone and wood building on a rise overlooking the entire cantonment, was quickly converted into a small fort. Major Cotton's wife, in the finest tradition of women who live on the fringes of empires, made tea and cut sandwiches for the defenders as they watched through the long night—and chided them for swearing.

The following morning, at first light, a scratch force of civilian volunteers of various nationalities (including a clutch of Methodist ministers who were in Singapore for a conference), naval ratings, and garrison gunners were assembled under Lieutenant-Colonel Charles William Brownlow, a Royal Artillery Officer who had seen active service in Burma and on the North-West Frontier. One hundred and seventy-six strong, armed with a Gatling gun and an assortment of rifles, they piled into cars and set off for Alexandra Barracks to relieve the siege of Lieutenant-Colonel Martin's bungalow.

Brownlow halted his motor column just outside the barracks and deployed his men in open order. Under heavy fire, they swept through the cantonment area to the bungalow. Feeling that it could not be adequately defended from a determined attack, Brownlow brought away its defenders. In this operation he lost two men killed and four wounded; eleven mutineers were killed.

Most of the mutineers now began to have second thoughts, particularly as it became clear that, contrary to their expectations, there was no German or Turkish warship in the harbour to take them away. At police stations in and around Singapore, singly and in small groups, they began to surrender.

In the next few days Ridout received a stream of reinforcements. A French cruiser landed ninety men and two machine guns; a Russian cruiser put one hundred forty sailors ashore; the Japanese Navy weighed in with seventy-five ratings from one of their warships; and the Sultan of Johore came himself with one hundred fifty of his soldiers, rocketing down on the Penang mail train. The following Sunday the 4th Battalion of the King's Own Shropshire Light Infantry arrived by steamer from Rangoon, but by this time all danger was past. In all, nearly a hundred people had been killed.

The mutineers who had fled or had gone into hiding were soon rounded up by patrols organized by Ridout. Dyak trackers imported from Borneo were sent into the Johore jungles to flush out those who had fled in that direction. By 31 March, only fifty-one were still at large. Officers and loyal VCOs and NCOs sorted through those captured and selected 202 for court-martial.

Lieutenant-Colonel Brownlow was named president of the court-martial, which first met in secret on 23 February and quickly condemned two men to death. They were shot the same day. Then, in a surprise move, the courts-martial were thrown open to the public, a most unusual step for the army in time of war. Ridout explained his reason to the War Office: "It would be seen that the men were being tried for mutiny and shooting with intent to kill and not, as alleged, for refusal to go to Turkey."

The executions, which took place over several weeks, were carried out at first inside the Outram Road Prison. Later they were held outside the walls where the first attracted an estimated six thousand Europeans, Malays, Chinese, and Indians who gathered to watch. At one mass execution of twenty-two mutineers, the crowd was estimated at fifteen thousand.

In every case the mutineers were led out, the sentence of each was read in several languages, and those condemned to death were tied to stakes, without blindfolds. They were shot by firing squads found by units which had suffered casualties in the fighting. As many of these were volunteers with little musketry training, there were a number of botched jobs in which the victims suffered more than was necessary.

Of the 202 men court-martialed, all but one were convicted. By 17 May forty-seven mutineers had been executed and the remainder sentenced to varying terms of imprisonment. Sixty-four were sentenced to transportation for life, a sentence to be served in the penal colony which had been established on the Andaman Islands in 1858.

The 5th Indian Light Infantry was reconstituted and sent to fight in Africa, first in the Cameroons and then in the East African campaign. As soon as the sepoys discovered that the Germans ate pork sausages and therefore could not be Muslims, they performed creditably. The regiment was disbanded in 1922.

Reports of the mutiny were heavily censored. The casualty figures, even the number of mutineers executed were suppressed. Until the facts were made public, the mutiny seemed nothing more than a bit of war-time excitement even in Singapore itself, where the Chinese festivities had continued unabated.

Within a few days of the collapse of the mutiny a court of inquiry was appointed under the direction of Brigadier-General Frederick Aubrey Hoghton of the Indian Army, recently arrived in Singapore from Burma. In addition to gathering evidence for the courts-martial, it examined the causes of the mutiny. The court sat for forty-three days and on 15 May 1915 produced a thorough and comprehensive

450-page report. It was not released to the public for fifty years.

What was revealed most clearly was the dirty linen of the regiment. Feuding and backbiting had occupied the officers, who seemed united only in their dislike of their commanding officer, for whom not one had a good word. Lieutenant-Colonel Martin, for his part, claimed that most of his officers had "joined in a cabal against him." Indeed, two of his junior officers, who had been refused permission to transfer out of the regiment, had taken the most unusual step of calling on Sir Arthur Young, the governor of the Straits Settlements, to warn that the 5th Light Infantry was on the verge of mutiny. Sir Arthur had ignored them, for he had been given Martin's assurance that the regiment was loyal.

The sepoys, too, had been disgruntled and restless. They had squabbled among themselves and had divided bitterly over the controversial promotion of a havildar to jemadar. They had found fault with their food: chicken had been substituted for their accustomed goat meat and they had not been receiving as much milk as they thought they deserved. It was clearly an unhappy regiment.

Martin came in for some stiff questioning from the court of inquiry, which eventually concluded that the principal cause of the mutiny was "the very unsatisfactory state of discipline which had prevailed in the 5th Light Infantry apparently for some time." He was castigated for barricading himself in his bungalow and "for marked weakness throughout." Others, too, British and Indian officers, were charged with "unsatisfactory conduct." There was, in fact, a "lamentable want of initiative and resource by all ranks" to quell the mutiny: "The time-honoured maxim of 'l'audace, toujour l'audace' when dealing with Orientals was apparently lost sight of. We believe that resolute action by a formed body of Europeans would . . . have exercised a marked effect upon the course of the mutiny."

The court noted, too, that the lack of British troops in

Singapore at the time was "not without its influence in bringing off the emeute." It found a major contributory cause had been the exposure of the men to "the evil influences of seditionists who were passing to and from the Far East and America." In the words of the court, the "gullibility and credulity" of the mutineers was "almost beyond belief."

The men of the 5th Light Infantry had indeed been suborned by outsiders. At a mosque near Alexandra Barracks the imam, Nur Alam Shah, had regularly preached anti-British propaganda, proclaiming that it was sinful to help the Christian British fight the Muslim Turk and declaring that the Germans, too, were Muslims. Furthermore, the sepoys had listened with interest to the exhortations of anti-British Indian nationalists known as Ghadrites, some of whom were returning from North America where they had found themselves unwelcome.

The *Ghadr* movement was founded by a brilliant but bitter young man named Har Dayal, whose interest in forcibly ejecting the British from India attracted the attention of the police when he returned home from Oxford, and he was forced to leave India. He went to the United States and in San Francisco founded the Hindu Association of the Pacific Coast and edited a publication in Urdu and Gomulki called *Ghadr (Revolution)*. Har Dayal's anti-British sentiments became widespread among Indians on the West Coast, both in the United States and in Canada.

The Germans found the *Ghadr* movement interesting and German embassies and consulates around the world helped distribute Dayal's publication. In July 1914 Dayal moved to Geneva and then, at the invitation of the German government, he set up headquarters in Berlin. With the aid of German money his operatives were soon spreading throughout India and the East, including, of course, Singapore, where a number of Indians working there responded sympathetically to Dayal's message.

The Singapore mutiny had, in fact, been part of a master plan hatched by Indian revolutionaries who hoped to provoke a revolution. Their intent was to overthrow British rule in Singapore, Malaya and Burma. From this south-eastern Asia base, they dreamed of an invasion of India, a general uprising, and a violent end to the British raj. The aborted Singapore mutiny was as close to success as they came.

Twenty-seven years later, on 15 February 1942, the exact anniversary of the mutiny, Singapore fell to the Japanese and a new breed of Indian revolutionaries saw a fresh opportunity to overthrow the British raj. Again, numbers of Indian soldiers—this time some twenty thousand, nearly all prisoners of war—were persuaded to break their loyalty oaths and turn on their former masters, to join the "Indian National Army" and to fight against their former comrades.

18

World War I

Britain in 1914 was pitifully unprepared for a major European war. The Government of India was even less prepared, for it had never been anticipated that Indian troops would be seriously involved in a major war in Europe. They were neither trained nor equipped to play such a role. But in those first critical months of the war, trained soldiers of any description were urgently needed in Flanders to stop the German juggernaut. Aid from India was invaluable and a corps of two divisions—the Meerut and Lahore divisions—was speedily assembled and shipped off. Each division consisted of two infantry brigades, each with four battalions, one British and three Indian. One brigade was dropped off at Suez to defend the Canal; the others sailed on to France. By the end of 1914 there had debarked at Marseilles 21 cavalry regiments, 68 battalions of infantry and 204 field guns. They were so sorely needed by the hard-pressed Allies that no time could be allowed for the men to become acclimatized or to be equipped with clothing for a European winter or even to be issued with the proper weapons to fight a European war. Indian brigades were rushed forward with the few machine guns they possessed, without howitzers, without trench mortars and without hand grenades. Signalling equipment and medical supplies were sadly lacking. An Indian division carried only thirty field guns; an English division had seventy-six.

While obsolete weapons, when used by gallant and disciplined men, served well enough for the campaigns in Burma and on the North-West Frontier, they could not suffice to meet the superbly armed, highly disciplined and equally courageous Germans. Nevertheless, the Indian troops were at once thrown into the hard-pressed lines at Messines and into the frozen trenches south of Ypres. There they performed heroically, but the Germans decimated them with massed artillery, hand grenades and trench mortars.

On 31 October 1914 the 57th Wilde's Rifles, in trenches near Messines, was attacked by nine German battalions. In one part of the line a platoon of Dogras was enfiladed and died fighting to a man. Rather than be taken, the last man left alive, Jemadar Kapur Singh, shot himself with his last cartridge. In another trench, Havildar Ganga suffered six wounds while killing five Germans, using first a bayonet and, when that bent, a sword he snatched up. He lived to receive the Indian Order of Merit and the Russian Order of St. George, 4th Class.

Brigaded with Wilde's Rifles in the Lahore Division at this time was the 129th Duke of Connaught's Own Baluchis,* entrenched near the village of Hollebeke, Belgium. When the Baluchis received the full force of a savage German attack, one of their two machine-guns was knocked out by a shell and the machine-gun officer was severely wounded. Five of the six-man crew of the remaining gun

---

* The title of this regiment was a misnomer, for it contained no Baluchis. The 129th was, like most infantry regiments in the Indian Army at this time, a one-battalion regiment; it consisted of two companies of Punjabi Muslims, three of Mahsuds and three of other Pathans. It had served outside India once before: against Arabi in Egypt in 1882.

were killed, but twenty-six-year-old Sepoy (later Subedar) Khudadad Khan, although himself grievously wounded and without support, fought his gun until he lost consciousness. He was left for dead, but managed to crawl back to his own lines. He became the first native-born Indian to win the Victoria Cross.

The story of the 129th Baluchis is typical of many Indian battalions in France. It had arrived in the harbour of Marseilles in a convoy of troopships on the morning of 26 September 1914 with a fighting strength of 9 British officers, 19 Viceroy Commissioned Officers and 790 other ranks. Laughing, sunburnt young officers leaned over the bulwarks and called out to ask if the war was still on, for throughout the voyage they had feared it would be over before they arrived. Told that the fighting still raged on the Western Front, they cheered. Within six months nearly all were mutilated or dead.

During the first ten days in the trenches the battalion fought well, but it lost three British officers; three Indian officers were killed and two wounded. Of the other ranks, 26 were confirmed dead; 67 missing, of whom most were, in fact, also dead; and 138 were wounded.

As with other Indian regiments, it was not easy for the 129th Baluchis to find replacements. Of those sent from the Reserve in India, one third were physically unfit for the rigours of a European winter. It was even more difficult to find Britons who could speak the appropriate languages and were familiar with Indian troops to replace the fallen officers. The attempt just before the war to establish an Indian Army Reserve Corps had been a feeble effort, and the problem was exacerbated when the 257 Indian Army officers who were on leave in England at the outbreak of war were siphoned off by Kitchener to help train the masses of men he was enlisting to form new battalions.

The possibility of commissioning educated Indians was raised, but when the idea was suggested to General Sir

James Willcocks, commanding the Indian Corps in France, he wrote to Lord Crewe, Secretary of State for India:

> No one has greater admiration for the Indian soldier and offi-
> cer, when he lives up to it, than I have. He's generally brave,
> nearly always loyal—but he is seldom, *if ever* fit to replace the
> British officer. . . . The Indian is simply not fit to lead his men
> against Europeans. . . . It is the presence and natural instincts
> of the white man which the Indian officer can *never* replace.
> . . . The Indian has not the instincts which make leaders in
> *modern* war.

Keeping Indian troops supplied with their accustomed food, or any food that their religions did not prohibit, taxed the commissariat. As the conditions under which they lived and fought deteriorated, as casualties were replaced by half-trained men, and particularly as British officers, VCOs and Indian noncommissioned officers were killed or hospitalized, morale declined, and with it the fighting spirit and efficiency of the troops.

A prime indicator of morale in extended combat is the number of self-inflicted wounds, usually toes shot off or wounds to the hand, particularly the left hand. As of 3 November 1914, of 1,848 Indian soldiers admitted to hospitals for wounds, 1,049 were hand wounds, most sustained in the first two weeks of combat. Senior officers at first stoutly refused to believe that their sepoys, all selected from the "martial races," were actually shooting themselves to escape the horrors of the trenches. However, a comparison of hand wounds in British and Indian Infantry battalions convinced the most reluctant. The statistics were striking and could not be ignored. On 15 August 1915 the three British infantry battalions with the highest number of hand wounds were the Connaught Rangers (54), 1st Manchesters (38) and 1st Highland Light Infantry (25). The three Indian infantry battalions with the highest number were the 47th Sikhs (479), 129th Baluchis (318) and 15th

Sikhs (236). Faced with the facts, General Willcocks requested that the proportion of British to Indian troops be increased to one battalion of British infantry to two (rather than three) Indian battalions.

On 19 December 1914 units of the Lahore Division near Givenchy supported a French attack. The following morning the Germans exploded a huge mine under trenches held by the Sirhind Brigade: a double company of the 1/4th Gurkhas and a company of the Highland Light Infantry were blown skyward or buried alive in their trenches. A German infantry attack immediately followed the explosion and the Indian battalions broke.

First to flee were the sepoys of the 129th Baluchis. A British officer saw them streaming back from the front: "Many of them had thrown away their rifles and they said that all their officers had been killed." Other Indian units joined the flight. Both the 1/4th Gurkhas and the 9th Bhopals retreated in some order, but without orders; the British battalions stood fast. All who reported on this disaster agreed that the principal cause of the panic had been the loss of the British officers.

By the end of 1914 the Meerut and Lahore divisions had suffered 653 British and 944 Indians killed, and 2,000 British and 6,182 Indians and Gurkhas wounded or missing.

Dr. Jeffrey Greenhut in a brilliant essay on the Indians in France concluded that their disappointing performance was the result of "the most severe imaginable form of culture shock," a trauma that also explains their excessive dependence on their British officers, their only interpreters of the alien environment.

After a brief period of rest in billets, the Indians were again put into the line, and again their morale plummetted. Although they went on to perform creditably at Neuve Chapelle in March 1915, it was evident that the Germans were more than a match for them. They had arrived in France with about 220 British officers, 325 VCOs and 14,000 other ranks. They had taken part in most of the ferocious battles of late 1914 and early 1915 and had been heavily reinforced. Their total losses were nearly five hundred British officers and an equal number of VCOs, and more than twenty thousand other ranks. Very few indeed of the original contingent remained.

After fourteen and a half months in France, almost a year of which was spent in the fighting zone, the 129th Baluchis were withdrawn. They had fought at First and Second Ypres, Givenchy and Festubert. There had served with them 41 British officers, of whom eight were killed and 15 wounded; 48 Viceroy Commissioned Officers, of whom eight were killed and 25 wounded; and 2,547 other ranks, of whom 146 were certain dead, 119 missing (mostly dead), and 944 wounded. Of the original regiment there remained only four British and five Indian officers; less than two dozen of the other ranks were still alive and fit.

Over the objections of Willcocks and even Kitchener, now Secretary for War, it was decided to withdraw the entire Indian Corps from France. Because "fear of unrest" prevented their return to India (there had been a few minor mutinies and political unrest was building in the Punjab), the corps was broken up and units were distributed around to other theatres of war. In spite of the initial reluctance to send Indian Muslims to fight Turkish Muslims, most Indians serving overseas found themselves in Mesopotamia.*

The 129th Baluchis was built up to strength and sent off to East Africa to fight a nasty war in the jungles of Tanganyika. There it served beside the reconstituted 5th Light Infantry, which had redeemed its reputation fighting in the Cameroons. The 129th, however, failed to regain the reputation it had earned in the early fighting in France, and in January 1918 it was sent back to India.

On 5 November 1914 Turkey went to war against Britain. Anticipating this, the British had already put to sea an expeditionary force from India which landed the next day

---

* Indians served in three main theatres of war: 138,000 went to France, 144,000 to Egypt and Palestine, and 675,000 to Mesopotamia.

at Fao, a port on the western Persian Gulf near the mouth
of the Shatt-al-Arab, and it at once began an advance up
the river. Reinforced, it beat the Turks in several sharp
engagements, and on 22 November it occupied Basra. On 9
April 1915 General Sir John Eccles Nixon arrived and took
command of the force, which now included the 6th and 12th
Indian divisions. His instructions were to protect the oil
fields and refineries of the Anglo-Persian Oil Company,
occupy the entire Basra Vilayet, and to prepare for an
eventual march on Baghdad.

On 12, 13, and 14 April the Turks were defeated in a decisive action that took place at Shaiba—known as the "mir-
acle of Shaiba." (Here the first Victoria Cross of the
Mesopotamian campaign was won, posthumously, by Major
George Godfrey Massey Wheeler of the 7th Hariana Lancers.) A Turkish counterattack was repulsed and the Turks
retreated to Kut-al-Amara. Basra was now secure, but Nixon
pushed on. Al Qurna was taken on 3 June and Nasiriya on
25 July.

Although no real strategic purpose would be served by
capturing additional territory, Simla approved Nixon's plan
for an advance on Kut-al-Amara, 180 miles into the heart
of enemy territory, and in early August the 6th (Poona)
Division under Major-General Sir Charles V. F. Townshend
(1861–1924) moved up the Tigris, making a feint at the
Turkish right flank while launching its main attack on the
Turkish left flank on the right side of the river. The plan
was nearly spoiled when deserters, a Punjabi havildar and
some of his men, revealed Townshend's intentions to the
Turkish commander, who, fortunately, refused to believe
them. The Turks were routed, and on 29 September Kut-
al-Amara was occupied. British cavalry chased the fleeing
Turks halfway to Baghdad.

Those directing the war in London now became ena-
moured of the notion that Baghdad—fabled Baghdad—a
great supply center and arsenal, could be captured. Such a
victory, it was reasoned, would offset the disaster at Galli-

A Gurkha sepoy and Indian soldiers stand ready to fight the Germans and Turks in World War I, on this music sheet. (National Army Museum)

poli. The news would set every bazaar in the Middle East buzzing and would have a splendid effect on the Punjab and the restless Pathans on the North-West Frontier, particularly the turbulent Mahsuds.

There could be no doubt that the capture of Baghdad would be a propaganda coup, but the British, lacking men, supplies, and, above all, effective leadership, were ill-prepared for such an adventure. Nevertheless, Townshend was ordered to continue his advance. In November the ill-advised operation began—and ended. The British were halted in their tracks a few miles south of Ctesiphon, where, with technical advice from the Germans, the Turkish forces— 19,000 regular infantry, 4,000 cavalry and 52 guns, plus 13,000 Arab irregulars—had dug themselves into a strong position astride the Tigris. Their trenches were deep, their wire was thick, and their guns were well sited. A British force of 10,200 bayonets, 1,000 sabres and 30 guns was pitted against them.

The British claimed Ctesiphon as a victory, but it was a victory which, in fact, marked the beginning of defeat. After a three-day battle in which 4,511 were killed or wounded, including 47 percent of the British officers, Townshend retreated. To deceive the enemy, tents were left standing. Large stocks of stores of all sorts were abandoned and the army scrambled back to Kut-al-Amara, reaching it on 3 December after a forced march of forty-four miles in thirty-six hours, made with little food or water and scarcely any sleep. When the Turks came up on 8 December, Townshend, instead of continuing his retreat, allowed himself to be invested. Neither Townshend nor Nixon was worried, for it was rashly believed that Townshend could easily be relieved before his supplies ran out.

This was not the first time Townshend had been besieged. In 1895, as a captain in the 2nd Central Indian Horse, he had found himself in command of a besieged garrison in a small fort in Chitral, in the extreme north-west corner of

India. He now telegraphed Nixon: "I mean to defend Kut as I did Chitral."

Townshend was a singular officer. He was restless and ambitious, a man without friends, a misfit who never developed an attachment for any regiment or corps in which he served. He preferred the company of actors and actresses to other soldiers and he married the daughter of a French count; he played the banjo and prided himself on his talents as an entertainer and raconteur. His successful defence of the mud fort in Chitral, where he was finally relieved by the heroic efforts of several thousand men, thrust him onto the world stage for a brief taste of fame as "the Hero of Chitral." This had been the high point in his life. Now he seemed almost eager for history to repeat itself and cast him once more in the role of the commander of a beleaguered garrison.

Shut up with him in Kut-al-Amara were approximately four battalions of regular British infantry, one battalion of Gurkhas, twelve battalions of Indian infantry (five of which were Punjabis and three Mahrattas), two squadrons of Indian cavalry and various supporting units, mostly British.

Kut, as it was usually called, was a filthy little Arab town built of mud bricks with a population of about six thousand. Located in a deep loop on the left bank of the Tigris, it was easily defended: the river protected it on three sides and the fourth side was easily entrenched. On 10, 11, and 12 December, Nur-ed-Din (or Nureddin), the Turkish field commander, launched repeated attacks with four divisions against the narrow end of the loop not protected by the river. Failing to break through, he settled down to a long siege, taking the precaution of blockading the river to prevent supplies being brought in by river steamer.

In the middle of December the war-weary Lahore and Meerut divisions (now prosaically named the 3rd and 7th divisions) began to disembark at the mouth of the Shatt-al-Arab. From France they had been carried to Egypt, where they were to be refitted and rested; instead, they were quickly shipped to Al Qurna, on the right bank of the lower Tigris about forty-five miles from Basra. They arrived in a helter-skelter fashion without their horses, wagons, artillery or ambulances, but Lieutenant-General Sir Fenton Aylmer, who took charge of them as they disembarked, wasted no time. As soon as all were ashore he pushed them up the Tigris to the relief of Kut and threw them at the Turk's advanced positions at Ali Gharbi. The Turks were driven back, but after a second defeat they took a firm stand at Umm al Hanna, only twenty miles from Kut, where they resisted so stoutly, inflicting such severe casualties, that Aylmer was forced to pause and await reinforcements. During this and all other attempts to relieve him, Townshend sat quietly at Kut, making no effort to create diversions or to assist those fighting their way towards him.

Another division, which had suffered 60 percent casualties at Gallipoli and was resting, refitting, and taking on recruits in Egypt, was ordered to Mesopotamia, but the Turks were steadily reinforcing their own lines and Aylmer decided that he could wait no longer. On the night of 7/8 March he launched his attack. After losing six thousand men, he fell back, beaten. He was immediately relieved of his command and was succeeded by Major-General Sir George Gorringe, who prudently decided to wait for the reinforcements before renewing the attempt.

Meanwhile, conditions inside besieged Kut were deteriorating. Even in the best of times Mesopotamia was a miserable place to soldier. A much quoted Arab proverb declared that Allah created a hell, added flies and called it Mesopotamia. Boxed up at Kut, Townshend's force was subjected to the bombs of German aircraft and a continuing artillery bombardment. The failure of Aylmer's second attempt to relieve Kut filled them with dismay.

Flooding made everyone miserable as the Tigris overflowed its banks into the defenders' trenches; horses sank to their withers and guns to their axles in mud; and hundreds of Turkish corpses were washed out of their shallow graves. When the weather turned cold, many men suffered from frostbite.

Townshend now put everyone on half-rations. One officers' mess tried mule tongue in aspic; another, on the birthday of one of its officers, rose to roasted starlings on toast.

In a near-incredible act of folly, enormous mounds of barley—hundreds of tons—had been stored in the open in a British-held village just across the river. It was remembered too late. Before anyone thought to collect and store it properly, it had been spoiled by rain. A search for hidden grain was ordered and although large stocks were discovered concealed in the walls of Arab houses, it was of little use, for by this time there was no fuel. All of the wood from Arab buildings had been torn out, every tree cut down and every root dug up for firewood. Not until someone discovered a large stock of fuel oil were cook fires again possible. Food cooked over the fires had an unpleasant taste, but sepoys could now bake their chapatties and all could have hot food.

In spite of the shelling, the miserable weather and the intense hunger, morale remained astonishingly high among both British and Indian troops. A gunner with half his face blown off by a Turkish shell mumbled before he died to the officer kneeling beside him: "Give 'em hell, sir."

Only Townshend seemed demoralized. He exasperated his superiors by his unending complaints. He was outraged when he learned that several major-generals junior to him had been promoted over his head, and when he learned that Gorringe on succeeding Aylmer was promoted to lieutenant-general, he wept on the shoulder of an astonished staff officer. It occurred to some of his staff that he might be unbalanced.

He confounded his would-be rescuers by six times changing his estimate of how long he could hold out. Although he made no effort to fight his own way out and failed to exert himself to create diversions or put pressure on the Turks when the relieving force attacked, he sneered at the failure of their valiant efforts. He twice suggested that he make his escape and leave his men to surrender. Three times he suggested that negotiations be opened with the Turks to exchange Kut and its weapons for the release of the garrison.

Rations were cut back again on 20 January 1916 and again on 7 March, when troops were reduced to ten ounces of barley flour and four ounces of parched grain per day. This was soon reduced once more. Finally the horses were killed and their meat was issued to the British troops—and offered to any Indian or Gurkha willing to eat it. Muslim and Hindu religious leaders telegraphed their sanctions in vain. Rather than eat it, one Sikh naik shot himself. In two battalions, the 103rd Indian Infantry and the 2/7th Gurkhas, its consumption was made compulsory. When at last starvation drove some five thousand Hindus to force it down, they were too weak to digest the unaccustomed food.

Scurvy, dysentery and beri-beri began to take their toll. Mercifully, spring flooding (caused by melting snows in the mountains of Asia Minor) brought forth grass and Indian soldiers crept out at night to reap those they knew to be edible. British soldiers tried to emulate them, but, not knowing one kind of grass from another, they usually ended up with a bitter-tasting, foul mess they euphemistically called "spinach."

A British airplane dropped vegetable seeds and a garden was eagerly planted in what had been the Arabs' communal latrine, but, successful as it was, it could not provide fresh food for thirteen thousand. The yield of vegetables was reserved for the sick and wounded. The bread ration was reduced to five ounces per day. Groundhogs were pronounced edible; all cats disappeared and only a few dogs whose masters were generals remained alive. Townshend's own dog, Spot, was spared. Airplanes dropped a little food, but not nearly enough, and often it fell into the Tigris or into the Turkish lines. When an officer died and his effects were auctioned, any food or cigarettes he had been saving brought unheard of prices.

No British or Gurkha troops deserted, but a number of Indians did—or tried to. Some were shot in the river when they attempted to swim across; others were caught, stood against a wall and shot. Arabs who left Kut were shot by the Turks, who wanted the villagers to stay and eat the meagre food supply.

Again and again Gorringe attacked, throwing his men against the Turkish lines in spite of heavy casualties. The 1st Black Watch had only 48 men left out of 842; the 6th Jats had only 50 out of 125; and the 1st Seaforth Highlanders 102 out of 962. By April 1916 they were still twelve miles from the beleaguered town.

On 27 April, after a siege of 147 days, the longest siege in British history, Kut capitulated. Prior to becoming invested Townshend had sustained about seven thousand casualties. While besieged he had lost an additional 1,608 dead and 1,836 wounded. In the attempts to relieve him, twenty-three thousand casualties were suffered.

Townshend tried to negotiate, offering the Turks first £1 million and then £2 million in gold plus all his guns if he and his force could go free, but the Turks would have none of it. They demanded unconditional surrender. Townshend wired his superior in Basra: "My duty seems clear, to go into captivity with my force, though I know the hot weather will kill me, for the continuous strain I have suffered since August till now is more than I can bear." The British set about destroying all their arms and equipment, keeping only one rifle per company as a defence against the Arabs in the town. Messages, records and code books were burned, the last scraps of food consumed.

Then the Turks marched in and took over. The surrender was the worst disaster to British arms since General Cornwallis's surrender of seven thousand men at Yorktown in the American Revolution (1781) and no worse would occur until the fall of Singapore to the Japanese in 1942. In all, Townshend surrendered 13,309 men, many of whom were in hospital.

Although the Turkish commander had assured Townshend that "your gallant troops will be our most sincere and precious guests," the Turks brought no food when they marched into Kut-al-Amara; instead, they stole clothing and anything else they could get from their prisoners. Food, the prisoners were told, would be given them at Shamran, nine miles upstream, a long march for starving men. Officers and a handful of other ranks were carried by steamer. The sick and wounded were left behind.

At Shamran the prisoners of war found black goatskin tents, enough for half their number, but no food, no latrines, no organization, and nothing but the filthy water of the Tigris to drink. Their guards were coarse, brutal troops from Kurdistan armed with rifles and whips. At dusk some camels arrived and Turkish hardtack was unloaded and thrown on the ground. The biscuits were hard and fibrous with straw and dirt, and they were flavoured, it was said, with camel sweat. Nevertheless, most of the men managed to choke them down. There was nothing else to eat.

By morning men had begun to clutch their stomachs and froth at the mouth. Some died. Enteritis, said the doctors, and told them to soak their hardtack and then bake it, not an easy thing to do when there was only a bit of camel thorn with which to make a fire. Officers fared better. They had been allowed to bring tents and clothing, and the Turks fed them. Townshend found himself especially well treated. His sword was returned to him and when he begged as a favour that his dog, Spot, be sent downstream to the British lines to be returned to England, the Turkish commander courteously complied.

Back in Kut, the sick and wounded watched helplessly as the Turks robbed them of whatever took their fancy and hanged in Turkish fashion—by letting the victim strangle—every Arab who had cooperated with their forces. The Turks arranged an exchange of 345 British and Indian sick and wounded for an equal number of healthy Turkish prisoners of war, but most of those in hospital were sent up river to Shamran. All, or nearly all, were soon dead.

At Shamran Townshend was detached from his troops and, together with his aide-de-camp, principal staff officers, an Indian servant, a Goanese cook and two British orderlies, was sent upstream on his way to Baghdad. As his steamer churned past the camp at Shamran, his men flocked to the river banks to cheer. He was quite touched. "I shall never forget that cheer," he wrote later. "Tears filled my eyes as I stood to attention at the salute. Never shall I have such a command again." Indeed, he never did.

Townshend ought to have petitioned for some of his officers to stay with his troops, but this did not occur to him. Perhaps the Turks would not have permitted it in any case, for officers were soon separated from their men and sent first to Baghdad and later into Turkey. They did not have an easy time, but compared to the suffering of their men their lot was luxurious. They were allowed to take with them an orderly or a servant each (colonels were allowed two), and eventually arrived at Kastamuni, a town on a tributary of the Kizil Irmak near the Black Sea, about one thousand seven hundred miles from Kut. They had money, were allowed to cash cheques and so were able to buy food and little luxuries. They were even able to send and receive mail.

Only the colonel of the Gurkhas refused to leave with the other officers and the Turks allowed him to stay. He and the other ranks—nearly three thousand British and six thousand Indian troops and followers—made a death march across more than a thousand miles of desert to Baghdad and then to Turkey.

At Shamran, before they set out, they were issued rations

for three days: nine biscuits, three ounces of jam and a handful of dates. On this almost unvarying ration they were to march at least eight miles a day in temperatures that exceeded 100° F. On the march they died by hundreds, by thousands, of thirst, starvation, brutality and diseases. No doctors accompanied them, only Indian apothecaries with what few medicines they could carry. Those who could sold bits of clothing and equipment for food. Their guards stole from them while they slept and many lost their boots in this way and were forced to march barefoot, driven on with whips and rifle butts. A sixteen-year-old British bugler was bastinadoed for rejecting a guard's sexual advances.

When the ragged columns of prisoners shuffled at last into Baghdad, the shocked American Consul shamed the Turks into putting five hundred of the worst cases into hospital. To others he gave what money he could.

The British other ranks appear to have been treated more harshly than the Indian and Gurkha troops and consequently fared worse. Of 2,592 captured at Kut, only 837 survived; of 10,486 Indians and Gurkha soldiers and followers, 7,423 survived, in some part because each class— Jat, Sikh, Mahratta—looked after its own.

At the end of a sixty-day march, the Kut prisoners were, without respite, put to work building a railway. With no increase in food rations or improvements in medical facilities, hundreds more died.

The Turks made serious efforts to suborn the Muslim troops. In the days preceding the *id al-fitr*—the feast of the breaking of the Ramadan fast, or Lesser Bairam, one of the two major festivals in Islam—Muslim VCOs were taken to Constantinople for a month where they were well treated and given a considerable amount of freedom, but put under heavy pressure to defect. Two Indian nationalists worked on them assiduously and a few VCOs did, in fact, yield, but Subedar-Major Khitab Gul of the 120th Rajputana Rifles managed to get to the American Consul in Constantinople and earnestly begged him to tell the British government of these attempts to suborn the Muslim officers.

On the day of the *id al-fitr* the VCOs who had refused to defect were presented to the Sultan, who in a speech instructed them that they were honour bound to fight against the Christian unbelievers, and then presented each of them with a sword of honour—or tried to. Subedar-Major Khitab Gul, standing on the right of the line, took the sword offered to him and threw it on the ground. Standing next to him was his friend, Subedar-Major Muhammad Hasan of the 104th Rifles, who did the same. Their action was followed by each of the others. Both Khitab Gul and Muhammad Hasan were given harsh prison sentences. When Khitab Gul was at last released, he attempted to escape, but failed.

The Turks had better luck with General Townshend, who was conducted in comfort—indeed, luxury—to Constantinople, where he was supplied with the best of food, presented with books, allowed to go sight-seeing and to bathe in the sea, which he found "delicious." He met Enver Pasha, then the Turkish Minister of War, who solicitously asked if he would like to have his wife and daughter join him. Yes, of course. He was ensconced in a comfortable villa by the sea on an island near Constantinople. When in October 1917 he learned that he had been knighted (KCB), he grumbled that he ought to have been raised to the peerage and he still burned at the injustice of not being promoted to lieutenant-general. Indifferent to the fate of his own men, he spent four months trying to get himself repatriated and finally succeeded, after promising to help the Turks negotiate the best possible peace terms. Snug at home, he was retired from the army and after the war he became a member of Parliament, but because of his fervid pro-Turkish sentiments, his efforts to act as a negotiator between Britain and Turkey were curtly rejected by his own government.

For the 837 British other ranks and the 7,423 sepoys and camp followers who were released at the end of the war there was no recognition other than copies of a holographed letter from King George V. It was a kindly letter, which he had written with his own hand, welcoming their release from "the miseries and hardships" they had endured. From General Townshend and the other generals there was not a word.

19

Amritsar

The initial response of Indians of all classes to the call of the King-Emperor and his sirkar for help in subduing Germans and Turks had been most gratifying. Not only had the princes made significant contributions of men and treasure, but other Indian leaders, even those who had been most critical of the British raj, had come forward to do their part. Notable were the efforts of Mohandas Gandhi, whose energies were directed towards recruiting. So successful was he that a grateful sirkar awarded him the prestigious Kaiser-i-Hind Medal, given to those who "performed important and useful service in the advancement of the public service in India." The Kaiser-i-Hind came in three classes: third class in bronze, second in silver and first class in gold. Gandhi was awarded the gold medal.*

Indians were not asked to "make the world safe for

---

* This was not the first time that Gandhi had been rewarded with a medal for his service to the Empire. Because the Anglo-Boer War in South Africa (1899–1902) was considered a "white man's war," Indians were not permitted to enlist in combatant arms, so Gandhi, then living in Durban, organized a corps of stretcher bearers, which did good work on Natal battlefields in the early days of the war. He was given a medal for this work.

democracy," as were the Americans, or to fight "for King and country," as were the British; instead, they were rallied to enlist "in defence of right and peace," which perhaps made as much sense as the other slogans. For whatever reasons, Indians flocked to sign up by the tens of thousands. Most by far were peasants and villagers. (Out of ten thousand university students, only seventy enlisted; the professional classes, too, stayed home.) By war's end, 1,096,013 had served in some capacity overseas and their usefulness did not end with the armistice of 11 November 1918.

Major wars always leave residues of violence. In 1918 the British and Indian armies found themselves fighting revolutionaries in Persia (Iran), where the Germans had been successful in stirring up unrest. In Shiraz the British colony had been expelled in 1915 and other Persian cities had seen outbreaks of anti-British violence. In 1916 the British organized the South Persia Rifles to replace an unruly Persian gendarmerie under Swedish officers, most of whose members had deserted or gone over to the rebels. The situation grew worse in 1917 when, because of the revolution in Russia, the Cossacks who had kept order in northern Persia were withdrawn. By 1918 the country was lapsing into anarchy. Even the South Persia Rifles proved unreliable; robbers roamed the roads and, except at the ports, life and property were almost everywhere unsafe. Added to the chaos and terror was the virulent influenza which began to creep over the world. In Shiraz alone, within a matter of weeks, ten thousand out of a population of fifty thousand died of the disease. In the spring of 1918 large Indian forces were sent to Persia "to restore order," and they remained for more than a year.

Among the units sent was the 120th Rajputana Rifles, which again included the gallant Subedar-Major Khitab Gul, who had thrown down the Sultan's proffered sword of honour. Now an honourary captain with the added title of Sardar Bahadur, he had been awarded the Indian Order of Merit, the Order of the British Empire and the French Croix de Guerre. It was said that the only rebuke he ever received was from his colonel for recklessly exposing himself under fire.

In December 1920 the Venizélist government in Greece fell and the unfriendly King Constantine re-ascended the throne. The Greeks then ceased to be allies and the Indian Army was used to fight the Kemalists in Asia Minor. In Iraq, too, there was much fighting as the dismembered Turkish Empire collapsed into ill-defined pieces and reckless men took advantage of the chaos and confusion.

In India itself there was no real revolution, but unrest in the Punjab might well have broken into open rebellion had it not been for the brutal actions of a British brigadier-general at Amritsar in April 1919, an action which provoked, in the words of the *Daily Telegraph,* "one of the greatest controversies that ever followed the action of a British officer."

Recruiting in the Punjab, the major source for men of the martial races, was aggressive during the war; too aggressive and verging on compulsion, according to some Indians, who accused the sirkar of using "press gang methods." In the event, the Punjab, containing only one sixteenth of India's population, contributed 400,000 men, a quarter of the army's recruits.

There were other causes for discontent: food shortages, soaring prices, severe income tax assessments and, among Muslims, anxiety over the fate of Turkey, with whose Sultan most Muslims felt a kinship. In Amritsar, holy city of the Sikhs, a hot, dusty, crowded city of about 160,000 people and a trade centre, merchants had difficulty obtaining or moving goods because the army had commandeered too many vehicles. As is ever the case at such times, ugly rumours floated through the bazaars. It was said that while the people of Amritsar were forced "to sleep with stones on their stomachs," grain was being exported to Britain. Many local officials believed that the Punjab was ripe for revolution.

Not only in the Punjab but throughout India there was

serious political discontent. The British had often promised, usually sincerely, that India would someday be self-
governing, but that day was never the present nor could it
be seen in the foreseeable future. On 17 August 1917, Edwin
Montagu, Secretary of State for India, announced that the
government would aim for "the increasing association of
Indians in every branch of administration and the gradual
development of self-governing institutions with a view to
the progressive realisation of responsible government in
India as an integral part of the Empire," but the government moved with glacial slowness in implementing this
policy. Many educated Indians who had looked forward
eagerly to such political reforms felt betrayed when they
were not immediately forthcoming. By failing to allow
intelligent, capable Indians to occupy more than a handful
of positions of responsibility in the government, by refusing them commissions as combatant officers, and by denying them the respect they deserved, the British alienated
those whom they ought to have cultivated. In fact, many
stringent war measures remained on the books, the most
hated being the so-called Rowlatt Act.

In 1918, just before war's end, Sir Sidney Rowlatt, a justice of the High Court, chaired a committee which designed
and recommended two bills to replace the Defence of India
Act, which, to prevent sabotage and subversion, had given
war powers to the government. Their purpose was to give
the sirkar broader powers to deal with anarchy and revolution. The acts would have allowed trials of political prisoners by judges without juries and would have given
provincial governments powers to gaol people without trial.
Mohammed Ali Jinnah, then a member of the Imperial
Legislative Council, wisely warned: "If these measures are
passed, you will create in this country from one end to the
other a discontent and agitation the like of which you have
never witnessed." Although one of the bills was dropped
and never enacted and the powers of the other were never
invoked, the very idea of the remaining act inflamed polit-

ical opinion. Violence erupted throughout the Punjab. The small European population, isolated and fearful, recalled again old stories of the horrors of the Mutiny.

It was the Rowlatt Act which brought Mohandas Gandhi, sniffing the political air, to front and centre on the national stage. He returned his medals to the government, persuaded the Congress Party* to protest the Act, and in April 1919 organized his first great *hartal*, the first active step in his satyagraha (passive resistance) movement. Although hartal is often translated as "strike" or "general strike," Gandhi originally had something a bit different in mind. He envisioned a hartal ("soul force") as a time when Indians would quietly close their shops, leave their factories, fields and schoolrooms, and stay at home to pray and fast. Let India stand still and be silent for a day, he said.

Perhaps this first time Gandhi really believed people would simply sit in their homes and meditate. They did not. Bloody riots broke out in Lahore, Kasur and elsewhere. European civilians were killed and two British officers were dragged from a train and beaten to death by a mob. In Lahore public buildings were burned to the ground and rioting raged for days, urged on by a local newspaper which trumpeted: "This is the command of Mahatma Gandhi." When the secretary of the Satyagraha Sabha, Gandhi's passive resistance organization, falsely reported that Gandhi had been arrested, rioting flared in Calcutta, Bombay, Ahmadabad and other cities. (In Ahmadabad, the centre of Gandhi's power in the Bombay area, 28 were killed and 123 seriously wounded.)

---

* The president of the Congress Party, the political vehicle which was to carry Gandhi to power, was at this time Annie Besant, née Wood (1847–1933), an eccentric Englishwoman who had organized the matchworkers' trade union in England and had founded the Central Hindu College at Benares. She became a devoted pupil of theosophist Madame Blavatsky (Elna Petrovna Blavatsky, née Helen Hahn, 1831–1891) and adopted a young Madrassi whom she claimed was the Messiah. She once described herself as "an Indian tom-tom waking all the sleepers so that they may work for their motherland."

In Amritsar, rumours flew: that Indian troops had mutinied, that the Lahore fort was taken, that the Lieutenant-
Governor had been killed. By 10 April, excited mobs roamed
the streets yelling for "white blood" and crying, "Murder
the Europeans!" and *"Gandhi ki jai!* (Long live Gandhi!)."
The Telegraph Exchange, a girl's school, a sub-post office,
and the Religious Book Society were destroyed. An attempt
was made to stop the Calcutta mail train. The town hall
was burned. Telegraph and electric wires were torn down.
The telegraph master, dragged from his bed and savagely
beaten, was rescued by a party of the 54th Sikhs led by a
jemadar.

A British sergeant, the electrician at the Military Power
Station, was waylaid and his skull beaten in. Two European railway workers were bludgeoned to death at the rail-
road yard and it was said of one that his body, when
recovered, "bore no resemblance to a human being." The
European manager of the National Bank, who had been a
popular man, having done much for the Indian community, was beaten to death, as was his assistant. Their bodies
were thrown upon a pile of office furniture, saturated with
kerosene, and set on fire. The manager of the Alliance Bank,
after firing his revolver into a threatening mob, was seized
before he could reload and was clubbed to death. His battered body, thrown from the veranda of his bank, was soaked
with kerosene and burned. The bank was razed. The manager of the Chartered Bank was rescued just in time by the
police.

A mob, voicing its intention to butcher the Deputy Commissioner, threatened to spill into the civil lines of the cantonment, but was driven back by the shots of a detachment
of sepoys under a resolute young lieutenant.

The Zenana Hospital was vandalized. Lieutenant-Colonel Henry Smith, a surgeon, was performing a cataract
operation when he heard the first shots. He dashed out of
the operating room and, when an attempt to telephone the
Deputy Commissioner proved futile, loaded an ambulance

with nurses and sped to the safety of nearby Fort Gobind Garh, whose original garrison of a company of the Somerset Light Infantry, a half-company of garrison artillery and forty men from the 12th Ammunition Column, had been reinforced only the day before by elements of the 54th Sikhs.

Miss Manuella ("Marcia") Sherwood, the superintendent and manager of the City Missions Schools, who had spent fifteen years working for the Church of England Zenana Missionary Society helping Indians in Amritsar, was caught by young thugs as she cycled down a lane where she was well known and thought she would be safe. Dragging her down, they beat her unmercifully with cudgels. Several times she managed to struggle to her feet, but each time she was seized by her hair and flung down to be beaten again. When she once succeeded in gaining her feet and ran to the open door of a nearby house, the door was slammed in her face. Not until she fell unconscious and appeared to be dead did her assailants, shouting "Victory to Gandhi!", run off.

When they had vanished, a Hindu shopkeeper ventured out and carried her into his house and with home remedies did what he could to ease her pain. Before she could be moved to safety, word of her escape reached her assailants and they returned to finish their grisly work. They were turned away by a doughty old Indian woman who swore that Miss Sherwood was not there. That night, concealed in a cart, she was smuggled to her home, where a European doctor treated her and then moved her to the safety of Fort Gobind Garh.

A number of bungalows and buildings had been designated as collecting points for European women and children in case of trouble and now they came tumbling into them, sometimes with nothing more than the clothes they wore. As quickly as possible all were transferred to the small fort, which had been built by Rajah Ranjit Singh a hundred years earlier to house his treasure. It was filthy and too small for the one hundred thirty women and children who now crowded inside its walls, and, with no sanitary facilities, it soon became filthier. In the stifling weather the stench was overpowering.

Although some of the police behaved creditably, many went into hiding. While Amritsar burned, the two Indian officials most responsible for public order locked horns, the Muslim City Inspector refusing to take orders from the Hindu Deputy Superintendent.

On the morning of 10 April unexpected reinforcements appeared when a train bearing Captain G. P. Crampton and Second Lieutenant Frank McCallum, on their way from Dehra Dun to Peshawar with a detachment of about one hundred men from the 1/9th Gurkha Rifles, pulled into the station. The men were unarmed except for their kukris (the traditional Nepalese knife), but fifty were at once issued rifles from the fort. About 10:30 p.m. that same day a detachment of 125 men from the 2/6th Royal Sussex Regiment and 175 men from the 1/124th Baluchis came up from Lahore, thirty-two miles away. By this time it was generally agreed that the city was out of control. It was time for the army to restore order.

Throughout its history the British Army, at home and abroad, had frequently been called upon to aid the civil powers when the police could no longer cope. Chartists, Irishmen and American colonists all faced British regulars. In India such use of troops was frequent as various Indian communities clashed and force was required to separate them. It was not, however, a congenial occupation. As Lieutenant-General Sir Havelock Hudson, Adjutant-General of the Indian Army, said: "No more distasteful or responsible duty falls to the lot of the soldier than that which he is sometimes required to discharge in aid of the civil power. If his measures are too mild he fails in his duty. If they are deemed to be excessive he is liable to be attacked as a cold-blooded murderer." Unlike most police, who were armed only with lathis, troops carried deadly weapons to be used at the discretion of the officer in charge, who was the sole judge of what constituted the minimum force necessary to control the situation. However, words such as "minimum force" were difficult to define in the presence of an excited mob. Even when properly handled, mob control was a delicate weighing of values. And not every mob was properly handled.

Normally a magistrate, representing the district authority, had the right to call upon the army at his discretion, and he accompanied a military column sent to a riot area. His function was to call upon the mobs to disperse, and to warn them that if they did not do so the troops behind him would be used. Once he turned control over to the officer in charge, his authority ended; he could neither order troops to fire nor control the firing.

On the evening of 10 April, while Amritsar's European refugees were fleeing to the old fort and the fires of burning buildings lit the sky, the man whose name would ever be associated with Amritsar was quietly dining in Jullundur, only fifty miles south-east as the crow flies but a three-hour ride by automobile. Brigadier-General Reginald Edward Harry ("Rex") Dyer and his wife were giving a dinner at Flagstaff House. Earlier, at six o'clock that evening, Dyer had received a message from Lahore describing the situation in Amritsar and directing him to send troops there as quickly as possible. Not many troops were readily available, but he had ordered Major Frank Scamander Clarke, DSO, to proceed to Amritsar with 100 men of the 25th London Regiment, 230 sepoys, and a surgeon with staff. Shortly after nine o'clock that evening Clarke and his troops were on their way by train.

To his dinner guests Dyer gave no hint that he was in any way disturbed, although his aides kept him informed as news came in by telegraph and through the reports of refugees. Not until two o'clock the next afternoon was he ordered to take personal charge at Amritsar, and then he seemed in no hurry, perhaps because he wished to avoid travelling during the heat of what was the Punjab's hottest hot weather season within living memory. In any case, it was six o'clock before he left by car with Captain Frederic Cecil Currer ("Tommy") Briggs, his brigade major, and Captain John Southey, Royal Army Medical Corps.

Dyer, fifty-five years old, had been born in India, the sixth child and youngest son in a prosperous family. At age eleven he had been sent to school in Ireland and from there had gone on to Sandhurst, passing out in July 1884. He was soon sent to fight in Burma and subsequently took part in several campaigns on the North-West Frontier, including the relief expedition to rescue Captain (later Major-General) Charles Townshend and his men besieged at Chitral. He spoke Hindustani and Urdu fluently and he had studied Persian and Pushtu as well.

His father was a successful brewer in India and his mother was a formidably respectable British matron remembered for declaring, when her husband once admitted to having lit his cigarette from the cheroot of a Burmese girl, "That sort of looseness is what has peopled Simla with thirty thousand Eurasians." When, over the objections of his parents, Dyer married the perfectly respectable but fortuneless daughter of an Indian Army colonel, he was cut off with 100 rupees.

Although physically strong, he had recently been suffering from arteriosclerosis and was often in pain, which did not improve his quick, hot temper. Nevertheless, he had had some success recently in delicately handling local disorders. In the summer of 1918, when there had been friction between the sepoys and civilians at Jullundur, he was credited with restoring good relations. A few months later, when Muslim sepoys of two police battalions attacked Sikh police, he had again brought order without resorting to force.

When Dyer and his party arrived in Amritsar about nine o'clock that evening, they at once met with the superintendent of police and with Sir Miles Irving, Deputy Commissioner of Amritsar. Dyer was thoroughly briefed and given a description of the attack upon Miss Sherwood. Irving, who had served eighteen years in the Punjab but was new to his job in Amritsar, considered the mobs impenitently hostile and he was eager to turn over responsibility to Dyer. The meeting ended about midnight when Irving drew up a document to be passed out to leading citizens for distribution throughout the city:

> The troops have orders to restore order and to use all force necessary. No gatherings of persons or processions of any sort will be allowed. All gatherings will be fired on. Any persons leaving the city in groups of more than four will be fired on. Respectable persons should keep indoors.

As soon as the city was turned over to him, Dyer led a small force to the Kotwali (city police station). There he found the City Inspector, who had maintained a low profile during the violence but was eager and able to produce a list of about a dozen ringleaders, whom Dyer ordered to be found and imprisoned. From the Kotwali he went to the railway station, where he had made his headquarters, and spent the night.

At his disposal Dyer had 475 British and 710 Indian and Gurkha officers and other ranks, several machine guns and two armoured cars. At dawn he moved his headquarters to the Ram Bagh, a large garden near the civil lines which offered shade trees, fresh water and space for tents.

Meanwhile telegraph wires had been buzzing and the commissioner for the Lahore District had reported the situation to Sir Michael O'Dwyer, Lieutenant-Governor of the Punjab, who in turn had reported to the Viceroy. From Simla the word came down that if troops were used and they were forced to open fire, "they should make an example." When this message was passed to Dyer, he carefully entered it in his diary.

On Sunday morning, 13 April, church parade was held as usual for the British troops. Knowing that the soldiers were exercised over the outrages that had taken place, particularly the assault upon Miss Sherwood, Dyer warned his men that they must keep calm and not seek personal reprisals against Indians.

At 10:30 a.m., following church parade, Dyer led 125 British and 310 Indian troops in a march through the city. He had written a new proclamation declaring that no one could leave the city without a pass, that residents could not leave their houses after 8:00 p.m., and that any group of four or more men would be considered an unlawful assembly. His parade stopped at nineteen different points in the city where the proclamation was read aloud in Urdu and Punjabi. Those who gathered to hear were mostly young men who greeted it with jeers and spat to show their contempt. Some drummed on kerosene tins and shouted defiant slogans: "The British raj is dead!" and "Let them fire on us!"

Shortly after noon the column marched back to the Ram Bagh. The heat was intense and everyone's nerves were on edge. Curiously, the proclamation had not been read at the Golden Temple of the Sikhs or at the Jallianwala Bagh, where the crowds would have been large and the greatest number of people would have heard it. Even so, there must have been few who did not learn of its contents.

Now that the army seemed to have the upper hand, a general feeling spread among the Europeans that strong reprisals should be undertaken. Lieutenant-Colonel Henry Smith, the surgeon who had rescued the nurses from the hospital, suggested that the mobs be bombed by aircraft.

While Dyer was organizing his forces and making his plans, twenty-three-year-old Hans Raj, son of a bazaar prostitute, was busy as well. Hans Raj was clever and he had acquired sufficient education to qualify for a respectable job, but he had twice been fired for theft. He had taken up politics and was now feverishly circulating an announcement that a mass meeting was to be held at the Jallianwala Bagh where letters would be read from two popular Indian leaders, a Muslim barrister and a Hindu assistant surgeon, both of whom Irving had unwisely arrested and sent out of the city. A competent organizer, Hans Raj arranged for a speakers' platform to be erected, for sweepers to clean the area, and for bhistis to move through the crowd offering water.

The word *bagh* means "garden," but the Jallianwala Bagh, like most such baghs in India, was a garden in name only. It was simply a bare plot of uneven ground 200 yards long hemmed in by houses and walls. It held a well, a tall peepul tree, a few smaller trees, and the ruins of a shrine.

When the meeting opened that afternoon, the crowd at Jallianwala Bagh was estimated at between five and fifty thousand, the lower figure being the more probable. Not all were there for the political speeches. The city was full of visitors: some had come to Amritsar to celebrate Baisakhi, the Hindu New Year, and some to attend an annual horse and cattle fair. Many of these were accustomed to making their way to the Jallianwala Bagh to meet friends or to roll up in blankets and sleep on the ground. As the speeches began, there was some obvious nervousness among the seated crowd. When a small airplane flew overhead, a few panicked and fled.

Dyer was at his headquarters at the Ram Bagh when, about four o'clock, he was told of the meeting. An hour earlier O'Dwyer, proclaiming the districts of Lahore and Amritsar to be in open rebellion, had declared martial law, a legal nicety of which Dyer was then ignorant but which was later considered to be of some importance. Assuming that the assembly at the Jallianwala Bagh was a deliberate provocation, Dyer set forth to teach the agitators a lesson. He took with him twenty-five Sikhs and sixty-five Gurkhas; only twenty-five of the latter were armed with rifles, the rest carried their kukris. He himself rode in a car with Captain Briggs and Sergeant William Anderson of the 1/25th London Regiment, followed by a car filled with police and by the two armoured cars.

Just before sunset Dyer and his men arrived at the main entrance to the Jallianwala Bagh, a long passage, so nar-

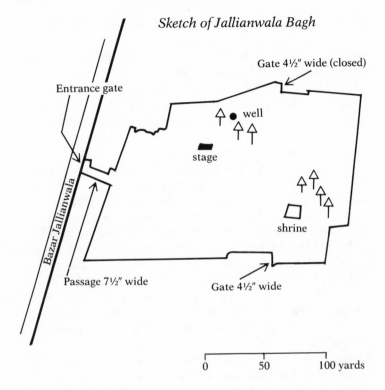

Sketch of Jallianwala Bagh

row that the armoured cars had to be left in the street with the police. In the street Dyer arranged his striking force: the Sikhs first, then the twenty-five Gurkhas armed with rifles, followed by the forty armed with kukris. He positioned himself in the rear with Anderson and Briggs. So formed they set off down the passage at the double.

At the sound of their pounding boots some of the crowd leapt to their feet and there were shouts: "They have come! They have come!" Hans Raj leapt forward, calling on them to sit down. "The sirkar will never fire on us," he cried.

But as Dyer's Gurkhas and Sikhs swung into the bagh, they immediately look up firing positions. Without calling on the crowd to disperse and without waiting to see if it was hostile, Dyer gave the order to fire.

"They are only blanks!" shouted Hans Raj just before he bolted.

There was now utter chaos. People tried to flee but could find no escape. The two narrow gates in the far walls were soon clogged by men struggling to force their way through and the firing soldiers barred the main egress. In a panic, men tried scaling the walls, tried sheltering behind trees, behind the ruined shrine. Only a few of the crowd were wise enough to lie down, although a couple of pensioned VCOs yelled for everyone to do so. No one tried to rush the soldiers and no one fired on them. The soldiers fired at will. When their magazines were emptied, they refilled them. Dyer, looking on, made no attempt to control the firing other than to direct it to points where the crowd was thickest. The firing lasted ten minutes, according to Dyer's estimate. Understandably, it seemed longer to those being shot at. It was long enough for Dyer to have, in his own words, "administered a lesson which would be felt through India." In all, 1,650 rounds of .303 Mark VI ammunition were fired. It was a massacre.

In his official report Dyer gave a curt explanation of his reason for opening fire without first giving warning: "On entering [the bagh] I saw a dense crowd, estimated at about 5,000; a man was on a raised platform addressing the audience and making gesticulations with his hands. I realized that my force was small and to hesitate might induce attack. I immediately opened fire and dispersed the mob." Later, he amplified this statement:

> I was faced with a dense mass of men evidently holding a seditious meeting. . . . The crowd appeared to be a mixed one, consisting of city people and outsiders. I did not see a single woman or child in the assembly. . . . There was no reason to further parley with the mob; evidently they were there to defy the arm of the law. The responsibility was very great. If I fired I must fire with good effect, a small amount of firing would be a crim-

inal act of folly. I had the choice of carrying out a very distasteful and horrible duty or of neglecting to do my duty, of
suppressing disorder or of becoming responsible for all future
bloodshed. . . . My duty and my military instincts told me to
fire. My conscience was also clear on that point.

Although there have been numerous accounts of the
casualties, the fact is that no one really knows the exact
number of dead and wounded. The figure of two thousand
killed is used by many Indian chroniclers, but this is
obviously absurd. The figure is probably closer to Dyer's
own estimate of "between 200 and 300" killed—a number
quite horrifying enough.

Several small boys were among the dead, and, it has been
said, one seven-week-old infant. Perhaps close to a thousand were wounded. Dyer made no attempt to collect the
dead or to succour the wounded, among whom was an
orphan boy, Udham Singh, shot in the arm, who grew up
to be the Ghadrite revolutionary who, in London in 1940,
murdered seventy-six-year-old Sir Michael O'Dwyer by
shooting him in the back.*

Leaving the ground littered with the silent dead and the
screaming and moaning wounded, Dyer marched his men
back to the Ram Bagh and filed his report. Michael O'Dwyer
responded with a personal message: "Your action correct
and Lieutenant-Governor approves." It did not occur to Dyer
that anyone would seriously question his move.

A great quiet fell over Amritsar in the days following.

---

* Udham Singh was tried, convicted, and then hanged at Pentonville
Prison. In India he is now much revered as a national hero. Thirty-four
years after his execution, his body was returned to India at the request
of the Indian government. On its arrival at Delhi the casket was draped
with the national flag and Prime Minister Indira Gandhi paid him
homage; his remains were taken on a tour of the country, there was a
memorial service for him at the Jallianwala Bagh and he was proclaimed a martyr. (For a fuller description of Udham Singh's life and
the honours accorded him after his death, see Alfred Draper's excellent
account in *The Amritsar Massacre*.)

Shops closed and business came to a halt. Dyer summoned the leading businessmen and harangued them in Urdu:

> You people know that I am a soldier. . . . For me, the battlefield of France or Amritsar is the same. . . . I have served in the army for thirty years. I understand the Indian sepoy and the Sikh people very well. You will have to observe peace or the shops will be opened by force and by rifles. You must inform me of the badmashes [bad characters]. I will shoot them. Obey my orders and open your shops or speak up if you want war.

All shops were soon reopened.

From the Europeans in Amritsar Dyer encountered nothing but praise. If anything, they felt that he had not done enough to compensate for the outrages they had suffered. Perhaps he paid too much attention to these voices, or perhaps the absolute power given him by martial law went to his head. For whatever reason, he lost whatever good sense he possessed.

In a series of orders designed to humiliate the innocent and the guilty alike, he decreed that Indians were to make salaam to any European they met; anyone who failed to do so was to be arrested, strung up on a tiktiki, a whipping triangle, and flogged. All bicycles belonging to Indians were confiscated. All tongas, tumtums, bail-gharris (ox carts) and other vehicles were ordered to be brought each morning to a designated place from whence they were detailed for various public duties. As it was the educated Indians, particularly lawyers such as Gandhi, Nehru and Jinnah, who were blamed as the troublemakers, Dyer drafted the ninety-three lawyers in the city to work as coolies and compelled them to watch the public floggings.

The police were given carte blanche and they used their authority to threaten, intimidate and torture. Major Sewallis Robert Shirley, the provost-marshal, later tried to justify their brutality: "The reluctance of the people of Amritsar

City to give evidence which would lead to the arrest and punishment of conspirators and rioters was very noticeable indeed, and if doubtful methods were used by the police, the inhabitants of Amritsar themselves are more to blame than anyone else."

On 19 April, Dyer paid a visit to Miss Sherwood, still swathed in bandages and in great pain. It was not yet certain that she would live. The sight of her suffering so inflamed him that he immediately issued his most reprehensible order.

Miss Sherwood had been attacked in a narrow, 156-foot-long lane known as Kucha Tawarian. Dyer posted pickets at each end of this lane and every Indian who used it was forced to crawl its length on hands and knees. Any who refused was instantly strung up on the tiktiki erected in the middle of the lane. Six courageous or foolish persons were whipped here. Never clean, the lane became filthy indeed as those who lived in its bordering houses threw their refuse into it, as was the custom, although sweepers refused to enter it. Water carriers no longer made their rounds and Indian doctors refused to attend patients living there. The infamous "Crawling Order" remained in effect until 24 April.

When six young men were arrested and charged with assaulting Miss Sherwood, Dyer did not bother with a trial. Acting as judge and jury, he ordered them to the tiktiki for thirty strokes each. In all, thirty-eight people were flogged in Amritsar. Similar punishment was dispensed in a summary fashion throughout the Punjab. At Gujranwala twenty-four were flogged, at Chuharkam forty, at Lahore eighty, and at Kasur eighty-five, including an entire wedding party which had broken the curfew. In Lahore it was said that British women urged the floggers to greater efforts.

At Lahore, where the railway station, the treasury, and other public buildings were attacked and two British officers killed, 1,500 British troops moved in and a martial law commission distributed justice with a heavy hand: 108 men were sentenced to death, 264 to transportation for life, and hundreds of others were given long prison sentences. Among those convicted was a man reputed to be one hundred fifteen years old and an eleven-year-old boy. News of the Amritsar massacre spread rapidly in ever-widening circles and Indians of all classes absorbed the sobering message: brutal as the British had been, Dyer had shown that they could be worse.

It is repugnant to civilized people to recognize that police brutality and crude punishments can be effective in restoring tranquillity to a restless population, but terror is often effective, it can at times overawe all dissent. So it was in the smouldering Punjab in 1919. Dyer's brutal massacre did exactly what he intended it should do. He had gone to the Jallianwala Bagh, as he later admitted, "to create a sufficient moral effect from a military point of view throughout the Punjab."

After 16 April not a shot needed to be fired in the Punjab. Throughout the province opposition was cowed and protest muted. Sir Michael O'Dwyer, who had believed the Punjab on the brink of open rebellion, told Lord Chelmsford, the Viceroy, that "the Amritsar business cleared the air, and if there was to be a holocaust anywhere, and one regrets there should be, it was best at Amritsar." Later he told a Disorder Inquiry Committee: "Speaking with perhaps a more intimate knowledge of the situation than anyone else, I have no hesitation in saying that General Dyer's action that day was the decisive factor in crushing the rebellion, the seriousness of which is only now being realized."

Lord Chelmsford reported the matter to Edwin Montagu, Secretary of State for India, and while conceding that Dyer's methods "have been most efficacious," he admitted that he had a twinge of conscience about it. Montagu had somewhat more than a twinge and wrote back to Chelmsford: "I feel very uncomfortable. I wish that you had not left so much to O'Dwyer. I wish O'Dwyer had not left so much to the military."

In any event, as Chelmsford said, the European community in India was "to a man a staunch admirer of O'Dwyer and the stern methods adopted in the Punjab." Indeed, in the officers' messes and in the English clubs of India, Dyer was hailed as the "saviour of the Punjab." Even many Indians welcomed the return of calmer days. Dyer was fêted by the Sikh priests of Amritsar and proclaimed an honorary Sikh.

Only when news of the massacre spread to the rest of the world were non-Indian voices raised in shock and outrage. The farther from the Punjab, the greater was the volume of disapproval. In the United States, Dyer, the British raj and British policies were universally condemned. In London, the affair was debated in the House of Commons, where Winston Churchill thundered: "This is an episode which appears to me to be without precedent or parallel in the modern history of the British Empire. . . . It is an extraordinary event, a monstrous event, an event which stands in singular and sinister isolation."

And in the House of Lords, Satyendra Prasanno Sinha, recently raised to the peerage as Baron Sinha of Raipur, reported that Dyer had shot down unarmed people who were merely "listening to a lecture." Finally a government committee was appointed, chaired by Lord Hunter, to investigate and report on the Amritsar affair. Lord Hunter, a Liberal lawyer and politician, a former Solicitor General for Scotland in the Asquith administration and afterwards a Senator in the College of Justice in Edinburgh, was a man unknown to India and unfamiliar with Indian affairs.

In India, Indian politicians and Indian newspapers were in full cry for Dyer's blood. The editor of the Bombay *Express* wrote: "The Jallianwala Bagh battue is an achievement which has created for Dyer a special niche in the gallery of frightfulness . . . it will go down in history as an indelible blot on British rule in India." Sir Rabindranath Tagore, the Indian novelist, poet and dramatist who had been awarded the Nobel Prize for literature in 1913, attempted to give up his knighthood in protest.

It was during this period that Jawaharlal Nehru, sitting quietly in a railway carriage, listened to Englishmen discussing with relish the details of the massacre. "This will teach the bloody browns a lesson," one exulted. Nehru ever after attributed to that moment the birth of his determination to throw himself behind Gandhi and the Congress Party. Within a year he was serving his first gaol term, establishing the bona fide required of every Indian nationalist.

Meanwhile, trouble was brewing in Afghanistan. During the Great War, Amir Habībollāh Khān had kept the country neutral in spite of the efforts of Turkish and German agents and the urgings of many of his own people, who argued that this was the time to attack while the British were preoccupied in Europe and elsewhere. On 20 February 1919, Habībollāh was murdered in his bed by his third son, Amānollāh Khān, who seized power, and—encouraged by the spirit of rebellion which then seemed to pervade the Punjab and by the paucity of British troops in India—sought to strengthen his precarious perch on the Afghan gadi by seeking to regain the North-West Frontier Province lost in 1820 to the Sikhs. On 3 May 1919 the Third Afghan War began when Afghan troops crossed the border at the west end of the Khyber Pass and occupied a village located at the source of water for Landi Kotal, then garrisoned by only two companies of Indian infantry.

The invasion was to have been timed with an emeute in Peshawar, but Sir George Roos-Keppel, serving his last days as Chief Commissioner of the North-West Frontier Province, acted with commendable speed. The 2nd Somerset Light Infantry was dispatched to the Khyber while troops and police sealed off the native quarter of Peshawar. The local ringleaders, the chief of whom was the Peshawar postmaster, were winkled out, and by dawn the next day Peshawar was secure.

More troops were rushed to the Khyber; three RAF airplanes (BE-2C's) made a spectacular bombing attack upon a gathering of hostile tribesmen on the Afghan side of the border; and two days later British and Gurkha troops drove the Afghans from their positions and the RAF harried their retreat.

The Afghans had also planned to attack at Quetta and in the Kurram Valley, but the British commander at Quetta made a pre-emptive strike across the border, captured the main Afghan fort and quickly stabilized his area. To the surprise and dismay of the British, the Wana Militia in South Waziristan and the Khyber Rifles were disaffected and there were mutinies and desertions, so these renowned Frontier Scouts were disbanded. In the Kurram Valley the invasion was successful and the Afghans besieged Thal, an important fort and communications centre on a plateau 100 feet above the Kurram River at the south end of the valley. If Thal fell, so would the important frontier city of Kohat, exposing the open plains of India to the invaders. Brigadier-General Dyer was dispatched with a brigade of two thousand men to effect its relief.

Dyer's brigade was a mixed lot, mostly Dogras, Punjabis and Gurkhas, and most were young, partially trained soldiers who had enlisted for the Great War. His only British battalion was the 1/25th London Regiment, a disgruntled territorial unit eager to go home now that the war had ended and unhappy that their demobilization was now delayed by the Afghans. Nevertheless, Dyer, although tired and ill, pumped new life into his brigade and under a blistering sun, with forced marches on little food and water, he pushed his men forward to rescue Thal and send the Afghans flying homeward. Dyer's superb handling of his guns and men was praised by General Sir Charles C. Monro, the Commander-in-Chief, India, for he had certainly saved Thal and possibly the Frontier. On 3 June the Afghans signed an armistice.

The war was a small one, many felt, only because Dyer

and O'Dwyer had managed to calm the Punjab before the Afghans attacked. Battle casualties amounted to only 236 British and Indian killed and 615 wounded, but cholera killed another 566.

In mid-October 1919, the Hunter Committee arrived in Delhi to investigate the Amritsar affair. Dyer testified on 19 November and was congratulated on his testimony by Sir Edward MacLagan, who had replaced O'Dwyer as Lieutenant-Governor of the Punjab. Nevertheless the committee, after twenty-six sessions over a six-week period, produced a majority report that condemned Dyer for firing without warning and for continuing to fire until most of his ammunition was expended.

Dyer appears not to have been overly concerned by the findings of the committee. Having gained well-earned laurels in the Afghan War, he was now in line for a major-general's post and he expected the promotion. When he was ordered to report to General Monro in Delhi, he pleaded illness; he was suffering from the effects of jaundice and from "gout in the head." In spite of his illness he was told to comply, but he had no suspicion that his career was about to founder.

His fellow officers had supported him and he had received the approval of his immediate superiors for his actions at Amritsar, so he was astonished when he met with General Sir Havelock Hudson, the Adjutant-General, the man who recently had publicly defended his actions, but who now bluntly told him that the Commander-in-Chief agreed with the verdict of the Hunter Committee and that he was therefore relieved of his command. He was then ushered in to see General Monro. It was a short interview. The man who had so recently praised him for the relief of Thal now confirmed that the government had no further use for his services. There was nothing for him to do but to pack his bags and return to the England he had left as a young man.

It was some solace to find at the Jullundur station, where

he was to board the train for Bombay, a crowd of Indian noncommissioned officers and VCOs assembled to bid him farewell. And at Bombay, a large crowd of Europeans came to cheer him as he boarded ship.

Back in England voices were raised in protest against Dyer's treatment and he found that he had many defenders. In July 1920 the House of Lords voted 129 to 86 in support of the statement that the House "deplores the conduct of the case of General Dyer as unjust to that officer, and as establishing a precedent dangerous to the preservation of order in the face of rebellion," an opinion which led Gandhi to declare that "cooperation in any form with the satanic British government is sinful."

On 8 July 1920 the *Morning Post* launched a drive to raise money for "The Man Who Saved India." Although the Government of India prohibited contributions from officers and officials, many contributed anyway and the money poured in. The Duke of Westminister gave £100; Gladstone gave 10 guineas; Kipling gave £10. In all, the fund raised £26,317 4s 10p, then a prodigious sum, and Dyer thus became a relatively rich man. Seven years later, as he lay dying of arteriosclerosis, he confided to his daughter-in-law: "So many people who knew the conditions in Amritsar say I did right . . . but so many others say I did wrong. I only want to die and know from my Maker whether I did right or wrong."

World War I was a watershed in the history of the raj. The socio-economic machinery of the Victorian and Edwardian era fell into obsolescence and political ferment grew. New Indian leaders, increasingly critical of British policies, clamoured for recognition and strove to instill a national consensus into the unhomogeneous Indian masses. In less than thirty years they succeeded, thanks in part, certainly, to Dyer. Nothing so exacerbated the raw emotions and racial intolerance of Briton and Indian as the Amritsar Massacre and its aftermath. Nothing could have more sharply exposed British apprehensions left over from the Mutiny of more than sixty years earlier, and nothing could have demonstrated more clearly to the Indian educated classes that no matter how much Western culture they absorbed, the British would never accept them as equals.

Most of the Western world has forgotten Amritsar, but Indians have not, and the Jallianwala Bagh is today a national shrine to the bitterness engendered there.

20

Indianization

I n 1858 Queen Victoria had proclaimed that "no native of India by reason of religion, place of birth, descent, colour, or any of them, would be disabled from holding any office or employment." It was a much lauded statement, but for more than half a century the Indian Army chose to ignore it, for almost the entire officer corps firmly believed that Indians could not effectively command other Indians in war. An Indian newspaper (*Friend of India*, 13 August 1876) pointed out the absurdity of this prejudice: "If that fine soldier, the Emperor Babur, were alive, we should make him a subadur in an infantry regiment, and put over him a public school boy."

In an attempt to overcome the acute shortage of British officers for the Indian Army during World War I, temporary officers were created at speed, often with the briefest of training. Predictably, regular officers were quick to note their professional and social shortcomings. Captain G. F. Paterson, a regular with the 34th Pioneers in the Sinai in 1918, wrote his wife that "there are some extraordinary things in the way of Officers in this camp, a lot of them going to the Indian Army Reserve; no wonder the Natives think they are fit to have commissions when they see some of the specimens sent to be officers over them."

In the middle of the war, to encourage recruiting among the martial races, Viceroy's Commissioned Officers (VCOs) were made eligible to receive the King's Commission, but this was never a practical matter; VCOs were too uneducated and too old to serve as subalterns. Of greater significance was the decision taken in 1917 and announced the following year that ten places would be reserved each year at Sandhurst for suitable Indians who, upon graduation, would receive the King's Commission. Those selected were to be "representatives of families of fighting classes which have rendered valuable services to the State during the war."

In addition to the Sandhurst appointments, a handful of King's commissions were given to selected noncommissioned officers, among whom was Iskander Mirza, who rose to the rank of colonel during the time of the raj and later (post-1947) major-general and soon after became President of Pakistan. Another handful was given to graduates of the Cadet College, Indore, and among these was K. M. Cariappa, who became the first Indian graduate of the Staff College, Quetta; the first Indian to command a battalion and an infantry brigade; and finally, the first Indian Commander-in-Chief of the Indian Army, by then (post-1947) the army of the new republic of India.

Overall, however, the scheme to send young Indians to Sandhurst was not a success and may actually have set back the cause of Indianization, for they were not properly selected. Perhaps it was impossible to do so, for Sandhurst was geared to educate products of the British public schools and it was nearly impossible for any young man who had not attended such a school to be a success there. Exposure to the normal lot of a cadet was a severe shock to most of the young Indians, who without exception came from wealthy families and had from their cradles lived in a degree of ease and luxury seldom attained in Britain. At Sandhurst they encountered staff sergeants who shouted at them; they were required to perform menial and distasteful tasks such as the daily cleaning of their leather accoutrements; and they were expected to submit to punishments they regarded as humiliating for minor offences. It is hardly surprising that many turned sullen and resentful.

Of the first twenty-five cadets, only ten were graduated and managed to succeed in the army. Ten failed their examinations, two resigned, two died, and one was deprived of his commission. Of the first eighty-five places filled by Indians between 1918 and 1926, almost all were the sons of Indian princes, nobles, wealthy landowners or planters. Of these, twenty-five, or 30 percent, failed, while only 3 percent of British young men did not make the grade.

Those few fortunate enough to be graduated were then, as were their British classmates who opted for the Indian Army, sent for a year to a British battalion or regiment stationed in India, during which time they commanded British troops. There appears to have been no objection to this on the part of the troops or from the British officers with whom they served. By this time, of course, they were completely anglicized and had absorbed British upper-middle-class manners and social and professional attitudes.

Like their British colleagues, the new Indian officers holding the King's Commission (KCOs) were more interested in sports and games than in politics, and, in general, they modelled themselves upon their colleagues and superiors. A few conformed only because they had to in order to survive, but certainly most, coming from aristocratic or landed families with conservative attitudes, conformed because they wished to. Even so, they encountered discrimination. Although they received equal pay, their allowances were not the same as those of their fellow officers. Among other allowances the British officer received extra pay for serving far from home, compensation, the authorities reasoned, the Indian officer was not entitled to receive. But the necessary expenses of an officer were the same, regardless of one's distance from home, and the British paid in bitterness for such cheese-paring.

Quite often the expenses of a young Indian officer exceeded those of his messmates, for while most British officers did not marry until they became field officers, many Indians married early in their careers, and thus had family bills as well as mess bills to pay. Some, too, had borrowed heavily to pay for their military educations. It became increasingly difficult for an Indian officer, unless he came from a wealthy family, to keep the servants, polo ponies and other luxuries expected in the regiments.

Indian officers frequently suffered socially. They overheard, and at times were meant to overhear, racial slurs. Their wives, not always sufficiently anglicized, some still in purdah, sometimes presented social problems, and the wives of British officers were not always understanding or helpful. The greatest barriers to social intercourse were the clubs which the British had established in India, as they had throughout the Empire. Indeed, it has been said that the debate over Indian membership in British clubs "almost split the Empire." A few commanding officers forbade their officers to join local clubs which banned Indian officers. During World War II the general commanding the Madras District refused to allow any European officers in his district to become members of the Madras Club. Some clubs, trying to compromise, exacerbated the problem and increased the humiliation by allowing Indians in the saloon bar and the billiard room, but not in the swimming bath. The last club to admit Indian officers was the Peshawar Club, which did not succumb until the colonel of an Indian cavalry regiment told the club committee that unless his Indian officers could be members, he would not permit any of his officers to join, and furthermore he would no longer hire out horses for hunting.

In spite of all the difficulties, financial, social and professional, the army acquired some splendid Indian officers and there were no major explosions. Many senior officers in Indian and Pakistani armies later remembered with gratitude individual British officers who gave them encouragement and helped them along.

A partial remedy for the failure rate of Indian cadets at Sandhurst was found in the establishment of the Prince of Wales Royal Indian Military College at Dehra Dun on 13 March 1922 on the site of Lord Curzon's Imperial Cadet Corps, which, deprived of Curzon's support, had collapsed. The new military school was not really a college, but an institution run along the lines of a British public school. Housing seventy boys at a time, it served as a preparatory school for Sandhurst, turning out "Brindians"—young Indian facsimiles of English public school boys who shared their manners and values.

Selection of the students proved to be a knotty problem. Political representatives of the martial classes claimed most of the places, reasoning that soldiers of their communities had most freely shed their blood for the Empire. In their favour was the military's dislike and distrust of the educated and urban Indian. Lieutenant-General Alexander Cobbe, Secretary in the Military Department of the India Office, thought the problem insoluble:

> It is an unfortunate fact that the fighting races of India, from which the Indian Army is recruited, are the very classes who are most backward as regards education, and on the other hand those classes whose intellectual qualifications are the highest are generally regarded as lacking in martial qualities.

Lord Rawlinson of Trent, Commander-in-Chief, India (1920–25), also had doubts, which he expressed in his diary:

> Will we ever get a young educated Indian to lead a charge of veteran Sikhs against a sangar held by Mahsuds and, if he did, would the Sikhs follow him? Will we ever get the sons of the landowners of the fighting races, who are brought up to despise the Babu . . . sufficiently educated to be trusted with the lives

of men in modern war? . . . It will take at least two, probably three generations to produce Indian officers of the right kind in sufficient numbers.

But the door had been pried open a crack, never to be slammed shut.

Indianization progressed more rapidly in the Indian Medical Service than in any other corps. All doubts and all prejudices were set aside when commissions for doctors were considered. Even in the late Victorian era, a few Indian doctors had been commissioned. One of the first, Bawa Jawan Singh, commissioned in 1891, rose to the rank of colonel and in 1918 was made a Commander of the Order of the Indian Empire (CIE). During World War I, although no Indians were commissioned in the combatant arms, nearly seven hundred Indian doctors were commissioned. In 1923, of 681 doctors holding the King's Commission, 150 were Indian, 102 of whom were recruited after 1915. Indian doctors even served with Gurkhas, whose snobbish regiments resisted Indian combatant officers to the end.

Indian political leaders, who were initially anti-army because of the part the army played in repressing civil disorders, soon came to realize that if or when India gained its independence, it would need this army and a strong cadre of competent Indian line officers, and pressed for speedier Indianization. Liberal British politicians agreed. In 1922 the Marquess of Reading, who was Viceroy from 1921 to 1926, told Viscount Peal, the Secretary of State for India, that Indianization of the army was "the crucial test of our sincerity in the policy of fitting India to advance toward the goal of self-government."

The greatest obstructions were the racial prejudices of British officers who were unwilling to serve with Indian officers and even more reluctant to serve under them. An article in the *Morning Post* (20 February 1923) put the matter bluntly: "To many of the most open-minded soldiers the idea of being under the command of an Asiatic is insuf-

ferable." Senior officers feared that if Indian officers holding the King's Commission were allowed into the army on
an equal footing, the supply of suitable British officers willing to serve would dwindle. Rawlinson wrote that "old officers say they won't send their sons out to serve under
natives."

In 1923 Lord Rawlinson announced the "eight unit
scheme," the designation of eight segregated units—five
battalions of infantry (out of 104), two regiments of light
cavalry (out of twenty-one), and one pioneer battalion (out
of seven)—in which Indian subalterns would be placed. It
was assumed that as Indian officers advanced in rank the
British officers would move out and eventually—after
twenty-two or twenty-six years, actually—the units would
be entirely Indian. The scheme was not a success. Borrow-
ing a term from the Americans, these units came to be called
"Jim Crow regiments." Of the first five Indian graduates
from Sandhurst, four refused to serve in a segregated regiment.

General Claude Auchinleck was later (1946) to say in a
letter to South-East Asia commanders:

> The policy of segregation of Indian officers into separate units,
> the differential treatment in respect to pay and terms of ser-
> vice as compared with British officers and the prejudice and
> lack of manners by some—by no means all—British officers
> and their wives, all went to produce a very deep and bitter
> feeling of racial discrimination in the minds of the most intel-
> ligent and progressive of the Indian officers.

In 1925 a committee composed of British officers and
Indian politicians, including Moti Lal Nehru and
Muhammed Ali Jinnah, recommended the abolition of the
eight unit scheme, the founding of a military college on the
lines Sandhurst, and a dramatic increase in the number of
Indian officers. Although the recommendations were unan-
imously approved by the committee, the government chose
to ignore them for several years, while the problem of a

burgeoning number of Indian junior officers was exacerbated by doubling the number of places reserved for Indians at Sandhurst.

In order to accommodate the numbers of Indian KCOs in the eight segregated units, the VCOs were eliminated. This was hardly a popular move; it was called "platoonism." Although the young officers knew that British subalterns commanded platoons in the British Army, they also knew that in commanding platoons in the Indian Army, a position held by VCOs elsewhere in the Indian service, they were serving at a lower level of responsibility than were their British counterparts. They could see as well that platoonism changed the odds of an Indian commanding a battalion (reaching the rank of lieutenant-colonel) from three to one to eight to one. In turn, the sepoys and sowars saw that in such a system they could never become VCOs.

Although Indianization was still regarded as an "experiment," the number of regiments to which Indian KCOs were admitted burst out of the eight units limits, and by 1928 12 percent of the army was open to them. On 10 December 1932, the Indian Military Academy (IMA) was established at Dehra Dun with a capacity for sixty Indians of the regular forces and twenty for the Indian State Forces. The length of the course was two and a half years, a year longer than Sandhurst at that date. The academic standards of Sandhurst were maintained and the professional training was in many respects superior. However, the anglicization was not as complete, and this caused some initial difficulties for the first graduates when they joined the messes of their regiments. The opening of the IMA was cheered by many Indian politicians, for they saw it as a clear indication that Britain really did not intend to stay in India.

Because an army commission carried great prestige, the competition to enter the IMA was intense. Probably the elite urban Indians from non-martial classes would have taken the vast majority of places had not the army made a point of reserving some for the martial classes, particularly from the army itself.

There were cheers from all ranks when a sepoy was selected for the IMA. The regimental history of the 16th Punjabis records the good news that in January 1934, "No. 6231 Naik Ghalam Mohd, son of Subedar Karam Khan had been selected as a Gentleman Cadet at the I.M.A. Dehra Dun. He was the first to be selected for this college from the regiment." (He rose to become a lieutenant-colonel and to command the 1st Battalion of the 16th Punjabis.)

By the late 1930s Indianization had become a political issue firmly linked to Home Rule and then to Independence, but throughout the Indianization period the government seemed to have had a positive knack for spoiling what good it did by attaching irritating or humiliating conditions. An IMA graduate was not to be the equal of a Sandhurst graduate. He was to be called an Indian Commissioned Officer (ICO) and his commission was valid only in India. Worse, his pay and allowance were considerably less than those of a KCO, and no more Indians were to be sent to Sandhurst. There would be no further Indian KCOs.

In 1940 Lieutenant-General Auchinleck, soon to become the last British Commander-in-Chief, India, wrote to Leo Amery, M.P., soon to be Secretary of State for India and Burma:

> In my opinion, we have been playing a losing hand from the start in this matter of "Indianization." The Indian has always thought, rightly or wrongly, that we never intended the scheme to succeed and expected it to fail. Colour was lent to this view by the way in which each new step forward had to be wrested from us, instead of being freely given. Now that we have given a lot we get no credit because there was little grace in our giving.

It was true enough, and the British suffered for their graceless tardiness in World War II when the shortage of officers for the Indian Army became a handicap that was never completely overcome. In 1919 there had been nine Indians holding the King's Commission; ten years later there were only ninety-one; and in another ten years, on the eve of World War II, there were only about 400 KCOs and ICOs out of a total officer corps of three thousand, and of these only a very few had attained field grade.

World War II rid Indianization of its invidious features. The VCOs returned and platoonism vanished. On 17 June 1940, the Government of India declared: "In effecting the expansion of the Army which is now at hand and the further expansion which is proposed, all units of the Indian Army (including Corps and Departments) will be thrown open to Indian Commissioned Officers."

Courses at IMA, Dehra Dun, were shortened to eighteen months and then to a year and in some cases to seven months. Its capacity was expanded to six hundred. Still another category of officer came into being: the Emergency Commissioned Officer (ECO). New officer schools were opened at Mhow and Bangalore, and all fees were abolished. Martial and non-martial classes were taken in, both as officers and as other ranks. Both British and Indian men, and a few women, were created ECOs, with generally good results. Although many educated Indians who would have made good officers were among those most politically conscious, i.e., nationalists, and refused to serve, the number of combatant Indian officers increased until by war's end there were 8,300, mostly ECOs. Where formerly there had been ten British to one Indian officer, there were by mid-1945 only four British to one Indian officer.

At the officer training schools for ECOs, cadets were rated by British officers. At one typical school 75.33 percent of the British cadets were rated average, compared with an almost equal number (76.84%) of Indian cadets, but 18.67 percent of the British cadets were rated above average and only 6 percent below average, while comparable figures for the Indian cadets were 8.96 percent above average and 14.2 percent below.

Interestingly, in view of the general pre-war belief that Indians could not command Indians, British commanders rated Indian ECOs superior to British ECOs in their handling of troops. This was not too surprising since many of the latter came straight from Britain with only an elementary knowledge of Urdu or of the habits and customs of their men. However, British commanders complained that their Indian officers lacked initiative and tended "to stick to the letter rather than the spirit of the instructions." Some grumbled that Indian officers put their personal comfort above that of their men and their personal interests above those of the regiment. But most had to agree that Indian officers performed far better than regular officers expected.

21

World War II

I n the final decade of the British raj, the Army in India faced four major crises: (1) the need to expand, reorganize and modernize for the exigencies of another world war; (2) the struggle to hold at bay the nationalists in India and to defeat the foes of Empire abroad, particularly the Japanese; (3) the problems presented by the Japanese-inspired Indian National Army; and (4) finally, the need ultimately to come to terms with the splitting asunder of the Indian Army by the political partition of the subcontinent and the independence of Pakistan and India. The British responses to these crises met with varying degrees of success.

In the mid-1930s, in spite of the belligerent activities of Hitler and Mussolini in Europe and the bloody beginnings in China of Imperial Japan's Greater East Asia Co-Prosperity Sphere, it seems to have occurred to almost no one that India might be involved in another world war. No plans were made for the expansion of the Indian Army or for its participation in another global conflict.

Throughout the inter-war years the money allocated to provide men and materiel for war had been steadily reduced.

Between 1922 and 1932, the Indian budget for military expenditures had declined dramatically, from Rs. 652.3 million to Rs. 474.7 million. In 1933, a slow reversal began when Britain granted an annual subsidy of £1.5 million, increased after the war started to £2 million, but it was a case of too little and too late. Highly professional but shabby, the Indian Army was sadly in need of repairs.

When World War II began, the Indian Army totalled 189,000 men, of whom 65,000 were needed for administration and service on lines of communication. There were thirty-seven battalions of British infantry and eighty-two Indian battalions stationed in India. Two Indian infantry battalions were in Hong Kong and two in Singapore, plus some Sikh and Punjabi gunners. Only two cavalry regiments had been partially mechanized; the remainder still trained and fought on horses.

There was an acute shortage of artillery and the guns available were mostly obsolete. There were no anti-tank units and there were only eight anti-aircraft guns in the entire country. Engineer and signal services lacked modern equipment; there was a serious shortage of motor vehicles; and the supply services were largely in the hands of civilians. An Indian Air Force had been formed, but it consisted of scarcely more than a dozen antiquated machines. The Royal Indian Navy owned only seven modern small sloops, three frigates, four corvettes, a miscellaneous collection of minesweepers, depot and store ships, trawlers, gun boats, and a variety of vessels in the coastal forces.

In the months just before the outbreak of war plans had been made to modernize and reorganize the infantry. A model battalion was to consist of 662 men of all ranks, including 12 officers (KCOs or ICOs) and 17 VCOs. Battalions were to be divided into a headquarters company and four rifle companies. The headquarters company was to be composed of an administrative platoon, a support platoon with light machine guns and 15-cwt trucks, and a signals platoon. Rifle companies were to be broken down into three platoons, each with three sections. In all, a battalion was

A subaltern and the colonel of the 7th Bengal Native Infantry on parade in India in 1938. (National Army Museum)

to have forty-four light machine guns, four mortars and six anti-tank guns. This was far better than in World War I and it all looked fine on paper, but almost no battalion was at full strength with a full complement of arms and equipment. Only a handful were fully motorized, and most, allotted only eight trucks, still relied on mules and other animal transport.

In spite of the dilapidated condition of the army and in spite of the awesome efficiency of Hitler's Panzers as demonstrated in Poland and of the ruthless power displayed by the Japanese in China, the authorities in India exhibited an astonishing lack of vision, and preparations for war proceeded at a stately pace. The generous leave taken by officers and other ranks in peace-time continued; officers regularly departed on weeks-long hunting and shooting trips. Although hundreds of thousands of Indians were eager to enlist, only 53,000 volunteers were accepted in the first *eight months* of the war, all from the "fighting classes." Foolishly, good VCOs and NCOs, invaluable for the training of an expanding army, were pensioned off when their peacetime service expired.

Soon after Britain declared war, General Sir Robert Archibald Cassells, Commander-in-Chief, India, inquired of His Majesty's Government in London what would be needed from India, and suggested that Indian Army units be trained for service abroad. He was advised that it was unlikely that Indian troops would be required. As a result of such lofty thinking, nearly a year of valuable time was wasted.

(Among the meagre military aid that was accepted from India at the beginning of the war were three mule transport companies manned by Punjabi Muslims. They were shipped to France and two were evacuated from Dunkirk from 26 May–4 June 1940; one was captured. For several years the evacuated Punjabis stayed on in Britain, first in western England and then in Scotland.)

In September 1939, when mobilization orders were opened, one of the first directives read: "Swords will be sharpened." In the same spirit, reserve officers recalled to the colours packed their dress uniforms and their sports gear; some shipped their polo ponies. It was not yet realized that the army's days of polo playing were nearly over; the need for men who knew horseflesh was past.

On the other hand, the day was distant when every officer would have his own car. In a few regiments officers had clubbed together to buy a motor car for the mess and it was used for excursions, but these were exceptions. In the Royal Deccan Horse not a single man knew how to drive. Even after the horses were gone, old commands endured. Trucks and armoured cars were taken to the "led-horse line" and a bugler blowing "Stable Call" summoned men to care for their vehicles.

Not yet recognized, but soon apparent, was modern warfare's need for soldiers with sophisticated skills. Punjabi peasants who understood horses, mules and bullocks but could not read directions or understand diagrams, charts

A sketch of a Jat lance daffadar's field service uniform in Italy during World War II. (National Army Museum)

or maps had now to be taught to use and maintain complex machinery. The attempts to form an Indian Armoured Corps out of Rajput horsemen were pitiful. Not only did the sowars lack mechanical and electrical skills, they lacked the mental framework for the new tasks. One man, cursed for his stupidity when he drove a 15-cwt truck straight into a large boulder, wrecking its axle and steering, mumbled morosely, "Well, a bullock cart would have gone over it." He was right, of course.

It was the obvious requirement for men with modern skills, or the capacity to master them, which led to the enlistment in great numbers, much sooner than in World War I, of the despised but clever Madrasis and Mahrattas, and even some Bengalis.

Fortunately for the Allies, most Indians gave generous support to the war effort. It is remarkable that at this period, only thirty years after the Amritsar Massacre, and at a time when Indian politicians were their most vociferous, young Indian men were enlisting in such numbers. There was no need for the high-pressure tactics used in the Punjab during World War I. The Indian Army grew to 2,644,323 men, all volunteers, the largest all-volunteer army in the history of the world. Nothing like it had ever been seen before, nor has it ever been seen since.

Recruits were easier to come by than equipment. India lacked the industrial base needed to supply a twentieth-century army in a major war. It had no motor car or airplane factories and no tankage to store strategic reserves of petrol, but slowly Indian industry began to make what it could for its own and British forces. Tent-manufacturing facilities were established in 1940, and soon other factories were turning out vast quantities of clothing, parachutes, blankets, footwear, webbing, and mosquito nets. Among the one thousand five hundred medical items manufactured were 336,000 ounces of castor oil, 160 tons of anti-mosquito cream, and 1.5 million water purification tablets.

The entry of the United States into the war soon brought a flow of American arms, equipment and supplies of all sorts. Thousands of engines and special chassis arrived from Canada and the United States, and bodies were manufactured in India; by the end of 1943, more than a hundred thousand vehicles had been assembled. Ordnance factories were opened, new steel mills began production, and India supplied ever more military needs as the war went on.

Some cavalry regiments, initially issued only trucks instead of armoured vehicles, made the best of them. The Central India Horse, for example, which had no armour when sent to fight in Africa as reconnaissance units, developed great skill in operating trucks behind enemy lines and in luring enemy tanks to follow them into positions where they could be destroyed by 25-pounder guns.

Indian politicians, occupied with local affairs and internecine quarrels, had paid scant attention to hostilities in distant Europe. Steps had been taken to create a more representative form of government; not soon enough, perhaps, but a 1935 Act for the Government of India had given considerable power to elected provincial assemblies, making them almost autonomous bodies in local matters, overseen by Indian ministers who were responsible to them. In 1938, eight out of eleven provincial assemblies were controlled by the Congress Party.

Accustomed now to having their advice sought and to making decisions affecting the welfare of their constituents, Indian leaders were shocked when, immediately after Britain's entry into the war, without consultation, discussion or debate, the Viceroy, the Marquess of Linlithgow, proclaimed that India was at war with Germany.

Only Sind and Bengal, where the provincial assemblies were controlled by Muhammed Ali Jinnah's All-India Muslim League, and the Punjab, where control was divided between Muslims, Sikhs and Hindus, offered support and cooperation to the sirkar. Hindu Congress leaders in eight provincial governments promptly resigned. It was a tactical error on the part of the Congress leadership, for the resignations broke forever the tenuous political bond of Hindu and Muslim.

Indian nationalists, mostly Hindus, were more interested in their quarrels with the British than in winning the war. Some actually conspired with Nazis and with the Japanese Army. Gandhi, now a national figure whose popular "hartals" resulted in increasingly bloody riots, called upon the British people to submit peacefully to the Nazis and Fascists. Jawaharlal Nehru, usually more level-headed, once remarked that the Japanese would be no worse than the British.

In the spring of 1942, during Britain's darkest days, Sir Stafford Cripps led a commission to India and offered Indian political leaders full dominion status at the end of the war if they would behave while the war was on; but Gandhi and other Hindu politicians renewed their demands for immediate independence. Accepting the Cripps proposal would be like drawing a cheque on a failing bank, Gandhi said.

Rejecting the peaceful road to independence, Gandhi launched a hate-British campaign. "Quit India!" was the slogan, and in one of his most absurd pronouncements, he sanctioned the destruction of railways, stations, bridges and other line of communication structures and facilities—provided they were destroyed in a non-violent manner. Not knowing how this could be accomplished, his followers blew up trains loaded with food and supplies destined for the hard-pressed army in Burma, attacked post offices, tore out telegraph lines, and cut great swaths of terror in which arson, murder and sabotage flourished. Two young Canadian Air Force officers who were caught by a mob at a railway station in Bihar were, quite literally, torn to pieces. Police did not always suffice and troops had to be used in some sixty incidents. "This is open rebellion," Gandhi proclaimed jubilantly. The British arrested him.

The violence intensified and ultimately fifty-seven battalions of infantry had to be diverted from the war for internal security duties. Although a small Muslim jihad incited by the Faqir of Ipi erupted on the North-West Frontier and a charismatic Muslim firebrand named Pir Pagaro stirred trouble among the Farqi Hurs in Sind, who even cut the Lahore-Karachi railway for a time, almost all the rioters and vandals in Northern India, where the worst violence occurred, were Hindus. Muhammed Ali Jinnah referred to the series of disorders as a Congress plot, and perhaps it was; certainly it drove still deeper the wedge between Hindu and Muslim leaders.

Because of war-time censorship almost nothing was known in Britain of these disorders, but among the British in India who knew there was a feeling of being stabbed in the back, of being kicked when down. The Hindus were not "playing the game." Bitter anti-Congress and anti-Hindu feelings came to be often allied with pro-Muslim sentiments. Although there were only nine Muslims to every twenty-four Hindus in India, they formed 65 percent of the troops who fought in North Africa, Italy, Malaya and Burma.

Interestingly, except for a few small incidents, these

uprisings had little effect upon serving troops or on recruiting. The Kirti Lehar ("Peasant Movement"), a Communist-inspired group, made valiant efforts to suborn sepoys and sowars—with little success. The affair of the Central India Horse was an exception, a minor failure in a war of vast proportions.

When the Central India Horse (21st King George V's Own Horse) were ordered to move from their station at Meerut to embark at Bombay for overseas, the sowars in the Sikh squadron made no objection, gave no sign of unrest or dissent; but when the troop train reached Bombay, instead of going straight to the dock, it was shunted onto a siding where the troops were kept idle for thirty-six hours. Here four Sikh sowars who had been converted by Kirti Lehar propaganda succeeded in persuading two thirds of the regiment to refuse to board their ship. It sailed without them. Courts-martial followed and the leaders were exiled to the Andaman Islands, where they were later freed by the Japanese. The Central India Horse went on to gain laurels as the reconnaissance regiment of the justly famous 4th Indian Division in North Africa and Italy.

As in World War I, the Indian princes eagerly volunteered their services. On the day war was declared (3 September 1939), the Maharaja of Jaipur, the polo-playing "Jai," wired the Viceroy begging to be allowed to fight with the Life Guards. To his chagrin, Linlithgow advised him to stay home and stick to his duties in his state. Even a cable from Jai to Buckingham Palace, placing his "personal services at the disposal of my beloved Sovereign," failed.

Some wondered why he did not go to war at the head of his own Sawai Man Guards, then serving in Baluchistan and later sent to East Africa and Italy, but Jai considered his own guards as imitations; he wanted to be a part of the real thing. All through 1940 he pestered the authorities, until at last he was given an emergency commission as a captain in the Life Guards and posted to the Household Cavalry Overseas Composite Battalion in Egypt. Overjoyed, he cabled his thanks to King George VI. Sadly, he served for only a few months; too many polo accidents and too many small plane crashes had rendered him unfit for the field.

Although none was more loyal than Jai, other princes gave more valuable support. The Nawab of Bhopal became an air commodore, sent two battalions on active service, and sold all his American investments to purchase a squadron of Spitfires. The Maharaja of Gwalior raised and trained seven thousand men. The Maharaja of Dewas served as a second lieutenant in a Mahratta regiment in Egypt, and the Maharao of Bundi, a handsome bon viveur, won a Military Cross in Burma. The sixty-year-old Maharaja of Bikaner carried his seventeen-year-old grandson off to war with him in North Africa. Jammu and Kashmir sent two battalions overseas and put others on the North-West Frontier. A battalion of Hyderabad infantry served in Mesopotamia, and the Nizam gave £170,000 to buy a corvette for the Royal Indian Navy. Eight princes presented their private airplanes to the Indian Air Force. By August 1941 the States Forces had expanded to 76,000 men.

Some of these units did well. A battery of Jammu and Kashmir artillery distinguished itself in Eritrea, particularly at the Battle of Karen, and the 1st Nabha Akal Infantry, which saw action in Italy, was described as "a very fine States Forces battalion." Some performed poorly and a few disgracefully. At the beginning of the Japanese counter-offensive in the Arakan in January 1944, a picket of the Gwalior Lancers in Burma, suborned by Indians who had joined the Japanese-sponsored Indian National Army, deserted to the enemy.

When at last it became apparent that Britain and its allies needed every man they could get and the Indian Army began to expand in earnest, there occurred, in general, a great mixing of classes; even Untouchables were recruited, though these had to be formed into units of their own. For the first time, Sikhs from different parts of the Punjab were mixed; Jats and non-Jats were mixed as well; and Dogras served with various Punjabi Hindus. All Madrasis, whether Hindu, Muslim or Christian, served together. The only single-class regiment was the 17th Dogras, all six of whose battalions fought in Malaya or Burma. (The 3rd Battalion of this regiment was sent to Singapore in November 1940 and claimed to have fired the first shot by the Indian Army against the Japanese.)

Among new units were "Boys' Battalions," composed of fifteen- and sixteen-year-olds who were paid ten rupees a month, given plenty of food with extra rations of milk, and trained to be soldiers. This proved to be an excellent scheme, for by the time they reached enlistment age they were already more than half trained and were demonstrably stronger and healthier than recruits who came straight from the villages.

A small Women's Auxiliary Corps (India) was formed. Most recruits were Christians, Anglo-Indians, or Burmese; only a few were Hindu and fewer still were Muslim. Women in the corps handled administrative work, freeing men to fight; a few were taught to drive. Enlistment could be for "Local Service" or for "General Service." Those in the latter category agreed to serve overseas.

The war proved educational for nearly all classes, including the British. When General Wavell arrived as Viceroy in October of 1943 there was famine in Bengal and he instituted rationing, but this proved complicated, for it had to be different for Hindus, Muslims, Christians, et alia, and it was believed that it had to be differentiated according to social class. Here the prejudices and misconceptions of the British authorities created problems. Because they believed that only upper-class Indians drank tea, the sugar ration for lower classes was reduced. According to Francis Yeats-Brown, the authorities were "frankly unbelieving" when told that "the wives of the shoemakers with the army liked their tea every morning, and with plenty of sugar in it!"

In rural Bengal there was only one doctor for every thirty thousand people, but with the army's help, 9 million were inoculated for cholera and smallpox over a six-month period. The army's own medical arrangements improved greatly in the course of the war. In 1943 there were one hundred twenty men in hospital as a result of tropical diseases for every wounded patient. By 1945 this ratio had dropped spectacularly to ten to one.

In the course of the war the Indian Army participated in campaigns in Syria, North Africa, East Africa, the Middle East, Malaya, Greece, Sicily and Italy (where twenty-year-old Sepoy, later Subedar, Kamal Ram of the 8th Punjabis became the youngest Indian ever to win the Victoria Cross).

The officers and men of the Indian Army earned no fewer than thirty-one Victoria Crosses, twenty of them in Burma, and a total of 4,028 awards for gallantry in action. Twenty-eight of the thirty-one Victoria Crosses were won by Indians and Gurkhas, three by a single battalion, the 2/5th Gurkhas, in the 17th Division.

Handsome twenty-three-year-old Second-Lieutenant Premindra Singh Bhagat of the Corps of Indian Engineers was the first Indian officer to win the Victoria Cross. In February 1941, the Italians in Eritrea were fleeing to Gondar with the British in hot pursuit. Speed was essential if the Italians were to be prevented from regrouping, but pursuit was held up by thousands of mines the Italians had planted. Lieutenant Bhagat and his men were given the task of clearing a track through the mine fields. For forty-eight hours non-stop Bhagat carried out his perilous task. Twice his carrier was blown up. Both his eardrums were damaged, but he carried on with what has been called "the longest continuous feat of sheer cold courage," clearing no fewer than fifteen mine fields and an incredible fifty-five miles of road before he collapsed from exhaustion and shock. Bhagat remained in the army after the war and, serving the Republic of India, earned yet another award for bravery and rose to the rank of lieutenant-general.

The war waged by the British against the Italians in Ethiopia has received little attention from historians. It was a campaign which had its own peculiarities, for the British worked with, or tried to work with, Ethiopian partisans, known as Patriot Forces. Major J. D. Guille of Skinner's

Major (later General) Premindra Singh Bhagat, Indian Engineers, the first Indian Victoria Cross of this war. He won the
award for clearing minefields at Gondar, Abyssinia, in January
1941 when a subaltern. (National Army Museum)

Horse described the planning for an attack on Debra Tabor,
a town east of Lake Tana on the Dessie-Gondar road:

> Before the plan of attack could be discovered, an agreement
> had to be made between the Patriot forces and our own troops
> as to the division of the loot. The conclusion of this agreement

was of far more importance to them than the capture of the town. Agreement having been finally reached, discussion could then begin as to how the town was to be captured. . . .

Just before zero hour a breathless and angry liaison officer came up to say that the attack was off. The Patriot leader, Hupta Selassie, was having his hair dressed, and would not be ready in time. The attack was therefore postponed to the following night. Once again Guilleforce [Major Guille's command] took up its position. Shortly after it began to rain; it was a pitch black night and though uncomfortably wet, the conditions were ideal. The Patriot forces Commander thought otherwise. He had had his hair done the previous night, and had no intention of getting it spoilt by going out in the rain, and so once again the attack was called off.

Soon after, the Italians at Debra Tabor surrendered without a fight. It is possible that the Patriot Force commander was not as vain as he seemed.

From the war's beginning until August 1945 the Indian Army suffered the following casualties:

Killed	24,338
Wounded	64,354
Missing	11,754
Prisoners	79,489
Total	179,935

Most casualties occurred in South-East Asia, for this was the primary battleground of the armies of India. Out of a total of a million Allied troops who fought there, 700,000 were Indians or Gurkhas. The Fourteenth Army in Burma, which had a 700-mile battle front, was the largest in the world. It was fortunate to be led to victory by General Sir William Joseph Slim, a product of the Indian Army, who was certainly one of the finest generals on either side in the war.

Slim was exceptional in almost every way. He did not come from a military family; his father had been an iron merchant in Bristol and could not afford to send his son to Sandhurst. During World War I Slim enlisted as a private in the Royal Warwickshire Regiment and was soon given a temporary commission. He was severely wounded at Gallipoli and again in Mesopotamia, where he won the Military Cross. He was finally awarded a regular commission in the West India Regiment, which ranked socially at the bottom of all British Army regiments. In 1919 he managed a transfer to the Indian Army and served with the 1/6th Gurkhas, whose officers did not at first welcome a man with his antecedents, but Slim had the intellectual abilities, character and charm to win both respect and friendship.

In 1935 he was only a major and because of his relative poverty he considered resigning his commission until he discovered that he could sustain himself by writing pulp magazine fiction under the name of Anthony Mills. A forty-seven-year-old brevet lieutenant-colonel in 1938, he rose rapidly during the war, commanding a brigade in East Africa (where he was again wounded), the 10th Indian Division in the Middle East, and in March 1942 he was sent to take command of a corps in Burma. In October 1943, following an unbroken series of Japanese successes in South-East Asia, he was given command of the newly formed Fourteenth Army. An unassuming man, he combined a sense of gentle humour with remarkable fortitude and determination. A brilliant and literate man, he wrote the most readable and human accounts of his campaigns of any general in the war.

Unlike many of his contemporaries, Slim had a high opinion of the Asian soldier. Comparing him to a British Tommy, he said that he is "at least equally brave, usually more careless of death, less encumbered by mental doubts or humanitarian sentiment, not so moved by slaughter and mutilation." With the ability to inspire trust and confidence in all of his soldiers, Asian and European alike, Slim was in every respect a remarkable soldier. And for the war in Burma an extraordinary soldier was needed.

chapter 22

War and Peace
in South-East Asia

S ome of the severest British losses of the war were suffered in late 1941 and early 1942 in South-East Asia
as the Japanese swept all before them. Most casualties were
soldiers in the Indian Army. At Hong Kong in December
1941 the 5/7th Rajputs and the 2/14th Punjabis, two fine
battalions, as well as several batteries of artillery and medical and transport units, were surrendered. More than sixty
thousand British and Indian troops were lost on 15 February 1942 when, in the greatest and one of the most humiliating disasters to British arms in history, Singapore fell to
a numerically inferior Japanese Army.

The triumphant Japanese scarcely broke stride before
attacking Burma from Siam (Thailand) along a wide front.
British defences rapidly melted. In the light of the previous
confusion over responsibility for the defence of Burma, it
is hardly surprising that military plans were neither clear
nor consistent.

The British seemed unable to decide where to place Burma
in the imperial scheme of things and unable to decide

whether or not it should be ruled by the Government of India. In consequence of this uncertainty, measures for its defence were never well defined. In April of 1937 it was separated from India and its own military command was established. In the next four years responsibility for its defence was shifted to Far East Command, Singapore, then back to India; to South-West Pacific Command, with headquarters in Java, then back again to India. Its peace-time garrison consisted of four battalions of the Burma Rifles, two battalions of British infantry, and the Burma Frontier Force, a kind of gendarmerie recruited mostly in northern India. Shortly before the Japanese attack on Pearl Harbor it was augmented by two Indian Army brigades.

In July 1941 General Sir Archibald Percival Wavell became Commander-in-Chief, India, succeeding General Sir Claude Auchinleck. Briefly, between 17 January and 7 March, 1942, General Sir Alan Fleming Hartley, took command. On 8 March Wavell was back and in command until 20 June 1943, when Auchinleck returned to serve as the last British Commander-in-Chief, India.

The forces in Burma, commanded by Lieutenant-General Sir Thomas J. Hutton, were organized into an army corps of two divisions: the 1st Burma Division (13th Indian Brigade and 1st Burma Brigade) under Major-General J. Bruce Scott; and the 17th Indian Division (2nd Burma Brigade and 16th, 46th, and [later] 48th Indian Brigades) under Major-General Sir John G. Smith. A professional soldier with the look of an affable accountant, Smith had proved the quality of his physical courage in World War I by winning both the Military Cross and the Victoria Cross; in Burma he was to prove that he possessed as well the moral courage needed to make difficult decisions.

In 1941 three fighter squadrons and three bomber squadrons were supplied by the Royal Air Force, and also available, thanks to Generalissimo Chiang Kai-shek, was the group of American volunteers which became known as the "Flying Tigers." The generalissimo's generosity was rooted in self-interest, for the Burma Road was his fragile life-line through which poured supplies from the United States. And all supplies landed in Burma had to come through the port at Rangoon. Hutton's first responsibility was to protect Rangoon.

On a map Burma resembles an amoeba protruding a long tail. The tail, called the Tenasserim, is the 400-mile-long stretch of land, only thirty to sixty miles wide, that separates Thailand from the Andaman Sea. The main body of the country is drained by three great rivers running north and south. In the east the Salween flows into the Bay of Bengal at Moulmein; fifty miles west of it is the Sittang; and a hundred miles farther west the mighty Irrawaddy, a thousand miles of navigable water, empties into the bay through a many-mouthed delta, on the eastern rim of which sits the great port and city of Rangoon.

The Japanese had little trouble capturing the Tenasserim. The Siamese gave them their support, as did many Burmese. It is almost impossible, as the British were to discover, to defend a people against their will, and most Burmese, with the exception of the hill tribes in the north and north-east, hated British and Indians alike and decidedly did not want to be defended. The Burma Rifles, a newly raised corps, fought well in their first battle at Moulmein; but soon after, deciding that they had best look after their own homes, many of the corps abruptly decamped. At the same time the Japanese had no trouble raising and arming a Burmese National Army to help them shove the British out of Burma. Everywhere the British were defeated and driven north and east.

At the end of January, the 48th Infantry Brigade disembarked at Rangoon. It was badly needed. The 7th Armoured Brigade dispatched as reinforcement from the Middle East was still at sea and Rangoon had to be held as long as possible. The natural barrier to the Japanese advance was the wide and fast-flowing Sittang River. It was crossed by two bridges: one three miles from its mouth, and a second at

Toungoo, 110 miles upstream. It was the first of these that was closest to Rangoon and considered vital. To defend the town General Smith had the 16th and 46th brigades, the tattered remnants of the 2nd Burma Brigade, and the newly arrived 48th Brigade, which consisted of three excellent Gurkha battalions.

Fighting all the way, these units were retreating westward towards the Sittang Bridge, where sappers were laying explosives to demolish it when the last Allied soldier had crossed. The exhausted but still fighting 48th was only sixteen miles from the bridge on the east side when its Gurkhas were shaken by vicious air attacks, not from the Japanese but from the RAF and the American Flying Tigers. By the morning of 22 February the Japanese had worked themselves into positions north of the bridge on the flank of the retreating British brigades.

At ten-thirty on that morning Brigadier N. Hugh-Jones, commanding the 48th Brigade, took personal charge at the bridgehead, and sent the 1/4th Gurkhas to assist the 4/12th Frontier Force and a company of the Duke of Wellington's Regiment in holding the east bank.

The battered brigades were retreating in relatively good order, but first to the bridgehead came the stragglers and those who had left the fighting too soon, and these carried exaggerated stories of lost battles. Hugh-Jones had lost radio contact, and the work of preparing the steel-girder bridge for demolition was behind schedule. Proper demolition materials were lacking and it was difficult to lay charges while men and vehicles were passing over the bridge. By one o'clock in the afternoon the Japanese had the bridge under long-range small arms fire; by three o'clock the charges were laid.

Uncertain if the bridge could be held into the following day, Hugh-Jones turned for advice to Major Richard C. Orgill, the Royal Engineer officer in charge. Orgill thought that even if it could be held—and he doubted it could—the job was so intricate and the Japanese so close that the demolition would have to be done under the cover of darkness. That, at least, was Hugh-Jones's understanding.

That night, still unable to decide on a course of action, Hugh-Jones called a meeting of his available battalion commanders to discuss the situation. Curiously, Major Orgill was not invited to take part. It was of vital importance that the bridge not be captured intact. It was doubtful if a strong Japanese attack the next day could be beaten back. On the other hand, thousands of British, Indian and Gurkha troops were still on the east side of the river. Finally, Hugh-Jones and the battalion commanders agreed that the bridge should be blown just before dawn.

Still irresolute, Hugh-Jones decided to pass the fateful decision on to Major-General John Smith, his superior. Smith was awakened in the middle of the night and the situation was explained to him. More than half of his command was on the wrong side of the Sittang, as Smith well knew, but, given the facts presented to him, he made without hesitation the only correct decision: "Blow it!"

It is difficult to be critical of Smith or of Hugh-Jones and his colleagues at the bridgehead. They carried heavy responsibilities, they were exhausted from strain and lack of sleep. Still, their action was criticized and many unanswered questions surround the decision. In the event, the first charge was detonated electrically from behind an abutment on the west bank, not by Major Orgill, but by Lieutenant (later Major) Bashir Ahmed Khan of the Malerkotla Sappers and Miners, and a span of the bridge dropped into the river—an action which could have been safely performed at the last minute in daylight.

Captain Bruce Kinlock of the 1/3 Gurkha Rifles was with his troops only a few miles from the bridge on the east side of the Sittang:

> Then, at 0530 hours, as the first light of dawn appeared in the eastern sky, from the direction of the river came the reverberating roar of three enormous explosions, and on the instant we

realized that the bridge had been blown and our lifeline cut. As the echoes died away, there was complete silence. All firing ceased, and every living thing seemed to be holding its breath. Then the Japanese, like a troop of excited monkeys, broke into shrill chattering. Believing that everyone else had crossed over and abandoned us to our fate, we were filled with anger.

A few men managed to swim or raft to safety, but most were taken prisoner. Only about thirty-five hundred were saved.

By blowing the bridge the British were able to hold Rangoon for two vital weeks, time enough for the 7th Armoured Division to disembark with its Stuart tanks. Without this reinforcement it is probable that none of the army in Burma would have survived. Nevertheless, General Smith was relieved of his command.

On 8 March 1942 a blackened and smouldering Rangoon, all of its military assets destroyed, fell to the Japanese. After pausing briefly to receive considerable reinforcements, they advanced north, up the Irrawaddy River towards Mandalay.

On 19 March William Slim was flown to Burma from the Middle East to take command of the British, Indian and Gurkha troops who had recently been reorganized into a corps called Burcorps. Reinforced by two Chinese armies (about the equivalent of two weak divisions), he established an east-west line about one hundred fifty miles south of Mandalay, but the Japanese slipped around it and captured the Yenangyaung oil fields, though not before Slim had converted them into blackened ruins.

Three days after Slim's arrival there occurred near Toungoo the last cavalry charge to be led by a British officer. Lieutenant-Colonel Arthur P. Sandeman of the Central Indian Horse, commanding a squadron of mounted Sikhs in the Burma Frontier Force, was a brave, if muddled, man, and his eyesight left much to be desired; he had given up polo when he could no longer see the ball. Nevertheless, he was leading his squadron on a reconnaissance when he saw troops which, up to the moment that they opened fire on him with a machine gun, he took to be Chinese. Instead of wheeling about and galloping back with information about the Japanese presence, as he certainly should have done, he drew his sword, shouted "Charge!" and dashed at the enemy, his whooping Sikhs at his heels. Not one reached the Japanese machine gun. Only a handful of survivors, which did not include Sandeman, trotted back to Toungoo.

The British did their utmost to hold Mandalay, but the Chinese forces on their left flank collapsed and it was wisely decided to draw back into the hills behind the Chindwin River, a major tributary of the Irrawaddy, to the Indian frontier. The march was long, an arduous two hundred miles, with the Japanese in close pursuit.

The Japanese had captured all of Burma and arrived at the gateway to India at a cost of not more then eight thousand men, but their supply lines were badly overextended and they were forced to halt at the Chindwin. The Chinese had lost more than fifty thousand men and the Anglo-Indian forces about thirty thousand, of whom nearly half were listed as missing. Most soon became prisoners of war, although a surprising number managed to elude capture and make their way back to India.

It was at this critical juncture in the war that Gandhi, now often called the Mahatma (the honourific of one revered for wisdom and high-minded selflessness), wrote, "I see no difference between the Fascists or Nazi powers and the Allies," and he launched his "Quit India" movement. Gandhi was "imprisoned" in the Agha Khan's palace in Poona where he was allowed to have with him a select coterie of family and followers. As a result of all this, troops badly needed on the North-East Frontier had to be redeployed to meet the internal disorders in India's cities, which Linlithgow characterized to Churchill as "by far the most serious rebellion since that of 1857."

This diversion of effort and the demands of other theatres of war prevented any substantial Allied operations in

Burma in 1943. Early in the year an abortive British offensive into the Arakan, an area of Lower Burma along the north-east coast of the Bay of Bengal, turned into a fiasco, and a sense of defeat and abandonment settled over the army on the Burma front.

Even when Slim was given full command of all the troops, now reorganized into the Fourteenth Army, the men called themselves the "forgotten army." It was true that the British press, reluctant to report defeats and retreats, gave little space to their operations.

In December of 1944 a second campaign opened in Arakan and enjoyed a modest success. Although of little strategic importance, the Japanese were driven from three formidable fortresses they had constructed and suffered their first defeats; the British and Indian troops learned that the Japanese soldier was not invincible.

The Chindit operations behind the Japanese lines, brainchild of the imaginative and flamboyant Major-General Orde Wingate, made dramatic headlines early in 1944. Wingate, who had little understanding of the Indian Army, insisted upon formations of his own design which did not conform to familiar or efficient patterns. (He seemed not to realize that Gurkhas did not understand either English or Urdu and needed to be under officers who could communicate with them.) Dashing, daring and romantic as the Chindits were, they made little difference in the scheme of things. The results achieved did not warrant the loss of life and the cost of the effort.

In mid-1944 the Japanese crossed the Chindwin and launched their Manipur campaign with an attack upon the Fourteenth Army's supply centres at Imphal and Kohima. Slim, determined to hold these bases at all costs, put fifty thousand men in them. When they were surrounded, he kept them supplied by air, three quarters of the supplies being flown in by the United States Army Air Corps. At the same time he assembled a corps at a railhead not far in the rear and began pushing back Japanese advance patrols. It was not easy. Slim later described the general scene at Imphal and Kohima:

> The prolonged and hard fought battle . . . swayed back and forth through great stretches of wild country, one day its focal point was a hill named on no map; the next a miserable unpronounceable village a hundred miles away. Columns, brigades, divisions, marched and countermarched, met in bloody clashes, and reeled apart, weaving a confused pattern hard to unravel.

The Japanese had not expected such stout resistance; they had, in fact, confidently intended to resupply themselves from the captured bases. When the monsoon rains arrived and washed out their lines of communication and supply, they fell back, suffering from starvation and disease, and were harassed by Allied air attacks.

In 1945 the British began a cautious advance into Burma. Setting up dummy headquarters, deceptive communications and feints, Slim duped the Japanese into believing that he was going to advance for a climatic battle in central Burma. Instead, he threw forces around the Japanese flank and cut their lines of communication. On 2 May, Rangoon fell; in the next four months the Japanese were pushed steadily back and out of Burma into Thailand, and pockets of resistance were efficiently mopped up. In all, the abortive invasion of India cost the Japanese 65,000 dead.

The immensely difficult reconquest of Burma was the most brilliant offensive campaign mounted by the British in World War II. Correlli Barnett has compared its sustained speed and *élan* with Wellington's destruction of the French armies in the Iberian Peninsula in 1813. In 1945 the British genius of this remarkable campaign, "Bill" Slim, became Commander-in-Chief of all Allied forces in South-East Asia. Three years later he was made Chief of the Imperial General Staff and promoted to field-marshal, becoming only the second man in British history to rise from private to field marshal. Lord Mountbatten called him "the finest general the Second World War produced." In 1960 this son of an ironmonger was created a viscount.

Even after the Americans dropped their atom bombs and the Japanese surrendered, much work remained for the armies of the raj; there was no peace in the former European colonies. Among other imperial tasks was the dispatch of an Anglo-Indian force into Thailand, then still called Siam, the only country in South-East Asia never to be ruled by a European power, although it had been occupied by the Japanese and the Siamese government had welcomed and assisted the Japanese Army. Nevertheless, the Anglo-Indian force was not an army of occupation; it was there to disarm and repatriate 125,000 Japanese troops, to release and repatriate 12,000 prisoners of war and 150,000 foreigners—mostly Javanese, Chinese, Indians and Malays—who had been imported as slave labour.

The Japanese cry of Asia for the Asians had struck a sympathetic chord and the subject peoples now demanded their freedom. A nationalist ferment boiled furiously from India to Indo-China. The most violent of the nationalist movements erupted in what was then still considered the Dutch East Indies. On Java, most of the defeated Japanese had turned over their weapons to those Indonesians who had collaborated with them and now called themselves nationalists. In this time of confusion, the thousands of Dutch men, women and children who had been interned by the Japanese were treated with even greater brutality by their former subjects and new warders, the Indonesians.

On 25 October 1945 the 49th Brigade under Brigadier A. W. Mallaby landed at Soerabaja in central East Java. Their mission was to disarm the Japanese, succour the Dutch internees, and, in general, restore order. The Dutch Army, almost nonexistent, could not hold their former East Indian possessions, and the inhabitants of the East Indies were united in their determination not to be ruled again by the Dutch. No one, least of all the British, wanted to make war on the Japanese-trained 12,000-man Indonesian Army, but Mallaby found himself in an impossible situation.

Three days after disembarking, a convoy of the 49th Brigade was ambushed: eleven officers and fifty other ranks were taken prisoner and shot. Another convoy, inadequately guarded by Mahrattas, was taking Dutch women and children to the docks when it was attacked and all were hacked to pieces. Mallaby arranged a truce, but it did not hold. Detachments of Mahratta and Rajputana Rifles guarding the gaol and the railway station were butchered to a man after fighting to their last cartridge. Mallaby himself was assassinated while trying to arrange a second truce. In three days the 49th Brigade lost 18 officers and 374 other ranks.

As the situation obviously required more than a brigade, the 5th Indian Division under Major-General E. C. Mansergh was dispatched to Java. Using tanks and strong escorts—and sometimes Japanese troops who had not been disarmed—some six thousand Dutch, mostly women and children, were safely brought out of the interior. Any European or Indian unfortunate enough to fall into Indonesian hands was mutilated and dismembered, usually in a public place.

Open warfare broke out in Soerabaja, and in a battle that lasted nineteen days the streets were finally cleared. Tragically, many men who had survived battles in East and North Africa or in Burma were killed in this "savage war of peace." Nevertheless, the British stayed on until early in 1946, when they were relieved by Dutch Marines.

Most troublesome of all the war's lees for the British were the former members of the Japanese-sponsored Indian National Army, officially referred to as Japanese Indian Forces (JIF), who came to be called "Jifs" by the Tommys and sepoys.

23

The
Indian National Army

During the war it seemed only logical to many of Britain's enemies, who hearkened to the outpourings of Gandhi, Nehru, Sardar Patel and other Hindu nationalists, that most Indian soldiers must be serving unwillingly in the British-officered Indian Army and would welcome an opportunity to fight against their British oppressors. They were encouraged in this belief by a remarkable Hindu politician: Subhas Chandra Bose (1897–1945).

Bose's father was a Brahman, a prominent lawyer and a member of the Bengal Legislative Council; Subhas Chandra was his ninth child and sixth son. Even as a boy, Bose had a strong military bent, but because of the army's prejudice against Bengalis and Brahmans, a military career was closed to him. During World War I, when the army lowered its caste barriers to include a regiment of Bengalis, Bose hastened to enlist, only to be turned down because of poor eyesight, first by an Indian doctor and then by a British doctor.

A brilliant but unruly student, he was expelled from Calcutta University for his part in the battering of a professor. Thanks to his father's influence, he was taken in by the Scottish Church College and there he succeeded in joining the university branch of the India Defence Force, a territorial unit. He loved the military training; it gave him a "feeling of strength and self-confidence."

In 1919, the tumultuous year of the Rowlatt Act and the Amritsar Massacre, Bose was graduated with first-class honours in philosophy. He was already an ardent nationalist, but he acceded to his father's wish that he go to Cambridge and study for the Indian Civil Service (ICS).

He enjoyed himself there. "What gives me the greatest joy is to watch the whiteskins serving me and cleaning my shoes," he wrote in a letter home. He was one of the brilliant and lucky few who passed the examinations that earned him a place in the elite ICS, but on his return to India he fell under Gandhi's spell and joined his Swaraj Party. Proud, fiery and ambitious, he rejected the glittering career open to him and became one of Britain's foes instead of one of its proconsuls.

Bose's rejection of an ICS career, an unheard-of event, brought him national attention. He organized the hartal protesting the visit of the Prince of Wales in 1921–22 and served on numerous party committees. Frequently in prison, he rose to be a political figure as important as Nehru, with whom in 1928 he formed the Independence for India League. He became president of the All-India Congress (1929–31) and in 1930 he was elected mayor of Calcutta.

Although a humourless man, Bose was said to possess considerable charm and a "magnetic, almost hypnotic, influence on others." He was undoubtedly the most popular Hindu in Bengal. Between 1933 and 1936 he travelled widely in Europe, regaining some of the health he had lost in British prisons and studying European revolutionary movements. After his return to India and still another spell in prison, he became, in 1939, president of the Congress. When he announced that he would stand for an unprecedented second term, he angered Gandhi, who had chosen his own candidate. He won and Gandhi never forgave him. Bose tried to heal the breach, but Gandhi, perhaps jealous of his growing influence, refused all reconciliation efforts and they remained enemies.

In December 1940, once again in prison, Bose escaped and made his way, disguised as a Muslim holy man, out of India to Kabul. From Afghanistan he travelled to Europe, where in 1942 he married the Austrian Emilie Schenkl, formerly his secretary. It was necessary to keep the marriage secret for it was widely believed that he had publicly vowed never to marry until India had achieved its independence. To make matters worse, he was known for his scathing remarks about Indians who adopted European manners and took European wives.

Bose met with both Mussolini and Hitler, and although he could not persuade either to promise freedom to India, he got permission to raise an Indian Legion of about two to three thousand men from Indian prisoners of war. Never entirely successful, the effort faltered from lack of encouragement when he and his would-be troops refused to swear allegiance to either Hitler or Mussolini. In 1942, Rommel refused to accept the services of the Indian Legion in North Africa and it was moved to Holland, where in 1943 it mutinied. Another Indian unit was raised in November 1944 from Indian troops captured in North Africa, but when ordered to Libya it refused to go.

Bose, having failed miserably with his legion in Europe, was sent by German submarine to Japan, where he had better luck, for there the Japanese under Major Iwaichi Fujiwara had already formed the Indian National Army with the aid of several Indian commissioned officers, notably Captain Mohan Singh and Captain Shah Nawaz Khan, both of the 1/14th Punjabis, who had been captured in Malaya.

Mohan Singh, a Sikh from the Sialkot District of the Punjab who joined the army in 1927, had been sent to the Indian Military Academy at Dehra Dun, where he distin-

guished himself as a cadet. He was commissioned (ICO) in
1934 and posted to the 1/14th Punjab Regiment, one of the
segregated Indianized regiments, then stationed on the
North-West Frontier.

In March 1941 the 1/14th Punjabis were sent to Malaya.
Although he was promoted to captain, Mohan Singh was
an unhappy man. Convinced that he had been discrimi-
nated against in the promotion process and smarting from
snubs he received from the European community, he nursed
his grievances.

Immediately after the surrender of Singapore in February 1942, the sepoys, VCOs and Indian officers were separated from the British officers and were subjected to the
blandishments and threats of Major Fujiwara. They were
informed that Britain had already lost the war and that the
Japanese, Asians like themselves, had been and would be
their staunch friends. Promised good treatment if they
cooperated, they were warned of harsh treatment indeed if
they refused. It is hardly surprising that many found the
Japanese proposition an offer they could not reject.

Mohan Singh, from the beginning an enthusiastic disciple of Fujiwara, was taken to meet Lieutenant-General
Tomoyuki Tamashita, commanding the Twenty-Fifth Army,
who assured him that Japan had no designs on India. Placed
in charge of all Indian prisoners, he conceived the idea of
forming an Indian National Army to fight alongside the
Japanese, an army that would free India of the British yoke.
He assured the sceptical Japanese that divisive influences
of religion, caste and language could be overcome by
instilling a patriotic desire for Indian independence,
although one of his most difficult tasks, as he later admitted, was convincing men that breaking their oath to the
British and taking a new one would be "a true and religious action."

Eventually about five battalions, the nucleus of the Indian
National Army (INA), were raised. The new army was egal-
itarian and caste-free, with common messes and canteens.

It had only one class of officer with one pay scale, VCOs were given regular commissions, and Mohan Singh, who styled himself "General," was liberal with promotions. Reasons for joining the INA varied. Some men simply wanted to escape the horrors of prison life. Others thought that joining might give them an opportunity to desert and return to their own lines. Many, perhaps most, who joined were young soldiers who had enlisted for the war and lacked the stiff discipline of the pre-war soldiers. Some were indeed true believers in the INA; they had heard the oratory of Gandhi and other Congress leaders and they had witnessed the example of many of their own Indian officers whom they had been trained to follow.

Mohan Singh wanted to lead his men in battle, but the Japanese had formed a poor opinion of the fighting qualities of Indians. They were used instead to guard concentration camps, build runways, and act as camp followers to the Japanese troops. Some were sent off to labour camps in Borneo, Celebes and Siam. Captured British rifles were the only weapons issued to them. Mohan Singh, who had dreamed of creating an army of a half million, was incensed when the Japanese limited the size of his force to one poorly equipped division and resisted his attempts to gain more control over it. Pushed to one side, he began to suspect that the Japanese merely wanted to replace the British. Annoyed by his suspicions and grievances, and tired of his constant complaints, the Japanese placed him under arrest and set to work disbanding the INA.

However, when Subhas Chandra Bose arrived in Singapore in October 1943, he rekindled the embers of Japanese enthusiasm, breathed new life into the scheme and a new INA was formed. Many who had never been proselytized by Mohan Singh threw in their lot with Bose and joined. South-East Asia had a large Indian population, and the new INA under Bose began to draw recruits from the civilian population of Singapore and Malaya as well as from prisoners of war. Many were influenced by Gandhi's "Quit India" resolution, which had passed the Congress in August and had been given wide publicity by the Japanese.

One of Bose's schemes was the formation of a unit of women soldiers, dubbed the Rani of Jhansi Regiment,* to be commanded by a woman doctor, Captain Lakshmi Swaminathan. Perplexed and annoyed, the Japanese, to whom the concept of women warriors seemed bizarre, dragged their feet and refused to provide a training site, but Bose's persistence finally pried one from them. When he wanted to send the women to the front, however, he went too far; the Japanese refused.

Bose did nothing to help the tens of thousands of Indian prisoners who remained in Japanese hands, nor did he press for Mohan Singh's release or even ask to see the other Indian officers who were imprisoned. He took no interest in the fate of those Indians who were being worked to death in Siam building the infamous Death Railway that was to stretch 262 miles through appalling jungle from Burma to Siam.

Estimates of the number of Indians who joined the INA vary widely. About 85,000 Allied troops had been taken prisoner by the Japanese in Malaya and Burma; of these, some 60,000 were Indians. All of these had been placed under Mohan Singh's control, and about twenty thousand, one third of whom were Sikhs, had enlisted in the INA during the first few months of its formation. They had sworn an oath to Mohan Singh. Under Bose this was changed and men swore an oath to the "Provisional Government of Free

---

* The Rani of Jhansi was a remarkable woman of great courage with considerable leadership abilities who, after her husband died, fought off all contenders to the gadi and retained control. She formed a small army that included women as troopers and gunners who fought beside the men. During the Mutiny of 1857–58 she was one of the few rulers of a princely state who sided against the British. At the start of the Mutiny she had promised safe conduct to the hapless European men, women and children living in Jhansi and had then seen them treacherously massacred. She was killed leading her forces into battle on 13 June 1868.

India," the head of which two months later was Subhas Chandra Bose, who took to himself as well the posts of "Minister for War and Supreme Commander of the Indian National Army," and spread the word that in future he should be called *Netaji* ("leader," to be used henceforth as the Germans used *Führer*).

The Japanese refused at first to approve of Bose's "Free India" (*Azad Hind*) movement, but when in October 1943 Bose established himself in Tokyo and declared war on Britain and the United States, the Japanese reluctantly gave their endorsement of the scheme and recognized the provisional government. Bose's government-in-exile was soon recognized by Germany, Italy, and several puppet Axis states as well. Eamon de Valera, President of Ireland, sent his personal congratulations.

Japanese senior officers had difficulty taking the INA seriously. The commander of the Japanese forces in Burma, when offered twenty-five thousand INA troops, accepted only three thousand. More than half were rejected as unfit for combat.

At least fifteen thousand prisoners, including a high proportion of Gurkhas, refused to join the INA, and these were subjected to considerable abuse. Indian and Gurkha VCOs endured particularly harsh treatment, alternated with periods of blandishments and privileges. Sikhs and Hindus were more easily suborned than Muslims. Of the officers who had cast their lot with Mohan Singh, most, like him, were ICOs; few KCOs had yielded. There were considerable differences between units. Two junior officers of the 3rd Indian Cavalry persuaded their men to stand fast and they did. As a punishment, one of the officers, Captain Hari Badhwar, was confined for weeks in an iron cage so small that he could neither lie down nor stand up. Sad to say, the British never rewarded or gave special recognition to those Indians and Gurkhas who suffered torture rather than betray them.

Men who broke their oath and served the Japanese were

subsequently acclaimed by their countrymen. A modern writer, Lieutenant-Colonel Bawa Sundar Singh, has expressed the view now widely held in India:

> The Japanese triumph in Malaya was an important epoch in military history. It struck a blow at British military power in Asia. . . . It mirrored to the technically superior Western nations that an Asian power had come of age. Singapore was for all Asian people a final vindication of what the Japanese had manifested at Port Arthur in 1905 that the white intruders who had humiliated Asia during the nineteenth century could be defeated. Under such conditions of bitterness was forged the Indian National Army which was the manifestation of the resistance of an India in bondage. . . .

> The British syllogism that the soldiers who crossed over to the INA had deserted a sinking ship and ratted on their oaths of allegiance was the coloured interpretation of an outworn colonial power.

In a memorandum directed to senior British officers in 1946, General Claude Auchinleck spelled out his own moderate view of those who so readily changed sides:

> Those who have served for many years with Indian troops, as I have done, have always recognized that the loyalty of our men was really to the officers of the regiment or unit. . . .

> In these officers their faith and trust was almost childlike. . . . It is true to say that in almost every case of serious discontent or indiscipline, and there have been remarkably few of them, which has occurred in the past fifty years, the cause could be traced to indifferent officers and bad man-management.

> The terrible tragedy of Singapore following on the fall of Hong Kong must have seemed to the great majority of VCOs and rank and file to be the end of all things, and certainly to the British "Raj." . . .

> Their British officers were taken from them and they were at once assailed by traitors. . . . Their Indian officers in many instances proved false to their trust. . . .

The strain and pressure to which these men, the majority of whom were simple peasant farmers with no cultural or educational background, were subjected is very difficult for any British officer . . . to visualize. . . .

It is quite wrong to adopt the attitude that because these men had taken service in a British-controlled Indian Army that, therefore, their loyalties must be the same as British soldiers. As I have tried to explain, they had no real loyalty or patriotism towards Britain, not as we understand loyalty.

Not all senior officers were as forgiving. Lieutenant-General Sir Francis Tuker, along with most other British officers, felt that "no soldier, even of a mercenary army . . . can ever condone the breaking of his pledged word of loyalty by any soldier of any caste, creed or race."

Although nationalist leaders did their best to cast the INA in an heroic mould, the entire affair was an inglorious episode. Certainly the INA did not do much fighting. Of twelve thousand INA soldiers sent to fight in the Second Arakan campaign, half quickly surrendered. INA men sent to raise a rebellion in Baluchistan surrendered the moment they arrived on Indian soil. In March 1945, two thousand INA troops in Burma surrendered without firing a shot. As Japanese fortunes turned in Burma, the INA looked more and more like a losing proposition—to the Japanese and to the Indians themselves. When the 1st Division of the INA joined the battle at Imphal, it was 6,000 strong, but 715 promptly deserted and 800 more soon surrendered. About 400 were killed fighting and some 1,500 died of diseases. Many had assumed that they had only to shout *"Jai Hind"* (Victory or Glory to India) or *"Chalo! Delhi!"* (On to Delhi) and the sepoys facing them would desert. They soon learned that this was not the case.

Most Indian, British and Gurkha soldiers held the "Jifs" in contempt, and General Slim reported that "Our Indian and Gurkha troops were at times not too ready to let them surrender and orders had to be issued to give them a kinder welcome." Captured INA soldiers sometimes received short shrift: nine were executed when captured and seven others received stiff sentences from courts-martial.

Shah Nawaz Khan, a former captain who became a major-general in command of an INA division in Burma, described in his diary his last days with the INA in the Chin Hills after the Japanese failure to capture Imphal. On 4 May 1945, he wrote: "Rained all day. The Japanese have left us completely in the lurch. They are running themselves and are not bothering about us." On 5 May, he wrote that "the Japanese have no further use for the I.N.A. and all liaison officers are withdrawn." Entries for the days that follow record the rapid deterioration of morale and discipline as officers and other ranks deserted. On 16 May, Shah Nawaz Khan was taken prisoner by the 2/1st Punjabis.

After the Japanese debacle in Burma, the INA was disbanded. Bose was in Singapore when, on 16 August 1945, he learned of the Japanese surrender. He scurried to Japanese headquarters in Saigon, where he persuaded Field Marshal Count Terauchi to send him by plane to Russia. He had now lost all sense of reality: he entertained some notion of transferring reconstituted INA units to Russia and of persuading the Soviets to invade India. He got as far as Formosa (Taiwan) in an overloaded Type 97-2 twin-engined bomber when, on 18 August, his plane, attempting to take off for Hsingan via Dairen, crashed and burned. Bose, soaked with petrol, leapt from the plane, a flaming torch. He died a few hours later in the hospital. His last words are said to have been: "India will be free before long." His old enemy Gandhi sent a message of condolence to his mother, praising her son in extravagant terms.*

---

* Many Indians refused to believe that Bose was dead. For years afterwards he was said to be in Russia, in Japan, in a remote Himalayan hideaway. Roads and parks in India bear his name. Every year his birthday, 22 January, is marked by parades and the many statues to him are garlanded. At 12:15 p.m., the time of his birth, the sirens of Calcutta blast a lament.

The INA presented a greater problem to the British after the war than it ever had during the fighting. While the war was in progress, those captured were treated as prisoners of war and put in separate camps, where their existence was concealed from the British and Indian publics; but at war's end the problem they presented could not be ignored. They were not prisoners of war to be repatriated as were the surrendered Japanese. Technically, every prisoner of war who had joined the INA had "waged war against the King-Emperor" and could be shot as a traitor, a rebel, at best as a deserter, but this was not like Singapore in 1914; the political climate had altered considerably. In any case, the British were incapable of trying and executing some twenty-three thousand Indians. After much debate, it was decided to divide them into three categories, classifying them according to their degree of guilt as white, grey or black.

There were some who had obviously joined the INA under compulsion or as a means of facilitating their escape and had done so at the earliest opportunity, but intent was difficult to prove, and these men, classified "white," finally numbered only 3,880. The vast majority, 13,211 men, were in the "grey" area. They had been credulous or they had merely wanted to avoid the harsh punishments for not joining or had despaired of any other solution to their plight. Certainly those who joined the INA had a better chance of surviving. Of those who remained true to the sirkar, 20 percent died of starvation, diseases and homicide, while less than 8 percent of those who joined the INA died after their capture. The 6,177 who were classified as "black" were the true believers, the ringleaders, particularly the Indian officers who had willingly changed sides and had actively aided the enemy. Also categorized as "black" were all those who had committed atrocities against British or Indian soldiers.

The whites were reinstated in the army without loss of seniority; greys, treated "with mercy and generosity," were dismissed from the army with forty days paid terminal leave; blacks were scheduled to face British justice. This whittling down of the numbers was obviously a wise procedure, but in failing to understand Indian political sentiments and the seriousness of the political ferment in which all India was now steeped, the army in its next step made two grave errors.

Seeking to avoid any charge of communal favouritism, the high command decided that the first three to be tried would be officers representing the three principal communities, Muslim, Sikh and Hindu: Shah Nawaz Khan (thirty-one), the former captain in the 1/14th Punjabis and former major-general in the INA; Gurbakhsh Singh Dhillon (thirty), former lieutenant in the 1/14th Punjabis and lieutenant-colonel in the INA; and P. K. Sahgal (twenty-eight), former captain in the 2/10th Baluchis and a lieutenant-colonel in the INA. The result was disastrous. Nationalists were quick to proclaim the INA soldiers patriots; the three disparate communities, in a rare show of unity, joined in their championship of all the accused. Gandhi praised the INA for its "self-sacrifice, unity irrespective of class and community, and discipline." The country was soon in an uproar.

Though the army's first mistake was an understandable, if misguided, attempt at impartiality, its second was simply stupid, a demonstration of its complete insensitivity to communal feelings. It was announced that the court-martial would be held in the Red Fort in Delhi. It possessed a good communications centre, it was convenient for witnesses, counsel, clerks, relatives and others concerned with the trial. It was "the most convenient from nearly every point of view." Unfortunately, from an Indian point of view its selection was provocative.

A former seat of the Mogul Empire, the Red Fort was for Muslims a reminder of the day when they, not the British, had ruled India. The Hindus venerated it as the place from which their own kings had ruled. All remembered that in 1857 Hindu and Muslim mutineers had died defending it.

Furthermore, a touch of irony not lost on the Indians, Delhi had been the goal of the INA soldiers who had so often shouted *"Chalo Delhi."*

The Indian press, extravagant in its praise of the INA, predicted reprisals if any of the accused officers were convicted. There appeared to be some danger of this. Posters appeared on the streets of Calcutta demanding the release of all INA soldiers and threatening that "twenty white dogs" would die for each INA veteran harmed.

On 5 November 1945 the court-martial opened. The court was composed of seven officers, the three junior of whom were Indian officers—a Muslim lieutenant-colonel, a Sikh and a Hindu who were majors. Major-General A. B. Blaxland was president; a British brigadier and two British lieutenant-colonels completed the court. All three defendants were charged with waging war against the King-Emperor. In addition, Gurbakhsh Singh Dhillon was charged with four counts of murder, P. K. Sahgal was charged with abetting the four murders, and Shah Nawaz Khan was charged with abetment in the murder of three others.

Seventeen defence counsels were present, including three former judges, a former member of the Viceroy's Executive Council, and Jawaharlal Nehru, who had first condemned the INA but, sniffing the political air, had quickly changed his views and put on his legal robe for the first time in twenty-five years. The defence began by challenging the legality of the court-martial, arguing that the accused had been officers in the Provisional Free Government and that subject peoples have a right to wage wars of liberation.

Throughout the two months of the trial, which ended on 31 December 1945, anti-British feelings were at fever pitch and INA veterans returning to their villages were welcomed as heroes. Outside the courtroom a one-day protest turned into a riot in which more than a hundred persons were killed or seriously injured. Rioting erupted in other cities, particularly violent ones occurring in Calcutta. Congress Party propaganda damned the British, apotheosized the three accused, and whipped up public opinion with inflammatory outpourings.

Nehru later wrote:

> The legal issues were important enough. . . . But behind the law there was something deeper and more vital, something that stirred the subconscious depths of the Indian mind. Those three officers and the Indian National Army became symbols of India fighting for her independence. All minor issues faded away, even the personalities of the three men being tried for an offence involving a death sentence became blurred in that larger picture of India. The trial dramatized and gave visible form to the old contest: England versus India.

After hearing thirty witnesses for the prosecution and twelve for the defence, the court closed and arrived at its verdict: All three officers were convicted of waging war against the King-Emperor and, in addition, Shah Nawaz Khan was found guilty of abetment. All were sentenced to be cashiered, to forfeit all pay and allowances, and to be transported for life. Many officers protested that the sentence was too light and they were exasperated when Auchinleck remitted the transportation for life. He feared, he said, that "To confirm the sentence of transportation would make them into martyrs and intensify the political campaign of bitterness and racial antipathy now being waged by Congress in connection with the INA trials." He was right, but he failed to see that any sentence, any decision, would now be unfortunate. Indians and Britons alike interpreted his action as an abject backing down in the face of Congress threats. All three defendants went free.

More trials followed. Fourteen more men, most accused of atrocities, including brutalities in prisoner of war camps, were tried before Auchinleck decided to end the proceedings. Only the worst cases were brought forward, but the realities of any crime were obscured by the political haze. Many of the fourteen were convicted, but to the indignation of most officers and British civilians, all death sentences were commuted to terms of imprisonment.

Interestingly, Captain Mohan Singh was never brought to trial.* Lieutenant-General Sir Francis Tuker later wrote:

> The leniency of the punishments handed out to these men was remarkable, especially to those who had committed acts of cruelty to our own captured soldiers, their brethren in captivity.

> The crimes were the more evil and sadistic because they were against helpless prisoners of war who had once been their comrades.

Gandhi paid a visit to Auchinleck to plead for the "poor misguided patriotic" INA prisoners. Auchinleck's unvarnished recital of the brutal crimes of which some were convicted failed to affect him.

Auchinleck's adviser, Colonel K. S. Himmatsinghji, a highly respected Indian officer, warned him:

> Never before has the entire country been in such a hostile mood against the British Government as it is today. This is due to political frustration. It is the only issue upon which there is agreement between the Congress and the [Muslim] League. The INA has aroused the imagination of all, including that of the Army. If any punishment is awarded to the INA personnel it will be denounced by all political parties. The future National Government will release all.

The conviction spread that the sirkar was now a paper tiger. As Lieutenant-Colonel Bawa Sundar Singh saw it later:

---

* The INA leaders gradually faded into oblivion. After Independence, all were released from confinement and there was a movement in Congress for the officers to be reinstated, but this was not supported. The INA had outlived its political usefulness. When Nehru became Prime Minister he agreed to their reinstatement but only at their rank at the time of their defection, i.e., as junior officers rather than as colonels and generals. Only one man took advantage of the offer. Mohan Singh was one of the leaders in the fight to have pensions awarded to INA veterans, and in 1974 Prime Minister Indira Gandhi gave state pensions of about £10 per month to an estimated sixteen thousand INA survivors.

"The White intruders from the mist-shrouded island of Britain saw that widespread pandemonium was the only alternative to the grant of immediate independence. . . . The INA stole the limelight in the sunset hour of British authority, and was responsible for the eventual retreat of a great Imperial system."

When in February 1946 a Captain Abdul Rashid was sentenced to seven years imprisonment on being convicted of incitement to murder and of cruelty to his own Indian soldiers, the Muslim League called for a public meeting in the centre of Calcutta to protest the sentence. There were three days of riots.

Congress formed an INA Relief Fund Committee which made relief payments to ex-INA soldiers and promised them civilian jobs, but employers were not eager to hire them, for many had proved to be indifferent employees. Businessmen in Calcutta were discovered bribing the secretary of the fund not to harass them.

Not surprisingly, morale in the Indian armed services sank as those who had resisted Japanese blandishments and had suffered for their loyalty went unrewarded while traitors and deserters walked free and were acclaimed by their countrymen. British soldiers, too, were restive. Many had enlisted for the war and now wanted to go home and to be discharged. Among the Indians the situation was reversed; many who had been taken into the service during the war had hoped to remain and were disappointed when they were denied a career in the army.

In January 1946, British airmen in the Royal Air Force units stationed at Dum-Dum (near Calcutta) mutinied. The miscreants were handled gently and the leniency shown them led other disgruntled service men, British and Indian, to believe, with some reason, that they could make trouble with impunity.

On 18 February 1946 a serious mutiny erupted in the Royal Indian Navy, which, like the Indian Air Force, was commanded by the Commander-in-Chief, India. The Indian

Navy had expanded at an excessive pace during the war—at one point by simply transferring two army battalions to the navy—and between 1942 and 1945 had suffered nine mutinies, but this was the most serious. It began in Bombay when ratings aboard HMIS *Talwar* complained of their food and of "the most outrageous racial discrimination" (their commandant had made derogatory remarks about Indian politicians) and refused to obey orders. Slogans like "Quit India," "Revolt Now," and "Kill the White Bastards" appeared on bulkheads. Ratings aboard twenty-four other ships in the Bombay harbour followed suit and two warships hoisted the Congress flag. Many sailors went ashore and paraded noisily through the streets, occupied public buildings, and tore down every Union Jack they encountered. In emulation of the INA, they proclaimed themselves members of the Indian National Navy (INN). Strikes were organized by civilians in support of the disgruntled sailors. Troops were called in and RAF Mosquitoes flew low over the city, lending colour to the increasingly warlike scenes in the streets. Three Indians were killed and thirty-two Indians and British were injured.

The trouble spread and in Karachi, too, sailors mutinied; at one time a ship in the harbour exchanged artillery fire with British shore batteries. Seven sailors were killed by gunfire. Within three days of the initial outbreak most of the Indian Navy's seventy-five ships and twenty shore installations were mutinous.

Both the Congress and the Communist Party initially lent support to the mutineers, but the Congress leaders became fearful of the havoc they had created and Sardar Vallabhai Patel, known as "the strong man of the Congress," begged the British to crush the mutiny. But the British were entering their last days as rulers; mutiny would no longer be crushed by brute force. The British grip on its Indian sword was weakening. On 23 February an officer and nine ratings were killed in a clash, but pleas by Nehru, Jinnah, and Patel and promises of better treatment and a fair hearing eventually achieved calm. By 3 March the mutiny was over and the sailors were back on their ships.

A commission of inquiry instituted to examine the causes of the naval mutinies found that inequalities between the food and pay of Indian sailors and that of British sailors and frustration over promotion opportunities were contributing causes, but equally important factors were the callousness of British officers and their lack of contact with and interest in their Indian sailors. The commission also concluded that nationalist propaganda had inspired the violence.

Lieutenant-General Tuker attributed the mutinies to the fact that " 'educated' boys were recruited, many actually from the universities," for "there is no more unbalanced and indisciplined body than the student class of Indian universities," he said. He sent out word to his subordinate commanders that the word "strike" was not to be used. "Mutiny was mutiny in the army no matter what it was called elsewhere."

There were also scattered mutinies or "strikes" in army units. An infantry battalion mutinied near Bombay; two pioneer units refused to obey orders and assaulted their officers; there was trouble at the Signal Training Centre at Jabalpur. None of these was regarded as serious, but they were symptomatic of the cracks that were beginning to develop in the armed forces of the raj.

It occurred to Indian politicians, rather belatedly, that the army they had been abusing would soon be *their* army. Independence was about to become a reality and, considering the internal security role which the Indian Army had always played, they would need that army, unpoliticized and in good repair. In May 1946 Nehru, now president of Congress, wrote to Auchinleck about army morale and discipline, exculpating his role in exploiting the INA trials for political purposes: "I suppose everyone who has given thought to the matter realizes that it is a dangerous and risky business to break the discipline of an army. It would obviously be harmful to do any injury to a fine instrument like the Indian Army. . . ."

Many British officers pointed to the creation of the INA and the behaviour of Indian political leaders as proof that Indians were still too irresponsible to govern themselves and they argued, with a touch of desperation, that the British were still needed to exercise control. But they were ignoring political realities. Efficient, honest, conscientious and far-seeing politicians and bureaucrats are desiderata of government, but they are by no means necessary. Independence for the people of India in the very near future had become a certainty. Those who thought otherwise were soon to depart its shores. There was haggling over the date until a brisk new Viceroy, Lord Mountbatten, fixed it at 15 August 1947—ready or not.

chapter 24

Last Days of the Raj

The British forces in India were in no way prepared for the strains and shocks they were to suffer in the final year of their existence. As late as March 1946 there existed not a single contingency plan to prepare the Indian Army for partition. Lieutenant-General Sir Francis Tuker, commanding Eastern Command, with clearer eyes than most, foreseeing that India would probably be divided into two countries each of which would want its own army, drew up a scheme for dividing the army along communal lines, but neither Viceroy Wavell nor Commander-in-Chief Auchinleck could bear the thought of splitting asunder the great Indian Army they knew and loved. Besides, they still believed there was a chance that India could be preserved whole. Staff officers, more pessimistic than their commanders, made plans for two other contingencies: "Madhouse" was the plan of action should the Indian Army become unreliable; "Bedlam" considered what could be done should it turn hostile.

On 23 March Sir Stafford Cripps arrived in Delhi as the key member of a three-man mission (all Cabinet members) to seek agreement on a formula for Indian independence.

Two days later he began a series of meetings with Indian leaders, the most important of whom was Gandhi, but Gandhi had no interest in even discussing any British plan. He was adamant in his demand for instant independence, an undivided subcontinent, and the abolition of the princely states. He spared Cripps only two hours of his time, telling him that he no longer had any official connection with Congress; that he had other plans and could not stay in Delhi to talk with him. He then went off to his ashram in Wardha, a small Hindu town on the Deccan Plateau, leaving Cripps aghast.*

Cripps had already made several unsuccessful trips to India. This was his last, and he again completely failed to obtain any agreement among the quarrelling Indians, or to correlate their views and the views of his own government with the wishes of the authorities in India.

It is perhaps not without significance that every Hindu and Muslim political leader was a lawyer. A Pathan chief echoed the sentiments of many when he asked incredulously: "Do you mean that after beating the Germans and the Japs, you are being chased out of India by Hindu lawyers?" Leonard Mosley said of these Indian leaders, Hindu and Muslim alike: "Words fell like drops of saliva from their tongues. They spoke like poets at their best and like Welsh Baptists at their worst; but one thing was certain, they were never at a loss for words or quotations. One by one they would troop in to see him [the literate but slow-spoken

---

* Cripps was neither the first nor the last British official to be baffled by Gandhi's doublespeak. Intelligent, honest, plain-speaking Wavell, when Viceroy, declared at the end of one interview with him: "He spoke to me for half an hour, and I am still not sure what he meant to tell me. Every sentence he spoke could be interpreted in at least two different ways. I would be happier were I convinced that he knew what he was saying himself, but I cannot even be sure of that." In Francis Wylie's summing up of Gandhi in *The Dictionary of National Biography*, he said: "He was not a profound but rather a muddled and wishful thinker, with a tendency to ignore facts when they failed to agree with his theories."

Wavell], Gandhi, Jinnah, Nehru, Azad and Liaquat, and they would spray him with jets of eloquent argument."

It became increasingly plain that the Muslims did not trust the Hindus and would not consent to any government in which Muslims would be a minority, for they feared, and with reason, that if the Hindu Congress gained control, as was inevitable, the fate of the Muslims would not be enviable. In spite of Gandhi, a separate Pakistan became increasingly a certainty.

Muhammed Ali Jinnah declared 16 August 1946 to be Direct Action Day: Muslims were to relinquish all titles they held from the sirkar and demonstrate to the world their determination to have a separate Pakistan. No one, probably not even Jinnah, understood exactly what kind of direct action was called for; violence was the result, and as with Gandhi's hartals, blood flowed in the streets.

The communal fighting that erupted in Calcutta was among the bloodiest in India's long history of bloody communal violence. For four days Muslims and Hindus slaughtered each other, with the Sikhs weighing in on the side of the Hindus. The exact toll will never be known, but 3,467 dead were counted in the streets, many more were carried away by friends and relatives; many died in hospitals, all of which were full to overflowing. Doctors operated continuously and nurses worked round the clock. Even medical students still learning anatomy were pressed into service. A plausible estimate put the casualties at six thousand people shot, stabbed, burned or hacked to death and another twenty thousand maimed. Scavengers were paid five rupees per corpse to dispose of the human detritus.

Added factors in any disturbance were the ubiquitous *goondas* (roughly translated as gangsters or thugs) who lived in the mud and thatch hovels called *bustees* in and around the city or in the streets themselves. Calcutta held hundreds of goonda gangs. Lieutenant-General Tuker, whose command area included Calcutta, described them:

They have an excellent Intelligence system and are prepared to turn their hands to any type of wickedness. They can be hired out for killings and stabbings and even shootings, throughout the town, supplemented, of course, by the occasional high grade terrorist. . . . During a riot they invariably know what is going on as they organize it. They keep the rioting going and immediately turn to looting.

Goondas and Sikh taxi drivers were credited with the most butchering.

European guests at the Grand Hotel in Chowringhee Square who looked out their windows, drawn by a shouting, laughing group of Sikhs, saw to their horror that they were engaged in dismembering and otherwise mutilating with their kirpans and knives a still-living Muslim. "I have a stomach made strong by experiences of a war hospital, but war was never like this," one witness observed.

The days and nights were hot and humid. There was no public transportation; sewers overflowed; streets filled up with the corpses and carcasses of animals; epidemics threatened. The police were overwhelmed. Calcutta ground to a halt. Nearby troops were called in and still others summoned from distant cantonments. The rioting soon spread to other cities in Bengal, the United Provinces and the princely states, where some of the princes indulged themselves in killing orgies. The Maharaja of Faridkot was the actual organizer of killing sprees, and Indians in Patiala remember still the days when "the trees were full of vultures and the canals full of bodies." In all, forty-five thousand troops were needed to restore order.

Direct Action Day and the three or four terrible days which followed became known as "The Great Calcutta Killing." Shahid Hamid, an Indian officer on Auchinleck's staff, noted that "Gandhi, the apostle of peace, kept away from the disturbances and made no effort to restore peace between the two communities. He always appears when conditions return to normal, and when law and order have been restored." But Gandhi was not the only leader to avoid the turmoil; neither Jinnah nor Nehru appeared in Calcutta or made any move to quell the violence. Indeed, at the end of Direct Action Day, Jinnah declared: "What we have done today is the most historic act in our history. . . . this day we bid good-bye to constitutional methods. . . . Today we have also forged a pistol and are in a position to use it." To Shahid Hamid, the Calcutta rioting seemed like a foretaste and a warning of what was to come—as indeed it was. Direct Action Day made one thing clear: neither Muslim nor Hindu would live peacefully in any nation governed by the other.

With the partition of India now a virtual certainty, the Sikhs, fearful of the Muslims, their traditional enemies, began, with reason, to worry about their own fate. Most of the nearly five million Sikhs in India lived in the Punjab and much of the richest, best-irrigated farmland lay in the western Punjab where Sikh-Muslim relations were badly strained, the sources of some of their differences going back several centuries. The most influential Sikh, revered as wise counsellor, elder statesman and religious mentor, was Tara Singh, seventy-one years old in 1947, a guru whose appearance was said to resemble a combination of an Old Testament prophet and a witch doctor. Tara Singh was against the partition of the Punjab and in favour of a separate Sikh nation carved out of what was projected to be the two countries. "Whatever is decided in Delhi will leave my people like no man's children in no man's land!" he predicted.

Perhaps no other community had prospered as well as had the Sikhs under the British raj: their farms had been watered by expensive canals and dams, their sons had been taken into the Indian Army in vastly disproportionate numbers, they had thrived as civil servants and merchants, and by acquiring urban skills they had become businessmen, clerks, taxi cab drivers and tram conductors. If the 250 million Hindus and the 90 million Muslims could each have their own nation, then why not the five million Sikhs? Not much more than a century earlier they had had their own state, which the British had snuffed out in two bloody wars. Now they set up a cry for their own country again, a Khalistan ("Land of the Pure"). But it was not to be—at least not yet.

The chiefs of the 565 princely states also fretted, wondering what their future was to be. In 1858 Queen Victoria had announced: "We shall respect the rights, dignity and honour of the Native Princes as our own." King George had told Mountbatten that he wished her promise to be kept as "their affection and loyalty are important assets for Britain," but in fact the princes were now merely a nuisance. A few years earlier they had formed a Chamber of Princes to represent their views and to present a united front, but, unable to agree amongst themselves or to coordinate their demands, they floundered helplessly and achieved nothing. Although nearly all enjoyed special treaties, Britain simply renounced their treaty rights and recommended that they join themselves either to Pakistan or to India.

All but four of the princes—Kashmir, Hyderabad, Junagadh (a small state containing the only lions left in Asia) and Travancore—had by 15 August reluctantly accepted constitutional guarantees for the retention of personal privileges and the payment of pensions free of income tax. (Immediately after signing away his state, one raja had a heart attack.) Travancore held out for only three more days. Junagadh soon caved in. But the Nizam of Hyderabad, the richest man in the world and commanding a sizable army, held out and refused to give up his state, telling Mountbatten: "I thought that I could safely rely on British arms and the British word." He soon learned otherwise. The British departed and Hyderabad was promptly invaded and conquered by the new Indian Army. So much for British treaty obligations. The Maharaja of Kashmir dithered, being the Hindu ruler of an essentially Muslim population. When

Pakistan tried to seize the state by force, the republics of India and Pakistan engaged in their first war.*

Leonard Mosley has described what the Indian political atmosphere was like in that final full year of the British raj:

> So much of the futile squabbling and litigious argument, the divagations of Congress, the mulishness of Jinnah, the cloudy idealism of Gandhi had no more effect on the eventual outcome than the chatter of birds in a thunderstorm. India in 1946 was a cauldron steeped in every ingredient calculated to produce the worst kind of noxious brew—obstinacy, venom, malevolence, anger, violence, jealousy and resentment. Absent in all hearts was the milk of human kindness.

Gandhi, demonstrating his talent for provoking violence while talking peace, demanded that the British leave at once and allow the political parties to settle matters among themselves—presumably by civil war. "Let the whole nation be in flames. We will not concede one inch to Pakistan," he declared. Over the objections of Wavell, and even though the Muslim League refused to participate, an interim Indian government was installed on 2 September 1946. The government in London distrusted the Viceroy and in February 1947 unceremoniously sacked him. "I have been dismissed as if I were a cook," he told Auchinleck. The calm, rocklike Wavell was replaced by the ebullient Viscount Mountbatten, who soon announced that India and Pakistan would become independent states on 15 August.

With the reluctant agreement of Muslim, Hindu and Sikh leaders, the actual division of the country was made by one

---

* It did not take long for the new governments to strip all the princes, one after the other, of their rights and privileges, and, of course, their troops and treasuries. The last to go was Mysore in May 1949. The States Forces were no longer considered "in tune with the changed conditions" and all were eventually absorbed into the Pakistani or Indian Army. In 1973 Indira Gandhi's government dissolved the last of the princes' privileges. So much for Indian constitutional guarantees.

man, Sir Cyril Radcliffe, Q.C. (later Viscount Radcliffe). Sir
Cyril, an able lawyer and art connoisseur, was considered
"one of the outstanding intelligences of his generation," but
he had never been to India and he knew absolutely nothing
about the country, its religions, its people or their problems. It was said that he could not tell a tamarind from a
peepul tree. Yet somehow this seemed to recommend him
to all those wallowing in the Indian political quagmire.

When he arrived in Delhi on 8 July 1947, he was told by
Mountbatten, to his utter astonishment, that he must finish the job in five weeks—and Nehru added that he hoped
it could be completed sooner. Sir Cyril, known for his skills
as a mediator, had expected that as the chairman of a committee he would simply preside over those more knowledgeable than himself who would devote themselves to the
problems of the division. But the Indian members of the
committee, Muslim, Sikh and Hindu, agreed on only one
thing: none would have anything to do with such an
unpopular task. All of the difficult decisions, none of which
would please everyone, must be Sir Cyril's alone.

In appalling heat and under constant pressure from an
unending stream of delegations with advice to offer, he did
the job of carving up the subcontinent single-handedly.
Through his thick-lensed spectacles he pored over the best
maps he could obtain without ever seeing the actual land
he was dividing.

When he suggested, not unreasonably, that the complex
division of water rights in the Punjab be settled by mutual
agreement between the two new nations, he brought down
on himself the wrath of Hindu and Muslim alike. Cooperation was anathema to all concerned. In the end, the fate of
millions of people, and of religious shrines, canals, dams,
railways, factories and cities, lay under his pencil and he
did the best he could. It was obviously impossible to satisfy
everybody. Although it seems unlikely that anyone else could
have done any better, he satisfied no one. When he had finished, he turned over his results to the Viceroy and left India

on the day it became two nations, before his work was made public.

The monument which, above all others, represented the suffering and endurance and bravery of the British during the Mutiny of 1857–58 was the ruins of the Residency at Lucknow, where so many soldiers and civilians, women and children, were so long besieged while gallant efforts were made to relieve them. It had been allowed to stand just as it was at the end of the eighty-seven-day siege, a shrine of the imperial British raj. Over the ruined Residency flew the Union Jack, and, as was known to every schoolboy, it was the only place in the British Empire where the flag flew legally both night and day. On the eve of Independence, a group of British soldiers led by Major-General Alfred ("Tiger") Curtis, marched quietly to the Residency and not only took down the flag but cut out the flagpole as well and cemented over the hole it had been set in, so that no trace of its presence was visible. At midnight, when a jubilant mob of nationalists, intent on taking down the famous Union Jack and raising the new flag of an independent India, arrived at the Residency, there was a near riot when they discovered that they had been forestalled. Auchinleck deplored Curtis's action, but most Britons cheered. The flag, sent to King George VI, now rests with other historic British flags in the museum at Windsor.

This was a difficult time for the last Commander-in-Chief, India. Auchinleck had got on well with Wavell, himself a soldier, but Mountbatten frequently angered him and drove him several times to threaten resignation. Mountbatten, for his part, would have gladly seen him off, but Auchinleck, darling of the Indian Army, was too popular.

Certainly the Commander-in-Chief's plate was piled high with trouble. Mutinies and so-called strikes threatened to undermine discipline in the armed services; Indian politicians were alternately begging him to release the INA prisoners and restore their status, or threatening him because he would not. The army was engaged in the unpalatable job of restoring order in an increasing number of riots and intervening in intercommunal fighting as communal emotions rose, and tensions increased; the Sikhs demanded a Khalistan; the Meos rose in rebellion and then demanded that British troops be sent to protect them. There was rioting in Dehra Dun, Bharatpur, Alwar, Meerut and Pilibhit. British soldiers clamoured to go home and no one seemed to know what was to be done with the Gurkhas, or with the surplus of British officers soon to be ejected from the Indian and Pakistani armies. There was a row when bitter British regimental officers demanded that the silver and other valuable properties of their messes be divided and the British share shipped to Britain. Intriguing and wrangling people beset him constantly. In the midst of all Auchinleck's woes, his wife suddenly deserted him and ran off with his "friend" and colleague, Air Chief Marshal Sir Richard Peirse.

In April 1947, Mountbatten assured Auchinleck that Pakistan was certain to come into being, but even then Auchinleck could not bring himself to believe that the Indian Army would be divided. Childless, deserted by his wife, it seemed that the Indian Army, all that was left that mattered to him, had become the plaything of Indian politicians. He fought desperately but futilely for its preservation. He argued that Pakistan would have all the important land frontiers and would require an army almost the equal of the armies of the British raj to defend it; that any talk of division would demoralize the army; that essential British officers would leave; that a fair division of assets such as stores, arsenals, workshops, laboratories, and ordnance factories was impossible; that the army must be preserved because it was the only stable and stabilizing institution in the country; and that division threatened to create politically oriented officers and men. Already some ambitious Indian officers were hobnobbing with politicians and jockeying for positions in the new armies.

Although all of the senior service officers in India supported Auchinleck's view that the Indian Army could not

be divided in the time available, Mountbatten ordered
Auchinleck to do it anyway, and in June the heartbreaking
task was begun.

The scrambling of races and religions, which had originally been a protective measure against another major
mutiny, now made the division of the Indian Army a task
of immense complexity. Nearly every battalion of infantry
and regiment of cavalry was a mixture, by company or
squadron or troop, of different communities. Now the Sikh
and Hindu companies and squadrons had to be separated
both organizationally and physically from Muslim units.
Muslim troops in Hindustan had to be sent to Pakistan and
Hindus and Sikhs in Pakistan had to be sent across the new
frontier to independent India. The partitioning of the Indian
Army was described by Field-Marshal Lord Ismay, Mountbatten's chief of staff, as "the biggest crime and the biggest
headache." A Muslim in the 1st Punjabis wrote: "What had
taken two hundred years to build was dismembered in three
months."

In many units there were touching scenes as comrades of
different religions parted forever. Men exchanged presents,
sang "Auld Lang Syne," and swore to remain friends. In
Delhi, the Hindu and Sikh officers gave a "Farewell Comrades" party for their Muslim counterparts and the senior
Hindu officer gave a toast, predicting, "we shall meet each
other frequently as the best of friends and in the same spirit
of good comradeship that we have had the good fortune to
enjoy all these years." The senior Muslim officer replied in
kind and all linked arms and sang, "For they are jolly good
fellows. . . ." Three days later, four Muslim officers who had
sung that night were among the one hundred fifty Pakistani officers and officials, with their families, who were
hacked to death by Sikh *jathas* (armed, lawless gangs) who
attacked the train carrying them to Pakistan.

The General Staff and almost all of the senior officers in
the army were British; Indianization had come too late and
had progressed too slowly. Out of 22,000 officers, 13,500

were British. Auchinleck considered that of the 8,500 Indian officers, many lacked the character, intelligence, personality and energy for senior appointments. Few of the younger officers had any peace-time experience. Only 2,800 British officers agreed to stay on until the end of 1947, primarily to help with the division of the forces. Auchinleck sent a policy note to his army commanders:

> It has been decreed, and in my opinion inevitably decreed, that we—the British officers—are to go. Before we go, it is our bounden duty to do all that we can to ensure the continued well-being and efficiency of our men and of the Army we have loved so well and served so long. We can do this only if we give freely and fully of our knowledge and experience to those who are to replace us in the higher commands and appointments.

A just and honest man, Auchinleck strove valiantly to do the right thing as best he could judge and as best he was allowed. He ordered that officers leave the regimental funds, mess silver and other assets for their Indian or Pakistani successors.

On 19 July the Defence Department was split into Indian and Pakistani sections and reconstituted under three main categories: personnel; movable stores and equipment, such as guns, tanks, vehicles, ammunition, and so on; and fixed installations, such as cantonments, arsenals and factories. The separation of troops by religion was the first important consideration. Overall, 30 percent of the Indian Army were Muslims and most of the remainder were Hindus and Sikhs, but this proportion varied with every regiment and every arm and service. Excluding Gurkhas, the class composition of the twenty-three infantry regiments was 9⅓ Hindus, 6¾ Muslims, 3⅔ Sikhs and 3¼ others. Demobilization had reduced the Indian Army to about 400,000 men. Of these, the new India received about 260,000 and Pakistan about 140,000.

Inevitably, the breaking up of units and the movement of battalions and squadrons brought confusion and often heartache. The 5th Royal Gurkhas, a Frontier Force regiment headquartered at Abbottabad for nearly a century, were given only a fortnight to pack up and leave for India.

In the first days of August two British generals were selected to head the two armies: Sir Rob Lockhart to be commander-in-chief of India's army and Sir Frank Messervy as commander-in-chief for Pakistan's army. For the time being, however, Auchinleck would remain in supreme command of both armies. Although Nehru had averred: "I would sooner have every village in India put to flame than to keep British troops after 15th August," Auchinleck and Mountbatten agreed on a slow withdrawal over a six-month period after Independence.

The Indian subcontinent celebrated its independence on the night of 14/15 August 1947. In Calcutta, cheering mobs tore down the street signs on the main thoroughfares and Clive Street became Subhas Road. There were joyous celebrations at Jullundur and in many other cities, but elsewhere it seemed that Independence gave license for one community to slaughter another. In Lahore, police did not interfere when fellow Muslims burned down Sikh *gurdwaras* (temples) and incinerated the crowds of innocents who had sought sanctuary there; in Amritsar, Sikhs stripped Muslim women naked and paraded them through the streets before raping them and then hacking them to death with their kirpans. Tara Singh at Amritsar's Golden Temple exhorted the Sikhs to slaughter all Muslims and the Sikh prayer, "First of all I worship thee, O Kirpan!" was now perfervidly intoned by Sikhs throughout the Punjab.

Calcutta knew that it was to be part of the new India and Lahore knew that it was to be in Pakistan, but millions of people elsewhere remained ignorant as to which new country was theirs. Not until the 17th was the boundary between the new countries announced, and then the Punjab exploded. Communal hatred and violence replaced all civil administration. Killing, mutilating, raping, looting, arson and every form of evil went unchecked in a mad violent fury. Millions tried to flee—Hindus and Sikhs from Pakistan and Muslims from the new India—but trains packed with refugees were stopped or derailed and all passengers slaughtered. Trainloads of dead Muslims—men, women and children—arrived in Pakistan in carriages on which were scrawled: "A present from India."

For the time being the British were forgotten as Indians gave vent to old prejudices and hatreds. Major-General J. B. Dalison, Deputy Quartermaster General, was on a train that was attacked by about five hundred Sikhs, who broke open the window of his carriage, dragged out his Muslim bearer and hacked him to pieces before his eyes. All other Muslims aboard were similarly dealt with. The attackers were well organized; their leader informed Dalison that he had orders not to harm the British "this time."

Major Clifford H. Williams reported: "I was driving down the Grand Trunk Road between Jullundur and Ludhiana, when I came across the scene of a recent atrocity. By the side of the road were the naked mutilated bodies of about forty women, only one alive. The common mutilations were breasts cut off, and stomachs of pregnant women slit open with their unborn babies beside them. While I gazed at this gruesome sight, a woman without breasts painfully sat up, saw me and sank back to die, and as she did so pulled over a piece of clothing to hide her nakedness."

Another officer, E. W. Robinson-Horley, was without a weapon when he came upon a group of Muslim women and children refugees who had just been waylaid by Hindu thugs:

In the flickering light from the bonfire, children and babies lay on the ground like so many rag dolls, their heads smashed against the wall of a small culvert. For them the night of terror was over, but not for the remaining mothers. . . . Knocked to the ground while others tore off their flimsy clothing, one after another the women were viciously assaulted. A member of the gang would thrust his *lathi* (six-foot bamboo pole surmounted by brass collars at both ends) right up the vagina as far as it would go and then, with a powerful heave, would tear the screaming woman wide open. How long it took them to die I do not know, but despite my experiences of the war, I had never felt so physically sick in my life. I had witnessed men die from terrible wounds, screaming in pain, but this butchery of innocent women and children was something my very soul could not stomach.

The communal war was not one-sided. A train of Sikh refugees from West Punjab was attacked by a Muslim mob west of Ferozepore and twenty-five people were killed, including three small girls who were hacked to death. More than a hundred passengers suffered stab wounds.

Refugee columns of bullock carts and people afoot, some twenty-five miles long, moving east and west, were attacked by armed gangs on the roads. Whole villages were surrounded and burned, their inhabitants tortured to death. It was a world gone mad with hatred and butchery.

Whatever peace and sanity existed, and it was precious little, was provided by a hastily organized unit known as the Punjab Boundary Force: 55,000 men under the command of Major-General Thomas W. ("Pete") Rees, a capable and experienced soldier, confident and energetic, who had commanded the 10th Indian Division in Iraq and North Africa in 1942 and the 19th Indian Division in Burma in 1944–45. His task was "to maintain law and order in the disputed area": 37,500 square miles containing a mixed population of Sikhs, Hindus and Muslims. As Mountbatten and Auchinleck had agreed that after 15 August British troops would not be used for internal security, the Punjab Boundary Force of Gurkhas and mixed regiments which had not yet been communally sorted and separated contained no British troops other than a high proportion of British officers. Although the force was inadequate for the task, it was, as Mountbatten's aide, Alan Campbell-Johnson, wrote in his diary, "probably the largest military force ever collected in any one area of a country for the maintenance of law and order in peace time."

Only a few weeks before, Mountbatten had confidently

reassured Muslim leaders: "I will see to it that there is no bloodshed and riot. . . . I shall issue orders to see that there are no communal disturbances in the country. . . . I will order the army and the air force to act and I will use tanks and aeroplanes to suppress anybody who wants to create trouble." The Punjab Boundary Force was designed to do just that.

General Rees established his headquarters at Lahore and distributed his troops on both sides of the Indian-Pakistani border in the Punjab. The army's normal internal security role was to support the civil powers, but in many areas there were no civil powers; the police were unreliable and law and order had collapsed. One of the first tasks was to try to save Muslim families from the fury of the Sikhs.

To make the most economical use of the meagre troops available, Muslims were concentrated in and around villages which had wells and troops were posted to defend them. Such villages often grew to become badly crowded refugee camps, some with as many as fifty-thousand people huddled in them. The civil authorities issued a few bags of flour, but starvation swiftly became common. Hindu soldiers guarding the camps refused to allow Muslims to slaughter their bullocks, so Muslims and their animals died together. Military hospitals were set up, but there was neither enough trained staff nor enough medical supplies; thousands died of septicaemia. Refugees from one side or the other of the border arrived in these camps with tales of fresh horrors seen or heard of, adding to the general panic.

Following a massacre of Muslims in Hoshiarpur (population 27,000), Brigadier Wheeler visited the town and found the gaol full of Muslims who had been arrested for carrying crude weapons. Not a single Sikh or Hindu had been arrested, although only Muslims had been slaughtered. He discovered that the police had actually assisted the mobs, directing troops rushing to the rescue to the wrong locations. When Wheeler demanded that the chief of police, a Sikh, be removed, the Hindu authorities refused.

Often the people of an entire village were slaughtered and their houses put to the flame before soldiers could arrive on the scene. Large Sikh jathas roamed the countryside, concentrating in strength to attack a Muslim village or a column of refugees. Lieutenant-Colonel P. S. Mitcheson wrote:

> Motoring from Beas to Lahore, at a time when 100,000 Mussulmans on foot were making their way westward through Amritsar, in the course of fifty miles I saw between 400 and 600 dead. One attack on the refugees went in from thick crops while I was nearby. In a few minutes fifty men, women and children were slashed to pieces while thirty others came running back towards us with wounds streaming.

It was not a proper military task that faced Pete Rees and his Punjab Boundary Force. On 17 August he reported that his men were behaving splendidly, "firm and rock-like as the united Indian Army always has been when called on," but a week later he had to confess that he feared his force would explode into its communal elements.

Soldiers of all faiths knew that the British officers would soon be gone and that they were steadily losing their influence. As men saw their co-religionists slaughtered, they became less inclined to protect those not of their faith. Hindu and Sikh soldiers alike were subjected to much political propaganda, some of it from former INA men, urging them to desert with their rifles and join in the killing, or at least to look the other way when their co-religionists were doing the massacring. In addition, every soldier worried about his own family, for many, if not most, came from the Punjab; many Muslims had wives and children in India and many Hindu soldiers came from Rawalpindi or Peshawar. The dependability of the most dependable was being eroded.

The problem was political: now was the time for the political leaders of all communities to show their mettle and exercise real leadership by disciplining their followers; but both Nehru and Jinnah were busy holding political

meetings and Gandhi sought to solve the communal blood-
letting by entering upon still another fast unto death. No
Indian or Pakistani leader came near the chaotic Punjab to
quell the slaughter and dampen the hysteria. Instead, they
continued to do what they had spent a lifetime doing: bitterly criticizing the British. They now carped and complained of the British efforts to maintain order, particularly
the work of General Rees and the Punjab Boundary Force.
A lifetime of censure, complaint and opposition to government had not prepared them to assume responsibility for
their rhetoric, to seize the reins of government and govern.

Auchinleck, realizing that the task of the Punjab Boundary Force was not only thankless but hopeless, demanded
that each of the two new countries assume responsibility
for its side of the border. On 1 September 1947 Rees's command was dissolved, ending the last active unified force of
the old Indian Army of the British raj, although not the
communal slaughter. Until the end, the discipline and the
traditions of the Indian Army had held firm—but just. The
British Army in India had already started to leave.

The first unit to embark for home after Independence was
the 2nd Battalion of the Royal Norfolk Regiment. Mountbatten and Auchinleck stood in drizzling rain to bid them
farewell while the troops paraded on the quay and the bands
played "Auld Lang Syne." Auchinleck had wished to keep
British troops on Indian soil until at least the beginning of
1948, but he was overruled. Still, the last British troops did
not depart until 28 February 1948.

The 1st Battalion of the Somerset Light Infantry—a regiment which had first served in India more than a century
earlier—formed up near the Gateway to India, that huge
ornate arch on the Bombay waterfront marking the place
where the Prince of Wales had first set foot in India in 1911.
Indian and Gurkha troops were drawn up and at the familiar command came to the salute as their band played "God
Save the King"; the British band responded with *"Bande
Mataram"* (Hail to Thee, Mother), song of the Congress Party

and now India's new national anthem. Nehru and Mountbatten, too busy to attend, sent messages to be read.* After presents and compliments were exchanged, the King's Colour and the Regimental Colour were trooped to the waiting *Empress of Australia* and the last British soldiers sailed away.

After more than three hundred years, it was over. Finished. There were no longer, and would never be again, armies of the British raj in India.

---

* Mohandas Gandhi was unable to savour the departure of the last imperial British legions. He had been shot by another Hindu in Calcutta the previous month, a victim of the turmoil he had in large part created.

Appendix A

Indian Army Ranks and Badges

Officers:

Cavalry	Infantry	British Equivalents	Badge
Rissaldar-Major	Subedar-Major	—	crown
Rissaldar	Subedar	—	2 stars
Jemadar	Jemadar	—	1 star

Warrant Officers and Noncommissioned Officers:

Daffadar-Major	Havildar-Major	Sergeant-Major	Royal Arms
Daffadar	Havildar	Sergeant	3 chevrons
Lance Daffadar	Naik	Corporal	2 chevrons
Unpaid Lance Daffadar	Lance Naik	Lance Corporal	1 chevron
Sowar	Sepoy	Trooper or Private	none

Appendix B

The Indian Salute States in 1931

Name of State	Area in Square Miles	Title and Religion of Ruler	Gun Salute
Hyderabad	82,698 (excluding Berar)	Nizam; Sunni Muslim	21
Mysore	29,528	Maharaja; Hindu	21
Baroda	8,135	Maharaja; Hindu	21
Jammu and Kashmir	85,885	Maharaja; Hindu	21
Gwalior	26,382	Maharaja; Hindu	21
Udalpur (Mewar)	12,915	Maharana; Hindu	19
Kalat	73,278	Wali, Brahui; Sunni Muslim	19
Travancore	7,625	Maharaja; Hindu	19
Indore	9,519	Maharaja; Hindu	19
Bhopal	6,902	Nawab; Muslim	19
Kolhapur	3,217	Maharaja; Hindu	19
Jaipur	16,682	Maharaja; Hindu	17
Jodhpur (Marwar)	35,066	Maharaja; Hindu	17
Bundi	2,220	Maharao Raja; Hindu	17
Bikaner	23,315	Maharaja; Hindu	17
Kotah	5,684	Maharaja; Hindu	17
Karauli	1,242	Maharaja; Hindu	17
Bharatpur	1,982	Maharaja; Hindu	17
Kutch	7,616	Maharao; Hindu	17
Cochin	1,418	Maharaja; Hindu	17
Rewa	13,000	Maharaja; Hindu	17
Patiala	5,932	Maharaja; Sikh	17
Bahawalpur	15,000	Nawab; Muslim	17

Name of State	Area in Square Miles	Title and Religion of Ruler	Gun Salute
Bhutan	18,000	Maharaja; Buddhist	15
Sikkim	2,818	Maharaja; Buddhist	15
Kishengarh	858	Maharaja; Hindu	15
Jaisalmer	16,062	Maharawal; Hindu	15
Alwar	3,213	Maharaja; Hindu	15
Tonk	2,586	Nawab; Muslim	15
Dholpur	1,200	Maharaj Rana; Hindu	15
Sirohi	1,964	Maharao; Hindu	15
Dungarpur	1,447	Maharawal; Hindu	15
Pratapgarh	886	Maharawat; Hindu	15
Banswara	1,606	Maharawal; Hindu	15
Orchha	2,079	Maharaja; Hindu	15
Datia	911	Maharaja; Hindu	15
Dhar	1,777	Maharaja; Hindu	15
Dewas (Senior)	449	Maharaja; Hindu	15
Dewas (Junior)	419	Maharaja; Hindu	15
Rampur	893	Nawab; Muslim	15
Idar	1,669	Maharaja; Hindu	15
Khairpur	6,050	Mir; Muslim	15
Jhalawar	810	Maharaj Rana; Hindu	13
Junagadh	3,337	Nawab; Muslim	13
Nawanagar	3,791	Jam Sahib; Hindu	13
Bhavnagar	2,860	Maharaja; Hindu	13
Porbandar	642	Maharaja Rana Sahib; Hindu	13
Dhrangadhara	1,157	Maharaja Raj Sahib; Hindu	13
Palanpur	1,769	Nawab; Muslim	13
Jaora	601	Nawab; Muslim	13
Ratlam	693	Maharaja; Hindu	13
Benares	875	Maharaja; Hindu	13
Cooch Behar	1,318	Maharaja; Hindu	13
Tripura	4,116	Maharaja; Hindu	13

Name of State	Area in Square Miles	Title and Religion of Ruler	Gun Salute
Jind	1,259	Maharaja; Sikh	13
Nabha	928	Maharaja; Sikh	13
Kapurthala	630	Maharaja; Sikh	13
Rajpipla	1,518	Maharaja; Hindu	13
Radhanpur	1,150	Nawab; Muslim	11
Morvi	822	Maharaja; Hindu	11
Gondal	1,024	Maharaja; Hindu	11
Pudukkottai	1,179	Raja; Hindu	11
Samthar	180	Raja; Hindu	11
Panna	2,596	Maharaja; Hindu	11
Charkhari	880	Maharaja; Hindu	11
Ajaigarh	802	Maharaja; Hindu	11
Bijawar	973	Maharaja; Hindu	11
Baoni	121	Nawab; Muslim	11
Chhatarpur	1,130	Maharaja; Hindu	11
Sitamau	210	Raja; Hindu	11
Sailana	297	Raja; Hindu	11
Rajgarh	962	Raja; Hindu	11
Narsingarh	734	Raja; Hindu	11
Jhabua	1,336	Raja; Hindu	11
Barwani	1,178	Rana; Hindu	11
Ali Rajpur	836	Raja; Hindu	11
Tehri-Garhwal	4,500	Raja; Hindu	11
Manipur	8,456	Maharaja; Hindu	11
Sirmur	1,198	Maharaja; Hindu	11
Mandi	1,200	Maharaja; Hindu	11
Bilaspur	448	Raja; Hindu	11
Maler Kotla	168	Nawab; Muslim	11
Faridkot	643	Raja; Sikh	11
Chamba	3,216	Raja; Hindu	11
Suket	420	Raja; Hindu	11
Janjira	377	Nawab; Muslim	11
Cambay	350	Nawab; Shia Muslim	11
Chitral	4,000	Mehtar; Muslim	11 personal
Shahpura	405	Raja; Hindu	9
Wankaner	417	Raj Sahib; Hindu	9

Name of State	Area in Square Miles	Title and Religion of Ruler	Gun Salute
Palitana	289	Thakor Sahib; Hindu	9
Dhrol	283	Thakor Sahib; Hindu	9
Limbdi	344	Thakor Sahib; Hindu	9
Rajkot	282	Thakor Sahib; Hindu	9
Wadhwan	243	Thakor Sahib; Hindu	9
Bagnanapalle	255	Nawab; Muslim	9
Baraundha	218	Raja; Hindu	9
Nagod	501	Raja; Hindu	9
Maihar	407	Raja; Hindu	9
Khilchipur	273	Raja; Hindu	9
Patna	2,399	Maharaja; Hindu	9
Mayurbhanj	4,243	Maharaja; Hindu	9
Kalahandi	3,745	Raja; Hindu	9
Sonpur	906	Maharaja; Hindu	9
Loharu	222	Nawab; Muslim	9
Baria	813	Raja; Hindu	9
Lunawada	388	Raja; Hindu	9
Sachin	49	Nawab; Sunni Muslim	9
Sawantwadi	925	Sar Desai; Hindu	9
Dharampur	704	Raja; Hindu	9
Bansda	215	Raja; Hindu	9
Chhota Udepur	890	Raja; Hindu	9
Balasinor	189	Nawab; Muslim	9
Sant	394	Raja; Hindu	9
Mudhol	368	Raja; Hindu	9
Sangli	1,136	Chief; Hindu	9
Jawhar	310	Raja; Hindu	9
Danta	347	Maharana; Hindu	9
Bhor	925	Pant Sachiv; Hindu	9
Bashahr	3,820	Raja; Hindu	9 personal

436 Non-Salute States

Selected
Bibliography

Allen, Charles, and Sharada Dwivedi. *Lives of the Indian Princes*. New York: Crown, 1984.

Allen, Charles. *Plain Tales from the Raj*. London: Futura Publications, 1976.

Anon. *The Army in India and Its Evolution*. Calcutta: Government printing, 1924.

———. *Frontier and Overseas Expeditions from India*. 7 vols. Compiled in the Intelligence Branch, Army Headquarters, India, Simla, 1907–13.

———. *India's Services in the War*. Reprint of 1922 ed. (2 vols in 1) Delhi: B. R. Publishing Corp., 1985.

———. *The Tiger Strikes*. Calcutta: Government printing, 1942.

Ballhatchett, Kenneth. *Race Sex and Class Under the Raj: Imperial Attitudes and Policies and Their Critics, 1793–1905*. New York: St. Martin's Press, 1980.

Barnett, Correlli. *Britain and Her Army*. London: Allen Lane The Penguin Press, 1970.

Barr, Pat, and Ray Desmond. *Simla: A Hill Station in British India*. New York: Charles Scribner's Sons, 1978.

Barthorp, Michael. *The North-West Frontier: British India and Afghanistan*. London: Blandford Press, 1982.

Beaumont, Roger. *Sword of the Raj*. Indianapolis: Bobbs-Merrill, 1977.

Becke, Maj. A. F., comp. *History of the Great War based on Official Documents: Order of Battle of Divisions*. Nottingham: The Sherwood Press, n.d. [first published 1934].

Beckett, Ian F. W., ed. *The Army and the Curragh Incident, 1914*. London: Bodley Head for the Army Records Society, 1986.

Bhatia, H. S., ed. *Military History of British India (1607–1947)*. New Delhi: Deep & Deep, 1977.

Bishop, H. C. W. *A Kut Prisoner*. London: John Lane, Bodley Head, n.d. (c. 1920).

Braddon, Russell. *The Siege*. London: Jonathan Cape, 1969.

Bristow, Brig. R. C. B. *Memories of the British Raj: A Soldier in India*. London: Johnson, 1974.

Broehl, Wayne G. *Crisis of the Raj*. Hanover, N.H.: University Press of New England, 1986.

Bruce, George. *The Burma Wars*. London: Hart-Davis, MacGibbon, 1973.

Callwell, Col. C. E. *Small Wars*. 3rd ed. London: HMSO, 1906.

Chandler, Edmund. *The Sepoy*. London: John Murray, 1919.

Chandra, Dr. Amil. *Indian Army Triumphant in Burma*. Delhi and Lucknow: Atna Ram & Sons, 1984.

Chaudhuri, Nirad C. *Thy Hand, Great Anarch! India 1921–1952*. Reading, Mass.: Addison-Wesley, 1987.

Cloude, Charles M. *The Military Forces of the Crown: Their Administration and Government*. 2 vols. London: John Murray, 1869.

Cohen, Stephen P. *The Indian Army: Its Contribution to the Development of a Nation*. Berkeley: University of California Press, 1971.

Collins, Larry, and Dominique Laspierre. *Freedom at Midnight*. London: Collins, 1975.

Colvin, Ian. *The Life of General Dyer*. Edinburgh and London: William Blackwood & Sons, 1921.

Conran, Maj. H. M. *Autobiography of an Indian Officer*. London: Morgan & Chase, 1870.

Copland, Ian. *The British Raj and the Indian Princes: Paramountcy in Western India, 1857–1930*. London: Sangam, 1982.

Corr, Gerald H. *The War of the Springing Tigers*. London: Osprey, 1975.

Crewe, Quentin. *The Last Maharaja: A Biography of Sawai Man Singh II, Maharaja of Jaipur*. London: Michael Joseph, 1985.

Cross, Colin. *The Fall of the British Empire, 1918–1969*. London: Hodden & Stoughton, 1968.

Curzon, Lord. *Frontiers*. Oxford: Clarendon Press, 1908.

———. *A Viceroy's India: Leaves from Lord Curzon's Notebook*. London: Sidgwick & Jackson, 1984.

Das, Maj. Gen. Chand N. *Traditions and Customs of the Indian Armed Forces*. New Delhi: Vision Books, 1984.

Das, S. T. *Indian Military—Its History and Development*. New Delhi: Sagar Publications, 1969.

Dasgupta, S., ed. *Adventures of British Soldiers in India*. Calcutta: B. Mitra, 1980.

Dibley, George. "The Maizur Affair, 1897–98," *Soldiers of the Queen*. Nos. 41–44, 1986.

Draper, Alfred. *The Amritsar Massacre: Twilight of the Raj*. London: Buchan & Enright, 1985.

Durand, Col. Algernon. *The Making of a Frontier*. London: Thomas Nelson, n.d.

Edwardes, Michael. *Bound to Exile*. London: Sidgwick & Jackson, 1969.

———. *High Noon of Empire: India Under Curzon*. London: Eyre & Spottiswoode, 1965.

———. *Playing the Great Game*. London: Hamish Hamilton, 1975.

Elliott, Maj.-Gen. J. G. *The Frontier, 1839–1947*. London: Cassell, 1968.

———. *Unfading Honour: The Story of the Indian Army, 1938–1945.* New York: A. S. Barnes & Co., 1960.

Forbes, Rosita. *India of the Princes.* London: The Book Club, 1939.

Fraser, John. *Sixty Years in Uniform.* London: Stanley Paul, 1939.

Ghosh, K. K., *The Indian National Army.* Meerut: Meenakshi Prakashan, 1969.

Greenhut, Jeffrey. "The Imperial Reserve: The Indian Corps on the Western Front, 1914–15." *The Journal of Imperial and Commonwealth History,* October 1983.

———. "Sahib and Sepoy: An Inquiry into the Relationship Between the British Officers and the Native Soldiers of the British Indian Army." *Military Affairs,* January 1984.

Gordon, Leonard A. *Bengal: The Nationalist Movement, 1876–1940.* New York and London: Columbia University Press, 1974.

Grimshaw, Capt. Roly. *Indian Cavalry Officer, 1914–15.* London: Sidgwick & Jackson, 1969.

Gutteridge, William. "The Indianisation of the Indian Army, 1918–1945." *Race, Journal of the Institute of Race Relations,* May 1963.

Haley, A. H. *The Crawley Affair.* London: Seeley, Service, 1972.

Hamid, Maj.-Gen. Shahid. *Disastrous Twilight.* London: Leo Cooper/ Secker & Warburg, 1986.

Harper, R. W. E., and Harry Miller. *Singapore Mutiny.* Singapore: Oxford University Press, 1984.

Hawkey, Arthur. *Last Post at Mhow.* London: Jarrolds, 1969.

Heathcote, T. A. *The Indian Army: The Garrison of British Imperial India, 1822–1922.* Vancouver: David & Charles, 1974.

Hennel, Col. Sir Reginald. *A Famous Indian Regiment, the Kali Panchwin (2.5 [formerly the 105th] Mahratta Light Infantry), 1768–1923.* Delhi: B. R. Publishing Corp., 1927, reprinted 1985.

Hibbert, Christopher. *The Great Mutiny: India, 1857.* London: Allen Lane/Penguin Books, 1978.

Holder, Lt.-Col. Denzil. *Hindu Horseman.* Chippenham, Wilts.: Picton Publishing, 1986.

Innes, P. R. *The History of the Bengal European Regiment, Now the Royal Munster Fusiliers, and How It Helped to Win India.* Printed by the Army and Navy Cooperative Society, Westminster, n.d. (c. 1885).

Jackson, Maj. Donovan. *India's Army.* London: Sampson, Low, Marston, 1940.

James, Lawrence. *Mutiny in the British and Commonwealth Forces, 1797–1956.* London: Buchan & Enright, 1987.

Jensen, Joan M. *Passage From India: Asian Immigration in North America.* New Haven: Yale University Press, 1988.

Judd, Dennis. *The British Raj.* London: Weyland, 1972.

Kaminsky, Arnold P. "Morality Legislation and British Troops in Late Nineteenth Century India." *Military Affairs,* April 1979.

Keats, Clifford. *A Soldier's India.* Chapel-en-le-Frith, Derbys: Caron Publications, 1986.

Keppel, Arnold. *Gun Running and the India North-West Frontier.* London: John Murray, 1911.

King, Peter. *The Viceroy's Fall: How Kitchener Destroyed Curzon.* London: Sidgwick & Jackson, 1986.

Lal, Shiv. *India's Freedom Fighters in South-East Asia.* New Delhi: Archives Publishers, 1985.

Lawford, Lt.-Col. J. P., and Maj. W. E. Catto. *Solah Punjab: A History of the 16th Punjab Regiment.* Aldershot: Gale & Polden, 1967.

Leasor, James. *The Boarding Party.* Boston: Houghton Mifflin, 1979.

Longer, V. *Red Coats to Olive Green: A History of the Indian Army, 1600–1947.* New Delhi: Allied Publishers, 1974.

Lutyens, Mary. *The Lyttons in India: An Account of Lord Lytton's Viceroyalty, 1876–1880.* London: John Murray, 1979.

MacMunn, George. *Vignettes from Indian Wars.* London: Sampson, Low, Marston, n.d. (c. 1932.)

———. *The Armies of India.* London: A. & C. Black, 1911.

Mains, Lt.-Col. A. A. "The Auxiliary Force (India)." *Journal for Army Historical Research,* Autumn 1983.

——. "Joining the Ninth Gurkhas in the Thirties" (unpublished).

——. "Military Organization in India" (unpublished).

——. *The Retreat from Burma: An Intelligence Officer's Personal Story.* London: W. Foulsham, 1973.

——. "Sorrowful Departure" (unpublished).

Mason, Philip. *A Matter of Honour.* New York: Holt, Rinehart & Winston, 1974.

Maxwell, Leigh. *My God—Maiwand! Operations of the South Afghanistan Field Force, 1878–80.* London: Leo Cooper, 1979.

Merewether, Lt.-Col. J. W. B., and the Rt. Hon. Sir Frederick Smith. *The Indian Corps in France.* London: John Murray, 1918.

Miles, Eustace. *Let's Play the Game, or the Anglo-Saxon Sportsmanlike Spirit.* London: Guilbert Pitman, 1904.

Moore, R. J. *Churchill, Cripps and India, 1939–1945.* Oxford: Clarendon Press, 1979.

Moorhouse, Geoffrey. *India Britannica.* London: Paladin Books, Granada Publishing, 1983.

Morris, James [Jan]. *Heaven's Command: An Imperial Progress.* London: Faber & Faber, 1973.

Mosley, Leonard. *The Last Days of the Raj.* New York: Harcourt, Brace & World, 1961.

Palit, Maj.-Gen. D. K. *Jammu and Kashmir Arms: History of the Jammu and Kashmir Rifles.* Dehra Dun: Palit & Dutt, 1972.

Palmer, Roy, ed. *The Rambling Soldier.* Gloucester: Alan Sutton, 1985.

Perkins, Roger. *The Punjab Mail Murder: The Story of an Indian Army Officer.* Chippenham, Wilts.: Picton Publishing, 1986.

Pollock, Sam. *Mutiny for the Cause.* London: Leo Cooper, 1969.

Prasad, Sir Nandan. *The Expansion of the Armed Forces and Defence Organization, 1939–45.* India: Orient Longmans, 1956.

Rawlinson, H. G. *The History of the 2/6th Rajputana Rifles (Prince of Wales Own).* London: Oxford University Press, 1936.

Richards, Frank. *Old Soldiers Never Die*. London: Faber & Faber, 1933.

———. *Old Soldier Sahib*. n.p.: Harrison Smith & Robert Haas, 1936.

Roberts, Lord. *Forty-One Years in India*. 2 vols. London: Bentley, 1897.

Robinson-Horley, E. W. *Last Post: An Indian Army Memoir*. London: Leo Cooper/Secker & Warburg, 1922.

Rosenthal, Michael. *The Character Factory: Baden-Powell and the Origins of the Boy Scout Movement*. New York: Pantheon Books, 1986.

Rubin, Barnett. *Feudal Revolt and State-Building: The 1936 Sikar Agitation in Jaipur*. New Delhi: South Asian Publishers, 1983.

Sataw, Michael, and Ray Desmond. *Railways of the Raj*. New York and London: New York University Press, 1980.

Schofield, Victoria. *Every Rock, Every Hill: The Plain Tale of the North-West Frontier and Afghanistan*. London: Buchan & Enright, 1984.

Shakespear, Col. L. W. *History of the Assam Rifles*. Gauhati, India: Spectrum Publications, 1980 (reprint of U.K. ed. of 1929).

Sharp, Andrew. "The Indianisation of the Indian Army, 1918–1945." *History Today*, March 1986.

Sinclair-Stevenson, Christopher. *The Gordon Highlanders*. London: Hamish Hamilton, 1968.

Singer, Andre. *Lords of the Khyber: The Story of the North-West Frontier*. London: Faber & Faber, 1984.

Singh, Lt.-Col. Bawa Sundar. *Tradition Never Dies: The Genesis and Growth of the Indian Army*. Bombay: Lalvani, 1972.

Singh, Khushwant. *A History of the Sikhs*. Vol. 2: 1839–1974. Princeton, N.J.: Princeton University Press, 1966.

Skinner, Lt.-Col. M. A. R. *Sworn to Die*. New Delhi: Lancer International, 1984.

Smith, Vincent A. *The Oxford History of India*. London: Oxford University Press, 1923.

Spear, Percival. *A History of India*. Vol. 2. Baltimore: Penguin Books, 1956.

Stewart, A. T. Q. *The Pagoda War*. Newton Abbot, Devon: Victorian Book Club, 1974.

Swinson, Arthur. *Six Minutes to Sunset*. London: Peter Davies, 1964.

Trench, Charles Chenevix. *The Frontier Scouts*. London: Jonathan Cape, 1985.

Trevelyan, Raleigh. *The Golden Oriole*. New York: Viking, 1987.

Trollope, Joanna. *Britannia's Daughters: Women of the British Empire*. London: Hutchinson, 1983.

Tucker, Sir Francis. *While Memory Serves*. London: Cassell, 1950.

Tully, Mark, and Satish Jacob. *Amritsar: Mrs. Gandhi's Last Battle*. London: Jonathan Cape, 1985.

Warburton, Col. Sir Robert. *Eighteen Years in the Khyber, 1879–1898*. London: John Murray, 1900.

Warner, Philip. *Auchinleck, The Lonely Soldier*. London: Buchan & Enright, 1981.

Watson, Steven. "The British in India." *History Today*, IV (1954), pp. 92–101.

Western, Col. J. S. E. *Reminiscences of an Indian Cavalry Officer*. London: Allen & Unwin, 1922.

Wolpert, Stanley. *Jinnah of Pakistan*. London and New York: Oxford University Press, 1984.

Wylly, Col. H. C. *The Green Howards in the Great War*. Privately printed, 1926.

Yates, E. P. "General Dyer: Some Recollections." *Blackwood's Magazine*, December 1927.

Yeats-Brown, Francis. *The Lives of a Bengal Lancer*. New York: Viking, 1930.

———. *Martial India*. London: Eyre & Spottiswoode, 1945.

Younghusband, G. J. *The Story of the Guides*. London: Macmillan, 1909.

Index

italicized page numbers refer to illustrations

Abdul Rashid, Capt., 344
Abdur Rahman, amir of
    Afghanistan, 109
Abyssinia, conflicts with Britain,
    75–77
Act for the Government of India
    of 1935, 308–9
Addiscombe military college, 99
Aden, 19, 41
Afghanistan:
    boundary with India,
        determination of, 192
    British "forward policy" in, 108
    British Resident for, 108
    British-Russian competition for,
        105, 106
    conflicts with Britain, 106–18
    North-West Frontier, invasion
        of, 287–89
Afridis, 199, 200, 201, 203
Agror, Khan of, 68
Ahmadabad, 271
Akalkot, Raja of, 225–26
Allenby Field Marshal Edmund,
    99–100
All-India Congress, 330
All-India Muslim League, 309
Almora Akhbar (Hindu weekly),
    148

Alwar, Maharaja of (Jay Singh),
    164, 226
Amānollah Khān, amir of
    Afghanistan, 287
Amb, Khan of, 68
Amery, Leo, 300
Ampthill, Lord, 211–12
Amritsar, 182
Amritsar Incident (1919):
    army called in, 274–78
    British refugees, 273–74
    British reprisals against
        civilians, 283–85
    criticism of British actions,
        286–87
    discontent among Indians,
        causes of, 269–71
    investigation of, 289–90
    martial law, 279
    massacre of civilians, 280–82
    mass meeting of civilians, 278–
        80
    nationalist movement, impact
        on, 287, 290–91
    restoration of calm, 285–86
    rioting by civilians, 272–73
Andaman Islands, 19, 41
Anderson, Sgt. William, 279, 280
Andrew, Elizabeth Wheeler, 149

Anglo-Boer War (1899–1902), 191, 267n

Anglo-Indians, British attitude toward, 62

Anglo-Persian Oil Company, 254

Arbors, 70

Arrow War (Third China War), 73–75

asamis, 31

Atkinson, Capt. George Franklin, 95

atrocities and cruelty by soldiers, 59n, 205–7

Auchinleck, Field Marshal Sir Claude, 165–66, 319, 346, 354
  independence for India, 348, 356–58, 359, 360, 365
  on Indianization program, 298, 300
  on Indian National Army, 336–37, 342, 343

Aurungzeb (6th Mogul emperor), 16

Aylmer, Lt.-Gen. Sir Fenton, 258

Ayub Khan, 109–10, 111, 115, 118

Babus (educated Indians), 187–88

Baden-Powell, Lord, 102, 161–62

Ball, Capt. Lionel Plomer, 238, 242

Baluchis, 187

Barnard, Charles, 141

Barnett, Corelli, 326

Baroda, Gaekwar of, 71–73, 123, 226, 229

Barrow, Maj.-Gen. Sir Edmund, 214, 218, 219

Bashir Ahmed Khan, Maj., 322

Bawa Jawan Singh, Col., 297

Bawa Sundar Singh, Lt.-Col., 336, 343–44

Baxter, (batman), 101

Bengal, Nawab of, 17

Bengal Army, 25, 38–40, 43–45, 179

Bengal Presidency, 18, 19

Beresford, Lord William, 95

Besant, Annie, 271n

Bhagat, Gen. Premindra Singh, 314, *315*

bhistis (water carriers), 36

Bhopal, Begum of, 123, 234

Bhopal, Nawab of, 312

Bhopal Army, 233

Bhutan, 71

Bikaner, Maharaja of, 228, 312

Bikaner Camel Corps, 228–29, 232

Birdwood, Lord, 177

Black Mountain tribes, 68–69

Blavatsky, Elna Petrovna, 271n

Blaxland, Maj.-Gen. A. B., 341

Blood, Sir Bindon, 200

Blunt, Wilfrid Scawen, 141

Board of Control, 17

Bombay *Express*, 286

Bombay Army, 25

Bombay Presidency, 18

Bose, Subhas Chandra, 329–31, 333–35, 338

boxing, 166

"Boys' Battalions," 313

Boy Scouts, 102

Briggs, Capt. Frederic Cecil Currer ("Tommy"), 276, 279, 281

Bristow, Brig. R. C. B., 139, 183

British Army in India, 37, 54, 365–66
  see also regiments, battalions and divisions

British attitudes toward Indians:
  Anglo-Indians, attitude toward, 62
  arrogance and superiority in, 57–64
  British women and, 59–61
  government employment, Indians barred from, 63
  Mutiny of 1857, impact of, 63–64

other ranks, attitudes of, 167
"right to rule," 62–63
British Committee Against Vice,
151
British Empire, nature of, 17–18
British officers, 32–34, *91, 92, 94,
95*
arrogance of, 97
backgrounds of, 96
cantonments, 128–29, 131, *133*
children of, 132–33
clubs for, 97, 295
division of Indian Army and,
358–59
elites and lesser officers, 96
family life, 131–33
finances of, 90–93
hill stations for, 134–38, 140–41
holidays, celebration of, 103
homes of, *58*
homosexuality among, 141–42
as "Imperial class," 93
Indian culture, attitude toward,
138
Indian officers, reluctance to
serve with, 297–98
Indian service, avoidance of, 79
Indian soldiers, relations with,
97, 177
Jews, prejudice against, 102–3
marriage among, 101–2, 139–40
military education, 99–100
mistresses, native, 141
pay and allowances, 92–93
promotion, system of, 46, 79, 98
religious attitudes, 103–4
rules and customs, 93–95
servants, 131
sexual practices, 102, 138–42
social life, *130,* 131–32, *132,
134,* 137
soldiers, relations with, 100–
101
sports, involvement in, 157–58,
161

training for service in India,
97–98
Urdu, knowledge of, 98
vetting to regiments, 98–99
wives of, *60,* 131–33, 136, *136*
see also Crawley Affair
Broderick, St. John, 211–13, 214,
215
Brooke, Brig.-Gen. Henry Francis,
113–14, 115
Brooke, Col. James Croft, 227
Brownlow, Lt.-Col. Charles
William, 242, 243
Bryan, Florry, 225
Brydon, William, 106
Bundi, Maharao of, 312
Burma, 19, 141
annexation by Britain, 71
military responsibility for, 318–
19
World War II, 318–26
Burma Frontier Force, 319, 321
Burma Rifles, 319, 320
Burma Road, 320
Burmese National Army, 320
Burnell, A. C., 188*n*
Burrows, Brig.-Gen. George
Reynolds Scott, 110, 111–12,
114, 115
Burton, Richard Francis, 103
Bushnell, Kate, 149

Calcutta, 18
communal violence, 350–51
Camberley Staff College, 99
Cambridge, Duke of, 79, 81
Campbell, Gen. Sir Colin (Lord
Clyde), 47, 50
Campbell-Johnson, Alan, 362
Canning, Lord, 38, 48, 64
cantonments, 128–29, 131, *133*
Cantonments Act Amending Bill
of 1895, 150
Cardigan, Earl of, 88
Cariappa, K. M., 293

Cassells, Gen. Sir Robert Archibald, 306
castes, 171–72, 185
Cavagnari, Maj. Sir Pierre Louis, 96, 108
Cawnpore, 40
Central India Horse incident, 311
Ceylon, 19
Chamberlain, Sir Neville, 67
Chamber of Princes, 353
Chambers's Journal, 138
Chand, Tara, 43
Chapman, Maj.-Gen. Edward F., 146, 149
Charles I, king of England, 16
Charles II, king of England, 16, 25
Charter Act of 1833, 45*n*
Chelmsford, Lord, 285–86
Chiang Kai-shek, Generalissimo, 319–20
children of British officers, 132–33
China, conflicts with Britain, 32, 73–75
China War of 1859–60, 32
Chindit operations, 325
Chitral, Battle of (1895), 256–57
Christian missionaries, 39
Churchill, Winston S., 200, 286, 324
Clarke, Maj. Frank Scamander, 275
Clive, Robert, 17
clubs for British officers, 97, 295
Clyde, Lord (Sir Colin Campbell), 47, 50
Cobbe, Lt.-Gen. Alexander, 296
Cochin, Rajah of, 208
Collins, Larry, 129
Collis, Gunner James, 114
Collis, William, 147
Commander-in-Chief, India, office of, 27
Communists, 31, 345

Congress Party, 271, 309, 341–42, 345
Connaught, Duke of, 207, *208*
Conran, Maj. H. M., 103
Contagious Diseases and Cantonment Act of India of 1864, 144, 145
Copland, Ian, 198–99
Corfield, Conrad, 164
Cornwallis, Lord, 26
Cotton, Maj.-Gen. Sidney J., 67
Cotton, Maj. and Mrs. William L., 242
Cox, Gen. Herbert Vaughn, 237
Crampton, Capt. G. P., 274
Crawley, Lt.-Col. Thomas R., 81–84, 85, 86, 87–88
Crawley Affair (1861–63), 78
    aftermath, 88–89
    arrest of Smales, 86–87
    background of, 79–82
    court-martial of Smales, 84–86
    Crawley-Smales dispute, 82–84
    prosecution of Crawley, 87–88
Creagh, Gen. Sir O'Moore, 140, 170, 180, 182, 219
Crewe, Lord, 251
Crewe, Quentin, 225
cricket, 166
Crimean War, 79
Cripps, Sir Stafford, 309, 348–49
Cromwell, Oliver, 16
Ctesiphon, Battle of (1915), 256
Curtis, Maj.-Gen. Alfred ("Tiger"), 356
Curzon, Lady, 224
Curzon, Lord, 63, 141, *208*, 219
    atrocities by British troops, handling of, 205–7
    background of, 204–5
    durbar hosted by, 207–9
    Government of India, Kitchener's reforms for, 210–11, 212–14, 215

Indian Army, reforms for, 217–18

princes, policy toward, 223–24

resignation, 214–15

Dadu Dayal, 227

daffadars, 29

Daily Telegraph, 269

Dalison, Maj.-Gen. J. B., 361

Darjeeling hill station, 134

Dehra Dun Club, 97

Delgrada, Anita, 225

Delhi, 40, 147–48

Dewas, Maharaja of, 312

Dickens, Charles, 50

diet of soldiers, 37

Direct Action Day (1946), 350–52

Disraeli, Benjamin, 121

Diver, Maud, 132, 133

dog fighting, 161

Dogras, 187

dogs, regimental, 112–13, 16

Duff, Sir Beauchamp, 219

Dufferin, Lord, 146

Dungarpur, Maharawal of, 225

Durand, Col. Sir Mortimer, 192

Durand Line, 192

durbar in honor of Edward VII (1903), 207–9, *208*

Dutch East Indies, 327–28

Dyer, Alfred, 147–48

Dyer, Brig.-Gen. Reginald Edward Harry ("Rex"), 275–78, 279–85, 286, 288–90

economic exploitation of India, 57

educated Indians:
    recruited for World War I, 250–51
    rejected for military service, 180, 187–88

Edward VII, king of England, 59, 207

Edward VIII, king of England, 230

Egerton, Maj.-Gen. Charles, 214

"eight unit scheme," 298–99

Elgin, Lord, 203, 224

Elizabeth I, queen of England, 15

Elles, Gen. Sir Edmund, 211, 214

Emergency Commissioned Officers (ECOs), 301

Enfield rifle, 67

Engels, Friedrich, 43

The Englishwoman in India (Diver), 132, 133

Enver Pasha, 265

Ethiopian theatre in World War II, 314–16

falconry (hawking), 164

Faridkot, Maharaja of, 351

Farrell, Maj.-Gen. Francis Turnley, 83–84

Fateh Singh (Maharana of Mewar), 234–35

Fayrer, Joseph, *126*

field hockey, 157

Findlater, Piper George, 202

First Afghan War (1839–42), 106–7

"Fishing Fleet" (marriageable women visiting India), 61, *61*, 139–40, 160

Flying Tigers, 321

Fourteenth Army in Burma, 316, 317, 325

France, 26, 74–75
    World War I, 248–53

Fraser, Sgt. John, 161

Fraser, Lovat, 219

"Free India" movement, 334–35

Friend of India (newspaper), 292

From Sepoy to Subedar (Sita Ram Pande), 168–69

Frontiers, *see* North-East Frontier; North-West Frontier

Frontier Scouts, 55, 197, 198, 200, 288

Fujiwara, Maj. Iwaichi, 331, 332

Gandhi, Indira, 282n, 343n, 354n
Gandhi, Mohandas K., Mahatma,
    181, 219, 329
  assassination of, 366n
  Bose and, 330, 331, 338
  doublespeak by, 349n
  independence for India, 349,
    350–51, 354, 365
  on Indian National Army, 340,
    343
  passive resistance movement,
    271
  on princely states, 223
  "Quit India" movement, 324
  recruiting for Indian Army, 267
  World War II, activities during,
    309–10, 324
Ganga, Havildar, 249
Garhwalis, 186
George V, king of England, 266
George VI, king of England, 311,
    353, 356
Ghadr movement, 246
Ghalam Mohd, Naik, 300
Gibson (Englishman at Singapore
    Mutiny), 239–40
Gilgit Scouts, 55, 197
Gladstone, William, 108, 290
Goodwin, Col. Buster, 195
Goondas (gangsters), 350–51
Gopāl Krishna Gokhale, 218
Gorringe, Maj.-Gen. Sir George,
    258, 259, 261
Government Gazette, 224
Government of India, Kitchener's
    reforms for, 210–14, 215
Governor-General, office of, 17,
    27, 45
Govind Singh, Guru, 183, 185
Grant, Gen. James Hope, 74
Grant. Lt.-Gen. Sir Patrick, 50
Granth Sahib (Sikh holy book),
    183, 185
Gray, Lt. Douglas, 162–63

Great Tasmania tragedy (1860),
    48, 50
Greenhut, Jeffrey, 180, 252
Griffin, Sir Lepel Harry, 64
Grimshaw, Capt. Roly, 97, 101–2,
    103–4
Grimwood, Ethel St. Clair, 191
Guille, Maj. J. D., 314–16
Gurbakhsh Singh Dhillon, 340,
    341, 342
Gurkhas, 41, 52, 64, 186, 228
Gwalior, Maharaja of, 312
Gwalior Army, 227

Habībollāh Khān, amir of
    Afghanistan, 287
Hamid, Maj.-Gen. S. Shahid, 183
Hamilton, Lord George, 124, 141,
    207–8, 209, 218
Hamilton, Lt. Walter, 108
Hans Raj, 278–79, 280, 281
Har Dayal, 246
Hari Badhwar, Capt., 335
Hartley, Gen. Sir Alan Fleming,
    319
Hastings, Warren, 17
havildars, 29
Haynes, Lt. E. George, 157
Henn, Lt. Thomas Rice, 114
Hennell, Col. Sir Reginald, 58–59,
    74
hill stations, 134–38, 140–41
Himmatsinghji, Col. K. S., 343
Hindu Association of the Pacific
    Coast, 246
Hindu Congress, 309
Hinduism, 103, 171–72, 183
Hindu Kush range, 192
Hindus:
  conflicts with Muslims
    regarding independence, 309,
    310, 350–52, 360–65
  as sepoys and sowars, 171–72
Hindustani Fanatics, 66–67

Hitler, Adolf, 331
HMS *Cadmus*, 238, 242
Hobson-Jobson dictionary, 188n
Hoghton, Brig.-Gen. Frederick
 Aubrey, 244
homosexuality, 141–42, 145–46,
 217–18
Honourable East India Company,
 15–17, 45, 65, 174
Hooker, Sir Joseph, 69
Hope, Adm. James, 74
horse racing, *139*
hospitals:
 military, 38, 176–77
 for prostitutes, 146, 148
Hudson, Lt.-Gen. Sir Havelock,
 274, 289
Hugh-Jones, Brig. N., 321, 322
Hume, Allan Octavian, 218
Hunter, Lord, 286
Hunter Committee, 286, 289
Hutton, Lt.-Gen. Sir Thomas J.,
 319, 320
Hyderabad, Nizam of, 122, 207,
 234, 312, 353
Hyderabad Contingent, 233, 234
 id al-fitr, 264–5

Imperial Assemblage (1877), 120–
 27, *124*, *126*
Imperial Cadet Corps, 217–18
Imperial Service Troops, 227–32
INA, *see* Indian National Army
INA Relief Fund Committee, 344
independence for India, 347
 British Army in India,
  departure of, 365–66
 communal violence, 350–52,
  360–65
 Independence Day, 356, 360
 Indian Army, division of, 348,
  357–60
 interim Indian government, 354
 negotiations for, 348–49

partition, 350, 354–56
peace-keeping forces, 362–65
politicians' reaction to violence,
 364–65
princes' concerns about, 353–54
Sikhs' concerns about, 352–53
Independence For India League,
 330
Indian Air Force, 304, 312, 344
Indian Armoured Corps, 307
Indian Army, 18–19
 auxiliary units, 55
 cavalry-infantry ratio, 35
 class composition of regiments,
  32, 51
 Commander-in-Chief, 27
 Commissariat Department, 36–
  37
 contractors with, 36
 diet of soldiers, 37
 division of, at independence,
  348, 357–60
 European troops transferred
  from, 47–48, 50
 formation of, 25–26
 Imperial Cadet Corps, 217–18
 Indian and British soldiers,
  ratio of, 50–51
 infantry brigades, 38
 integration of regiments, 312–
  13
 medical services, 38, 176–77,
  297
 mercenaries in, 41, 169–70
 noncombatants with, 35–36
 noncommissioned officer ranks,
  29
 numbering of regiments, 52, 54
 presidential armies, 25, 26, 40
 profit-making by regiments, 31–
  32
 promotion system, 46–47, 54
 ranks, tier of, 28–30, 367
 recruits for, 26–27

Indian Army (*continued*)
 re-enlistment procedures, 34
 reforms under Curzon, 217–18
 religious instructors with, 36
 reorganization of 1858–61, 50–
  54
 reorganization of 1895, 40
 reorganization of 1902, 40–41,
  215–17
 "serve in any country"
  requirement of recruits, 54
 Sikhs' importance to, 185
 silladar system of cavalry
  regiments, 30–35, 52
 staff officers, 27
 transfer of power to Crown, 45–
  54
 transport facilities, 37
 uniforms, 32, 54, 77
 as volunteer army, 28
 weakness as fighting force, 41–
  42
 weapons for Indian troops, 54
 "White Mutiny" of 1859, 48
 World War II, failure to prepare
  for, 303–7
 see also British officers; Indian
  officers; "martial races"
  theory; Mutiny of 1857;
  regiments, battalions and
  divisions; sepoys and sowars
Indian Civil Service (ICS), 63, 93,
 330
Indian Commissioned Officers
 (ICOs), 300
Indian Distinguished Service
 Medal (IDSM), 173
Indian General Service Medal,
 174
Indianization program, 218
 British reluctance regarding,
  300–301
 Indian officers, training of, 292–
  302

in Medical Service, 297
 as political issue, 297, 299, 300
 World War II as impetus for,
  301
Indian Legion, 331
Indian Military Academy (IMA),
 299–300, 301
Indian National Army (INA), 303,
 328
 battlefield performance, 337
 Bose's accession to leadership,
  333–35
 British attitude toward, 336–38
 disbanding of, 338
 formation of, 331–33
 "Free India" movement, 334–35
 Indian attitude toward, 335–36
 Japanese attitude toward, 333,
  335
 nationalist movement's support
  for soldiers, 340–44, 346–47
 number of recruits, 334
 post-war treatment of soldiers,
  339–44
 POWs refusing to join, 335
 women soldiers, 334
Indian National Congress, 218
Indian National Navy (INN), 345
Indian officers, 174, 177–78
 battlefield performance, 301–2
 British officers' reluctance to
  serve with, 297–98
 clubs, membership in, 295
 discrimination experienced by,
  294–95
 military education, 217–18, 296,
  298, 299–300, 301
 segregated regiments, assigned
  to, 298–99
 training of officers as part of
  Indianization program, 292–
  302
 World War I, training for, 292–
  93

World War II, training for, 301
Indian Order of Merit (IOM), 173–74
Indian Staff College, 100
Indian State Forces, 232–35
Indore, Maharaja of (Tukoji Rao Holkar), 222
Indore, Maharaja of (Yeshwant Rao Holkar), 225
industry in India, 308
Ipi, Faqir of, 310
Irving, Sir Miles, 276–77, 278
Iskander Mirza, Col., 293
Islam, 103
    see also Muslims
Ismay, Field Marshal Lord, 358

jackal baiting, 161
jackal hunting, 159–60, *160*
Jagatjit Singh (Maharaja of Kapurthala), 225
Jaipur, Maharaja of (Sawai Man Singh II), 158, 165, 233, 311–12
Jaipur Army, 226–27, 233–34
Jallianwalla Bagh, 279–80, 282, 286
James I, king of England, 15
James, Cmdr. A. G. Trevenen, 160
James, Lionel, 202–3
Jammu Army, 233
Jang Bahadur, Rama Jodha (of Napal), 231
Japanese Indian Forces (JIF), see Indian National Army
Jats, 185
Jay Singh (Maharaja of Alwar), 164, 226
jemadars, 29
Jews, officers' prejudice against, 102–3
Jhansi, Rani of, 334n
"Jim Crow regiments," 298
Jinnah, Mohammed Ali, 219, 270,

298, 309, 310, 345, 350, 352, 364–65
Johore, Sultan of, 243

Kaiser-i-Hind Medal, 267
Kamal Ram, Subedar, 314
Kandahar, 110, *110*, 113, 114
    siege of (1880), 115–16, 118
Kapur Singh, Jemadar, 249
Kapurthala, Maharaja of (Jagatjit Singh), 225
Kashmir, Maharaja of, 353
Kashmir Army, 228, 233
Kathiawar peninsula, 72n
Khadir Cup, 162–63
khaki uniforms, 77
Khalsa (religious and military fraternity), 183
Khelat, Khan of, 121, 123
Khitab Gul, Subedar-Major, 264–65, 268–69
Khudadad Khan, Subedar, 250
Khudu Khels, 67
Khyber Pass, 200–203
Khyber Rifles, 55, 197, 200, 288
Kim (Kipling), 106
King's Commission Officers (KCOs), 30, 294
Kinlock, Capt. Bruce, 322
Kipling, Lockwood, 123, 135
Kipling, Rudyard, 106, 121, 123, 151, 222, 290
Kirti Lehar ("Peasant Movement"), 311
Kitchener, Lord, 100, 195, 206, 208–9
    departure from India, 219
    Government of India, reform of, 210–14, 215
    Indian Army, reorganization of, 40–41, 215–17
    on "martial races" theory, 217
    on nationalist movement, 218–19

Kitchener, Lord (*continued*)
  personality of, 209–10
  prostitution, policy on, 151–52
  World War I, 253
kotes (armories), 30*n*
Kumaonis, 186–87
Kumar Gopal Saran Narain Singh
  (Maharaja of Tikari), 231
Kurram Militia, 55, 197
Kut-al-Amara, Battle of (1915),
  256, 257–62

Lahore, 284–85
Lakshmi Swaminathan, Capt., 334
Lansdowne, Lord, 225
Lapierre, Dominique, 129
Lauterbach, Oberleutenant sur
  Zee Julius, 241
Lawrence, Maj. Stringer, 25
Legge, Col. Heneage, 207
Le Marchant, John Gaspard, 99
Lichfield, Bishop of, 148
Lilley, Clarissa, 85, 87, 88
Lilley, Sgt.-Maj. John, 85–86, 87
Linlithgow, Marquess of, 309, 311,
  324
Lockhart, Sir Rob, 360
Lockhart, Sir William, 201, 202,
  206
lock hospitals, 146, 148
Love-Montgomerie, Lt. J. H., 240
Lucknow, 40
Lumsden, Lt.-Gen. Harry, 77
Lushais, 71
Lytton, Edith, Countess of, 123,
  136
Lytton, Lord, 105, 108, 188
  background of, 124–25
  Imperial Assemblage, 120, 121–
    22, 123, 125–26, 127
  at Simla, 137, 140–41

McCallum, Lt. Frank, 274
MacLagan, Sir Edward, 289

M'Math, Capt. William Hamilton,
  112
MacMunn, Gen. George, 25, 44,
  128, 170, 180, 182, 201
Madras Army, 25, 180
Madras Club, 295
Madras Presidency, 18, 25
Magdala, 76
Maidan Valley, 202
Maiwand, Battle of (1880), 110–15
Malakand Pass, 200
Mallaby, Brig. A. W., 327, 328
Malta, 75
Mansergh, Maj.-Gen. E. C., 328
Mansfield, Maj.-Gen. Sir William,
  84, 85
Marshall, Mrs. D., 240
Marshman, John Clark, 106–7
"martial races" theory, 51
  British belief in, 179–82, 190
  classes considered martial, 186–
    87
  educated Indians and, 180, 187–
    88
  Kitchener's perspective on, 217
  modern pespective on, 187
  non-martial classes, battlefield
    performance of, 189–90
  northern men, superiority of,
    181, 182
  recruitment of martial classes,
    188–89
  Sikhs favored by, 182–86
  southern men, inferiority of,
    180–81
Martin, Lt.-Col. Edward Victor,
  238, 242, 245
Marx, Karl, 43
Mason, Philip, 93, 96, 129
masturbation, attitudes toward,
  145–46
Masuds, 68
Mayo College, 218
Mazhabis, 185–86

medals and awards for soldiers, 172–74
medical services, military, 38, 176–77, 297
Meerut Tent Club, 162
Mehmed V, sultan of Turkey, 236
Meinertzhagen, Richard, 164
Menpes, Mortimer, 209
Meos, 357
Mers, 187
Mesopotamian theatre of World War I, 253–54, 256–66
Messervy, Sir Frank, 360
Mewar, Maharana of (Fateh Singh), 234–35
Mianas, 71–72
Mias, 71–72
Miles, Eustace, 156
military education:
    for British officers, 99–100
    for Indian officers, 217–18, 296, 298, 299–300, 301
Minto, Lord, 215, 219
Miris, 70
mistresses of British officers, 141
Mitcheson, Lt.-Col. P. S., 364
Mohammed Aslam, Maj. Sardar, 200
Mohan Singh, Capt., 331–32, 333, 334, 343
Mohmands, 201
Monro, Gen. Sir Charles C., 288, 289
Monro, Col. W., 141
Montagu, Edwin, 270, 285
Monteith, Lt. Arthur Mackworth, 113
Montgomerie, Col. D., 58
Moore, William James, 145
Moplahs, 71
Morning Post, 290, 297
Mosley, Leonard, 349, 354
Mountbatten, Lord, 326–27, 347, 353, 354, 355, 356, 357, 358, 360, 362–63, 365, 366
Muhammad Hasan, Subedar-Major, 264–65
Mullane, Sgt. Patrick, 114
Muscat, Imam of, 123
Muslim League, 344, 354
Muslims, 183, 186
    conflicts with Hindus regarding independence, 309, 310, 350–52, 360–65
    Islamic religion, 103
    in World War I, 236–37, 244
    see also Singapore Mutiny of 1915
Mussolini, Benito, 331
Mussoorie hill station, 134
mutineers of post-World War II period, 344–46
Mutiny of 1857, 40, 44–45
    British attitudes toward Indians, impact on, 63–64
    causes of, 38–39, 44
    political aspects, 43–44
    in Yusafzai country, 65–66

Nabha, Rajah of, 208
Nagas, 71, 227
naiks, 29
Naini Tal hill station, 134
Nānak Chand, 183
Napier, Gen. Sir Robert, 75–77
nationalist movement, 44
    Amritsar Incident as impetus for, 287, 290–91
    beginnings of, 218–19
    Ghadrites, 246
    INA soldiers, support for, 340–44, 346–47
    Indianization program and, 297, 299, 300
    princes, attitude toward, 222–23

Nationalist movement (*continued*)
  "Quit India" movement, 324,
    333–34
  representative government,
    movement toward, 308–9
  Rowlatt Act and, 270–71
  satyagraha (passive resistance)
    movement, 271
  World War II, activities during,
    308–11, 324
  see also Mutiny of 1857
Nawanagar, Jam Sahib of, (K. S.
    Ranjitsinhji), 222*n*, 231
Nehru, Jawaharlal, 219, 309, 329,
    330, 345, 355, 360, 366
  Amritsar Incident, influence of,
    287
  communal violence, response
    to, 352, 364–65
  INA soldiers, defence of, 341,
    342, 343*n*, 346–47
Nehru, Moti Lal, 298
Nepal, 41
Nepalese War of 1816–17, 69
Nesselrode, Count Karl, 106
Netherlands, 16
Newbolt, Sir Henry, 156*n*
Nicholson, Lt.-Col. John ("Lion of
    the Punjab"), 19, 66
Nightingale, Florence, 144–45,
    166–67
Nixon, Gen. Sir John Eccles, 254,
    256
North-East Frontier, 69–71, 191
North-West Frontier, 192
  administration of, 207
  Afghan invasion of, 287–89
  boundary determination, 192
  defence system for, 197–98
  independent tribal territory,
    193
  political officers in, 198–200
  roads, 198
  sport in, 160, 164

  tours of duty in, 195, 197
  tribes' relations with British,
    193–95
  warfare in, 65–69, 200–203,
    202, 287–89
Nur Alam Shah, 246
Nur-ed-Din, 257

O'Dwyer, Sir Michael, 277, 279,
    282, 285, 286, 289
officers, *see* British officers; Indian
    officers
Oghi, 68, 69
Ogilvie, Vere, 131
Okhamandal, 72–73
Ootacamund hill station, 134
opium trade, 69, 73–75
Orakzais, 201
Order of the Indian Empire, 121
Order of the Star of India, 121
Orgill, Maj. Richard C., 321–22

Pakistan, creation of, 350, 357
Palmer, Sir Arthur Power, 206
Panjtar, 66, 67
Parry, Lt.-Col. Frederick William
    Best, 146–47
Patel, Sardar Vallabhai, 329, 345
Paterson, Capt. G. F., 292–93
Pathans, 115, 160, 187, 237
  British attitude toward, 193–95
  conflicts with British, 65, 66–
    67, 69, 202–3
  relationships within tribes, 196
Patiala, Maharaja of, 225
Patiala Army, 233
Payn, Lt.-Col. William, 84
Peal, Viscount, 297
Peel, Maj.-Gen. Jonathan, 50
Peel Commission, 50–52, 54, 55
Peirse, Air Chief Marshal Sir
    Richard, 357
Persia, Indian troops in, 268

Peshawar Club, 295
Phayre, Lt.-Col. Robert, 226
pigsticking, 161–63, *162*
Pigsticking or Hog Hunting
    (Baden-Powell), 162
The Pioneer (English-language
    newspaper), 137–38
Pir Pagaro, 310
police forces, 55
political officers:
    in Afghanistan, 108
    in North-East Frontier, 191
    in North-West Frontier, 198–
    200
    in princely states, 225–26
polo, 157–59
Pondichéry, 26
"poodle-faking," 140
Prendergast, Brig. John, 157
presidencies, 18, 19
Primrose, Lt.-Gen. James, 110,
    115–16
princely armies, 55, 226–27
    commanders of, 228–29
    Imperial Service Troops, 227–
    32
    Indian State Forces, 232–35
    ranks, tier of, 233
    in World War I, 229–30, 231–
    32, 234
Prince of Wales Indian Military
    College, 296
princes:
    anglicization of, 223
    British military assistance to
        friendly princes, 71–73
    British policy toward, 220–21
    classes of princely states, 221
    Curzon's policy toward, 223–24
    deposed by British, 225–26
    at durbar honoring Edward VII,
        207–8
    at Imperial Assemblage, 121–
        22, 123

    independence, concerns about,
        353–54
    marriages to Europeans, 224–26
    as military commanders, 228–
        29, 230–31
    nationalists' attitude toward,
        222–23
    people's attitude toward, 223
    perquisites of European royalty
        denied to, 222
    political officers assigned to,
        225–26
    titles of, 222
    World War II, participation in,
        311–12
Prinsep, Valentine ("Val"), 121,
    122, 125, 126–27, 137
Prior, Melton, *208*
prostitution, military's regulation
    of:
    brothel conditions, 149, 153–54
    fees of prostitutes, 149
    Kitchener's policy, 151–52
    opponents of military policy,
        147–49, 150, 151
    recommendations for regula-
        tion, 144–46, 148, 150–51
    recruitment of prostitutes, 146–
        47
    separate facilities for British
        and Indian soldiers, 149–50
Pudukkottai, Raja of, 224
"pukka," meaning of, 131
pukhtunwali, 195
Punjab, 182
Punjab Boundary Force, 362–65
Punjab Irregular Field Force ("Pif-
    fers"), 27, 197

Quetta, 288
Quinsaps, 172
"Quit India" movement, 324,
    333–34

Radcliffe, Cyril, Viscount, 355–56
"raj," meaning of, 18
Rajputs, 187
Rangoon, 320, 323, 326
Rangoon Incident (1899), 205–6
Ranjit Singh, 184
Ranjitsinhji, K. S. (Jam Sahib of
    Nawanagar), 222*n*, 231
Rawlinson, Lord, 296–97, 298
Reading, Marquess of, 297
Red Fort, 340–41
Rees, Maj.-Gen. Thomas W.
    ("Pete"), 362, 363, 364, 365
Batalions, regiments and divi-
    sions:
  Bombay Sappers and Miners,
    114, 118
  Boys Battalion, 313
  Duke of Wellington's Regiment,
    321
  Escort for His Britannic Majes-
    ty's Envoy Extraordinary and
    Minister Plenipotentiary at
    the Court of Nepal, 41
  Gordon Highlanders, 202
  Highland Light Infantry, 251
  Jacob's Horse, 32
  Jacob's Rifles, 111
  Probyn's Horse, 32
  Queen's Own Corps of Guides,
    33, 66, 76, 77
  Queen's Own Madras Sappers
    and Miners, 172, *173,* 187
  Viceroy's Bodyguard, *33*
  1st Battalion of the Somerset
    Light Infantry, 365
  1st Bengal Cavalry, *33*
  1st Black Watch, 261
  1st Burma Brigade, 319
  1st Burma Division, 319
  1st Nabha Akal Infantry, 312
  1st Punjab Cavalry, *33*
  1st Seaforth Highlanders, 261
  1st Sikh Infantry, *33*

  1st Skinner's Horse, 32, 159
  1st West Kent Regiment, 205
  2nd Battalion of the East Kent
    Regiment, 147
  2nd Battalion of the Royal Nor-
    folk Regiment, 365
  2nd Burma Brigade, 319
  2nd Goorkhas (Prince of Wales's
    Own), *73*
  2nd Somerset Light Infantry,
    287
  3rd Baluch Regiment, *172*
  3rd Bengal Cavalry, *33, 173*
  3rd Indian Cavalry, 335
  3rd Light Cavalry, 40
  4th Battalion of the King's Own
    Shropshire Light Infantry,
    243
  4th Battalion of the Rifle Bri-
    gade, 147
  4th Gurkha Rifles, *33* 1/4th, 252,
    321
  4th Indian Division, 311
  5th Indian Division, 328
  5th Indian Light Infantry, 237–
    46, 253
  5th Royal Gurkhas, 360
  6th Gurkhas: 1/6th, 317
  6th (Inniskilling) Dragoons, 78–
    88
  6th Jats, 261
  6th (Poona) Division, 254
  6th Royal Sussex: 2/6th, 274
  7th Bengal Native Infantry, *175,*
    305
  7th Gurkhas: 2/7th, 260
  7th Rajputs: 5/7th, 318
  9th Bhopals, 252
  9th Gurkha Rifles: 1/9th, 274
  9th Lancers (Queen's Royal
    Lancers), 158, 206–7, 208–9
  10th Bengal Lancers, 171
  10th Hussars, 158
  10th Indian Division, 317, 362

11th Bengal Lancers, 32, *171*
11th Bengal Native Infantry, 40
13th Duke of Connaught's Bengal Lancers, *33*
13th Indian Brigade, 319
14th Murray's Horse, 32
14th Punjabis: 1/14th, 332 2/14th, 318
14th Sikhs, 166, *184*
15th Bengal Lancers (Fane's Horse), 32, *33*
15th Multani Cavalry (Curetan's), 32, 33
15th Sikhs, 251–52
16th Indian Brigade, 319, 321
17th Dogras, 313
17th Indian Division, 319
18th Bengal Infantry, *33*
19th Bengal Lancers, 32
20th Bengal Native Infantry, 40
21st King George V's Own Horse (Central India Horse), 308, 311, 323–24
25th London Regiment: 1/25th, 288
25th Punjab Cavalry, *229*
27th Light Cavalry, 34–35
28th Light Cavalry, 34–35
29th Punjabis, 166
33rd Punjabis, 41
34th Bengal Native Infantry, 39
34th Pioneers, 292
34th Poona Hobe, 101
39th Foot, 26
45th Sikhe (Ratlray's), 33
47th Indian Brigade, 319, 321
45th Sikhs, 251
48th Indian Brigade, 319, 320, 321
49th Bengalis, 179
49th Brigade, 327, 328
51st Regiment (King's Own Yorkshire Light Infantry), 145
55th Bengal Native Infantry, 66

57th Rifles (Wilde's), 249
62nd Punjabis, 51
66th (Berkshire) Regiment of Foot, 112–14
96th Foot, 67
103rd Indian Infantry, 260
103rd Mahrattas, 189
110th Mahrattas, 189
117th Mahrattas, 189
120th Rajputana Rifles, 264, 268
124th Baluchis: 1/124th, 274
129th Duke of Connaught's Own Baluchis, 249–50, 251, 252, 253
Renshaw, Capt. and Mrs. Richard William, 82–83, 88–89
Residency at Lucknow, 356
Rewa, Maharaja of, 229
Richards, Pvt. Frank, 149–50, 153–54, 161
Ridout, Brig.-Gen. Dudley Howard, 237–38, 243
Ridout, Mrs. Dudley Howard, 238, 240
rissaldars, 28, 29
Roberts, Field Marshal Lord, 76, 109, 116, 118–19, 146, 150, 177–78, 180–81, 211, 213
Robinson-Horley, E. W., 361–62
Rommel, Field Marshal Erwin, 331
Roos-Keppel, Sir George, 237, 287
Rose, Gen. Sir Hugh, 47, 80–81
Ross, Alexander Clark, 144
Rowlatt, Sir Sidney, 270
Rowlatt Act, 270–71
Royal Air Force (RAF), 160, 319, 321, 342, 344
Royal Army Medical Corps, 38
Royal Artillery in India, 36, 118
Royal Indian Army Service Corps, 37

Royal Indian Navy, 304
    mutiny of 1946, 344–46
Royal Regiment of Artillery, 37–
    38
the rupee, 27*n*
Russell, George, 150
Russell, William, 138
Russia, threat to India, 105–6,
    118–19, 227

Safed Koh range, 192
Sahgal, P. K., 340, 341, 342
Salisbury, Lady, 211, 218
Salisbury, Lord, 105
Salute States, 221, 368–371
Sandeman, Lt.-Col. Arthur P.,
    323–24
Sandhurst military college, 293–
    94
sanitary conditions around bar-
    racks, 166–67
San-ko-lin-sin, Gen. (Sam Collin-
    son), 74
Sarat Chandra Das, 106
satyagraha (passive resistance)
    movement, 271
Sawai Man Singh II (Maharaja of
    Jaipur), 158, 165, 233, 311–12
Schenkl, Emilie, 331
Scott, Maj.-Gen. J. Bruce, 319
Secretary of State for India, office
    of, 17
The Sentinel, 148
sepoys and sowars, 29, *33*, 37, 39,
    76, *171*, *172*, *173*, *175*, *184*,
    229
    barracks provided for, 174–75
    customs, importance of, 170–72
    enlistment, reasons for, 169–70
    Hindus, 171–72
    information sources on, 168–69
    language problem, 176
    loyalty to British, 170
    medals and awards for, 172–74

medical services for, 176–77
    as mercenaries, 169–70
    officers, relations with, 177
    peace-time service, 176
    polo ponies, training of, 158–59
    retirement and pensions, 174
    southerners, British attitude
        toward, 180–81
    training for, 177
    wages, 175–76
Seringapatam, Battle of (1791), 26
sexual practices of British officers,
    102, 138–42
sexual practices of soldiers, *see*
    prostitution, military's regu-
    lation of; veneral disease
    problem
Shahid Hamid, 351–52
Shah Nawaz Khan, Capt., 331,
    338, 340, 341, 342
Sher Ali, amir of Afghanistan,
    107–8
Sherwood, Manuella ("Marcia"),
    273, 284
Shirley, Maj. Sewallis Robert,
    283–84
shooting for sport, 159, 165–66
Shute, Lt.-Col. Charles Cameron,
    79, 80
Sikhs:
    conflicts with British, 184–85,
        206
    conflicts with Muslims at inde-
        pendence, 360–65
    independence, concerns about,
        352–53
    as martial race, 182–86
Sikkim, conflicts with British, 69–
    70
silladar system of cavalry regi-
    ments, 30–35, 52
Simla hill station, 134–38, 140–41
Singapore Mutiny of 1915, 237
    collapse of, 242–43

court of inquiry report, 244–46
execution of mutineers, 243–44
internment camp, capture of,
    240–42
murder of British citizens, 239–
    40
mutiny on ship, 237–39
revolutionaries' role in, 246–47
Singh, Sir Pertab, 97, 230–31
Singh, Sumer, 231
Sinha, Satyendra Prasanno, 286
Sita Ram Pande, Subedar, 168–69
Sittang River bridgehead, 320–23
Skinner, Col. James, 96, 199
Skinner, Lt.-Col. M. A. R., 32–33
Slim, Field Marshal Sir William
    Joseph, 316–17, 323, 325–27,
    337
Smales, Capt. Thomas, 82–83, 84,
    85, 86–87, 88
Smith, Lt.-Col. Henry, 272, 278
Smith, Maj.-Gen. Sir John G., 319,
    320, 322, 323
Smuts, Jan, 17
soccer, 166
South-East Asian theatre in World
    War II, 316, 317, 318–26
southern Indians, British attitude
    toward, 180–81
Southey, Capt. John, 276
South Persia Rifles, 268
South Waziristan Militia, 197
South Waziristan Scouts, 55
sowars, see sepoys and sowars
sport, 155
    boxing, 166
    British and Indian teams, com-
        petition between, 155–56
    British attitude toward, 156–57
    cricket, 166
    dog racing, 161
    falconry (hawking), 164
    field hockey, 157
    horse racing, *139*

jackal baiting, 161
jackal hunting, 159–60, *160*
pigsticking, 161–63, *162*
polo, 157–59
shooting, 159, 165–66
soccer, 166
swimming, 166
tent-pegging, 163, *163*
tiger hunting, 163–64, *165*
tug-of-war, 166
Stanley, Henry M., 76
Stansfeld, H. H., 59
Stewart, Lt.-Gen. Sir Donald, 109,
    116
Straits Times, 239
Stuart, James, 148
subedars, 28, 29
Suez Canal, 59, 61
Swaraj Party, 330
Swat, 200, 201
swimming, 166

Tagore, Sir Rabindranath, 286–87
Tamashita, Lt.-Gen. Tomoyuki,
    332
Tara Singh, 352, 360
tea production, 69
tent-pegging, 163, *163*
Terauchi, Field Marshal Count,
    338
Thailand, 327
Theodore, king of Abyssinia, 75,
    76
Thesiger, Capt. Charles Wemyss,
    80, 88
Third Afghan War, 287–89
Third Burma War, 71
Third China War (Arrow War),
    73–75
Tibet, 70
tiger hunting, 163–64, *165*
Tikari, Maharaja of (Kumar Gopal
    Saran Narain Singh), 231
The Times, 78, 88, 122

The Times of India, 199, 219
Tippoo Sahib ("Lion of Mysore"), 26
Tirah campaign (1897–98), 201–3, *202*, 228
Tochi Scouts, 55, 197
Tochi Valley, 201
Tomlin, Mrs. F. L., 240
Townshend, Maj.-Gen. Sir Charles V. F., 254, 256–57, 258, 259–60, 261, 262, 263, 265, 266
Travancore, Rajah of, 208
Treaty of Defence (British-Dutch—1619), 16
Treaty of Gandamak (British-Afghan—1879), 108
tug-of-war, 166
troopships, life on board, *49*
Tuker, Lt.-Gen. Sir Francis, 100, 154, 337, 343, 346, 348, 350–51
Tukoji Rao Holkar (Maharaja of Indore), 222
turbans, 184
Turnbull, Gavin Ainslie, 82–83, 86, 88

Udham Singh, 282
Umedwar (hopeful) book, 188
uniforms of soldiers, 32, 54, 77
Untouchables, 189–90
Urdu language, 98, 176

Valera, Eamon de, 335
varmas, 171
VCOs, *see* Viceroy's Commissioned Officers
venereal disease problem, 143–44, 145, 148, 150–51, 152–53
Viceroy, office of, 17, 19, 45
Viceroy's Commissioned Officers (VCOs), 28, 30, 177, 293, 299
Victoria, queen of England, 45, 112, 120, 203, 217, 221, 292, 353

Victoria Cross, 108, 114–5, 174, 231, 250, 314–5, 319
Vitai Lampada (Newbolt), 156*n*

Waghers, 72, 73
Wales, Edward Prince of, 124, 126
Wales, Edward, Prince of (later Duke of Windsor), 230–1
"wallah," meaning of, 62*n*
Wana Militia, 288
Warburton, Col. Robert, 67, 96, 199–200
warfare:
　in Abyssinia, 75–77
　in Afghanistan, 106–18
　British assistance to friendly princes, 71–73
　in China, 32, 73–75
　in North-East Frontier, 69–71, 191
　in North-West Frontier, 65–69, 200–203, *202*, 287–89
　against Sikhs, 184–85
　see also World War I; World War II
Warrant of Precedence (book on social precedence), 132
Wavell, Gen. Sir Archibald Percival, 221, 313, 319, 348, 349*n*, 354, 356
Wazirs, 68
Weir, Capt. Archibald, 80, 81, 86, 88
Western, Col. J. S. E., 101, 161, 164, 181, 197
Westminister, Duke of, 290
Wheeler, Brig., 363
Wheeler, Maj. George Godfrey Massey, 254
White, Gen. Sir George, 213
"White Mutiny" of 1859, 48
Willcocks, Gen. Sir James, 250–51, 252, 253
Williams, Maj. Clifford H., 361

Willingdon Sports Club, 97
Winchester, Mary, 71
Wingate, Maj.-Gen. Orde, 325
wives of British officers, *60*, 131–33, 136, *136*
women in Indian National Army, 334
Women's Auxiliary Corps (India), 313
Women's Christian Temperance Union, 149, 150, 151
Woolcombe, Mrs. Gordon, 239
woordy majors, 29
World War I, 34, 36, 189
  African theatre, 253
  captivity for British and Indian troops, 261–66
  educated Indians recruited for, 250–51
  European theatre, 248–53
  heroism of Indian troops, 249–50
  Indian officers trained for, 292–93
  Indians' enthusiasm for fighting in, 268
  Mesopotamian theatre, 253–54, 256–66
  morale problems, 251–52
  Muslim soldiers, problem of, 236–37, 244
  see also Singapore Mutiny of 1915
  princely armies in, 229–30, 231–32, 234
World War II, 190
  battlefield performance of Indian troops, 312, 314. 316
  "Boys' Battalions," 313
  Central India Horse incident, 311

  Ethiopian theatre, 314–16
  homefront in India, 313–14
  Indian Army's failure to prepare for, 303–7
  Indian officers trained for, 301
  industry's contribution, 308
  integration of regiments, 312–13
  political impact on India, 308–11
  princes' participation in, 311–12
  Sikh troops, 182
  South-East Asian theatre, 316, 317, 318–26
  volunteers for the military, 307–8
  Women's Auxiliary Corps (India), 313
  see also Indian National Army
Wylde, A. B., 157
Wylie, Francis, 349*n*

Yacht Club, 97
Yakub Khan, amir of Afghanistan, 108, 109
Yeats-Brown, Francis, 90–91, 103, 138, 162, 181, 182, 185, 313
Yeshwant Rao Holkar (Maharaja of Indore), 225
Young, Sir Arthur, 245
Young, Mackworth, 207
Younghusband, Maj.-Gen. Sir George, 95, 98
Yule, Col. Henry, 188*n*
Yusafzai country, uprising in (1857), 65–66

Zahīr-ud-Dīn Muhammad (Babur), 15
Zhob Militia, 55, 197